FOOD LOVERS'

FOOD LO

GUIDE

NEW ORLEANS

The Best Restaurants, Markets & Local Culinary Offerings

1st Edition

Becky Retz & James Gaffney

gpp

Guilford, Connecticut

Copyright © 2012 Morris Book Publishing, LLC

Editor: Kevin Sirois
Project Editor: Lynn Zelem
Layout Artist: Mary Ballachino
Text Design: Sheryl Kober
Illustrations © Jill Butler with additional art by Carleen Moira Powell and MaryAnn Dubé
Maps: Daniel Lloyd © Morris Book Publishing, LLC

ISBN 978-0-7627-7354-1

Printed in the United States of America
10 9 8 7 6 5 4 3 2 1

All the information in this guidebook is subject to change. We recommend that you call ahead to obtain current information before traveling.

Contents

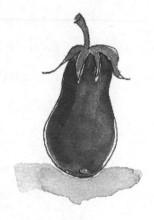

I dedicate this book to the hard-working men and women of the New Orleans food-service industry, who save us all every day.

—B. Retz

This book is dedicated to the indefatigable spirit of the people of New Orleans, who built this city out of a swamp, rebuilt it twice more after conflagrations, and again most recently in the aftermath of Katrina. It must be the food that keeps us all here.

—J. Gaffney

About the Authors

Becky Retz is the coauthor of *Insiders' Guide to New Orleans* (Globe Pequot Press) and a contributor to *National Geographic Traveler: New Orleans*. Becky also spent two decades working for *The Times-Picayune* newspaper, where she wrote stories on dining, education, health, and entertainment, as well as penning a weekly automotive column. She's also spent many exhausting but rewarding days working the front of the house in a busy New Orleans restaurant.

Becky is the proud mom of poet Chris Freeman. She is also a blushing bride. After completion of this current project, Becky plans to finally honeymoon with her new husband, Steve. The two live in the Gentilly neighborhood of New Orleans.

James Gaffney is a veteran travel journalist and has been a book, magazine, and newspaper writer since 1985. A cultural explorer at heart, he has traveled the world writing about diverse topics ranging from the aboriginals of Far North Queensland and Mayan burial caves in Honduras's storied Mosquito Jungle to the Byzantine and Ottoman legacies of modern-day Istanbul. Since 1989 he has served as national affairs editor for a syndicated news service covering international travel and aging issues. Television credits include cowriting the thirteen-episode series *Quest for Adventure* for The Travel Channel. He is the author of *Keys to Understanding Medicare,* published by Barron's; coauthor of *The National Geographic Traveler New Orleans,* published by The National Geographic Traveler; author of *Day Trips from New Orleans* and coauthor of *Insiders' Guide to New Orleans,* both published by Globe Pequot Press. His award-winning photography has been exhibited at professionally juried local and national galleries. He works at New Orleans' daily newspaper *The Times-Picayune* as an automotive writer and photographer.

Acknowledgments

Living through Hurricane Katrina gave a lot of us here in New Orleans a much deeper appreciation of the people in our lives whom we can count on. And no one in the past five years has fit that description more than my hard-working husband, Steve, who continuously inspires me through his passionate commitment to his work and his loving support of me. I thank him for that, as well as for his superior insights into and his voluminous knowledge of the local food-service industry. Without that, and his uncanny ability to make me laugh, I could never have completed this project.

My son Chris, with his always-churning creative energy, continuously challenges me to examine and reexamine my view of the world rather than simply allowing the inertia of middle age to set in. I really don't think I'll ever turn into an old lady with him around.

My extended family and friends have been so gracious every time I've had to cancel or postpone plans because I had to work on this book. I thank them for that and plan to make up for it, when the work is all done, with good meals, cold cocktails, and long leisurely chats.

I gratefully acknowledge James Gaffney, my old friend and colleague. He's a true professional and the only person I would have wanted to work with on this project. He is a talented writer, an insightful collaborator, and he always has my back. I couldn't ask for anything more, either personally or professionally.

Thanks go also to Amy Lyons and Kevin Sirois of Globe Pequot for thinking of me for this project and for being so easy to work with.

Finally, I want to thank my fellow New Orleanians who have worked so hard to rebuild our beloved city. Nearly six years ago we returned to mud-caked neighborhoods we couldn't even recognize and a town on the verge of extinction. But instead of giving up in the face of this almost insurmountable task, they sang out in one clear voice, "Won't bow down. Don't know how." I'm proud to count myself among them and honored to live through this historic time with them. Who Dat!

—B. Retz

To Cathy, my wife, love of my life and traveling companion nonpareil, thank you for keeping my head from exploding during the stress-filled months spent researching and cobbling together this writing venture. And for sacrificing countless nights and weekends for info-gathering prowls and endless dine-a-thons, which included your eating a record five Dreamsicle snowballs in a row one afternoon for a taste comparison of this icy New Orleans tradition. Without you none of this would have been possible.

To Larry and Claire Dejean, my beloved relations, dear friends, and "Katrina evacuation family," thank you for introducing me to the true Cajun Country fare of Opelousas and St. Landry Parish, from kolaches (with my godchild Tyler James) and deep-fried boudin patties to cayenne-dusted cracklins so fresh and juicy the flavorful, salty fat literally squirts into your mouth at first bite.

To my sister Lynn, thank you for all those evenings in my youth when you cooked your delicious oven-baked, homemade enchiladas and reminded our family that true Mexican fare doesn't originate from a frozen dinner or drive-thru window. To my still best mate from high school, Larry Cataldo, thank you for showing me in our adolescence how your preparation of a simple, hearty soup for your family is an act of love.

To Xavier Laurentino, thank you for your friendship and for sharing with me over the years the passion, knowledge, and consummate cooking skills you bring to Catalan food, truly one of the world's great cuisines, both as a master chef and imaginatively creative human being.

To the chefs and cooks around the world this travel writer has had the pleasure to meet during the past quarter-century spent as a wide-eyed wanderer with notepad, camera, and fork, thank you for opening my mind, heart, and palate to the stories your cultures have often revealed in a single dish.

To my longtime coauthor Becky, with whom I am always proud to share a book credit, thank you for selflessly taking the lead role by narrowing down more than 1,200 restaurants metropolitan-wide to a succinct and insightful best-of list.

To Kevin Sirois and Amy Lyons, thank you for being great team captains and editors who not only stewarded this enterprise but also reminded me just how fond I've grown of my Globe Pequot Press "family" over the years.

To New Orleans, thank you for adopting this Los Angeles ex-pat and teaching him the simple blessing of a dripping-to-your-elbows, roast-beef po-boy enjoyed at City Park on a triumphantly perfect spring day. Outsiders can say what they will about my beloved city and its residents, but when it comes to food, to paraphrase Lou Reed, our week is their year.

—James Gaffney

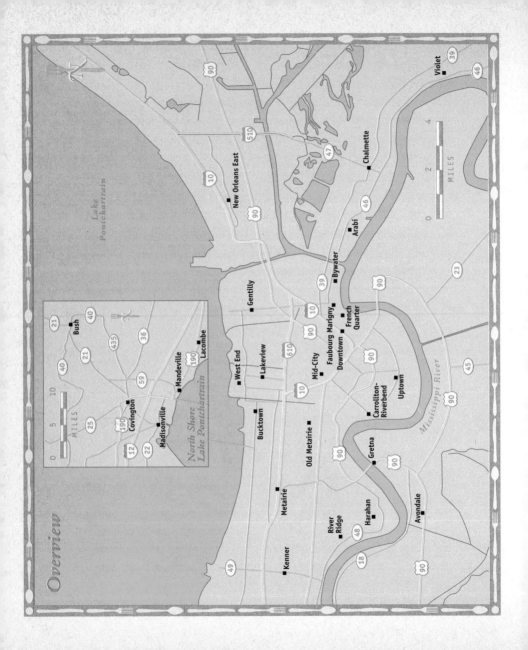

Overview

Lake Ponchartrain

Violet

Chalmette

Arabi

Bywater

New Orleans East

Gentilly

Faubourg Marigny

French Quarter

Downtown

Mid-City

Lakeview

West End

Carrollton-Riverbend

Uptown

Bucktown

Gretna

Old Metairie

Metairie

River Ridge

Harahan

Avondale

Kenner

Mississippi River

Inset map

North Shore
Lake Ponchartrain

Bush

Lacombe

Mandeville

Madisonville

Covington

MILES

0   5   10

Introduction

Bienvenue! Welcome to New Orleans. I hope you're hungry, because this little subtropical metropolis boasts more than 1,200 restaurants ready to feed you. And just to make it easier, in the following pages, we've narrowed down that number to the city's very best dining experiences. Whether you're in the mood for white tablecloths and superior service or an overstuffed po-boy and a scoop of homemade potato salad, you're in the right place.

It's truly our pleasure, because, you see, we're obsessed with food. Of course, who wouldn't be, when it's this good? I remember a day almost 20 years ago when I was part of a bus tour for local writers, designed to show off all the new projects around town that were going to push New Orleans forward in the film, arts, and tourism industries. The day was a disaster. Virtually all of the sites we visited were either behind schedule or work had been stopped completely. By midday, I was starting to get depressed. I was sitting on the bus thinking, "Why would anybody even come here?" as I absently bit into a sandwich from the bag lunch I had been handed. Then something remarkable happened. There was an explo-

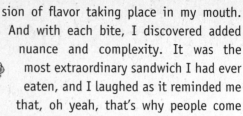

sion of flavor taking place in my mouth. And with each bite, I discovered added nuance and complexity. It was the most extraordinary sandwich I had ever eaten, and I laughed as it reminded me that, oh yeah, that's why people come here. It turns out the sandwiches had been made by Susan Spicer, the now nationally renowned chef, then the newest rising star. Nearly two decades later, I couldn't begin to tell you what was on that sandwich, but I still clearly remember how it made me feel. Tasting that sandwich filled me with nothing less than joy. And that's why I, like pretty much everybody else who lives here, am obsessed with food.

That's why it's common for our lunch conversation to center around dinner. And it's why, if you ask anyone who has relocated here how they ended up in New Orleans, their answer will undoubtedly sound something like: "I came for a visit, started eating, and never left." And it's why, when many parts of the city are still struggling to rebound from Hurricane Katrina and we're in the midst of a national economic recession, New Orleans now has 50 percent more restaurants than it did before the storm. (What can I say? For us, when in doubt, eat.)

So, thank you for coming to New Orleans and giving us the chance to share our gastronomic glee with you. All you have to do is relax and stroll through these pages until you come across something that piques your interest.

How to Use This Book

New Orleans has always been a city of distinctive neighborhoods, so that's how we've organized this book. The vast majority of restaurants are within the city limits. Those are divided into neighborhoods. Additionally, there are a handful of suburban eateries to round out the coverage. Because there are fewer of those, they are generally grouped by larger geographic areas than the city restaurants.

Each chapter features a **Neighborhood Map** showing where the restaurants are located. Within each chapter, you'll find listings organized alphabetically under the following categories:

Foodie Faves

This section focuses on restaurants that have perhaps not been long-standing establishments in their respective communities but still manage to serve a good meal.

Landmarks

The restaurants in this category are institutions in the local culture either due to their longevity or contribution. They deserve much recognition for helping put New Orleans on the culinary map.

Specialty Stores, Markets & Producers

Helping you navigate all of the artisan bakeries, butcher shops, and specialty markets, we give you a list of must-visit food shops.

Learn to Cook

New Orleans is home to a respected group of nationally acclaimed chefs, and we explain how, and where, you can hone your skills. If you want your love affair with New Orleans food to go on after your trip is over, check out these opportunities to learn to cook like a local.

Recipes

At the back of this book, we give new meaning to the phrase "continuing education" and help you create some of our favorite local dishes at home.

Price Code

Each listing uses a simple price code to indicate the cost of a single entrée. (Some of you may be pleasantly surprised to discover how inexpensive a lot of food in New Orleans is.) The code works as follows:

$	**Less than $10**
$$	**$10 to $20**
$$$	**$20 to $30**
$$$$	**$30 to $40**
$$$$$	**More than $40**

Because New Orleans is such an established food town, there are a number of reliable sources writing about and reporting on the state of eating. Following are some of the best.

Gambit Weekly (www.bestofneworleans.com): Gambit is the city's free alternative newspaper. Ian McNulty writes about food and drink. His articles can be found by searching the site.

The Times-Picayune (www.nola.com): *Picayune* reporters have covered New Orleans and its happenings since the 1830s. Brett Anderson is the newspaper's restaurant critic. His reviews appear in the Friday Lagniappe entertainment section. On Thursday, food editor Judy Walker writes about local food in general and prints lots of recipes. She also appears in weekly nola.com videos demonstrating cooking tips and kitchen tricks. Both writers' work generally can be found on the nola .com home page on the publication day or by searching the site. As of this writing, all nola .com content is free.

Tom Fitzmorris (www.nomenu.com): Tom Fitzmorris is the local godfather of food writing. He has penned a weekly restaurant review column since 1972, making it the longest-running restaurant review column written by one person in America. He's also been hosting a three-hour-a-day food and drink radio show since 1975. The broadcast airs weekdays from 3 to 6 p.m. and Sat noon to 3 p.m. CST. You can listen live at wwl.com. His website features the most reliable and comprehensive list of New Orleans restaurants, as well as his personal blog posts of eating experiences and formal restaurant reviews. The website is searchable and very user-friendly. Generally, the only knock people have against Fitzmorris is a distaste for what some see as a know-it-all attitude. But if you read his reviews and listen to his broadcasts, it's hard to argue that he doesn't know a hell of a lot about the local restaurant scene and cooking in general.

WWOZ 90.7 FM (www.wwoz.org): WWOZ is New Orleans' non-profit jazz radio station. On Saturday mornings, 7 to 8 a.m. CST, George Ingmire hosts a show about local food, festivals, and culture called "New Orleans All the Way Live." The hour features local music interspersed with features on New Orleans events and cuisine. Listen live online.

Festivals & Events

In a nationally renowned food city like New Orleans, it's only to be expected that we would celebrate food at the drop of a hat—er, oyster. At times it seems there is a festival to celebrate virtually every kind of favorite food under the sun. And, in fact, there is. But there are also fetes celebrating our devotion (Dr. Drew might say "addiction") to refreshing arboreal alcoholic beverages, plus one festival that celebrates the nation's reportedly oldest neighborhood of free African Americans, which naturally touts food—in this case, "some of the best gumbo to be found anywhere." For a current list of events in New Orleans, contact the New Orleans Convention and Visitors Bureau at www .neworleanscvb.com (800-672-6124).

March

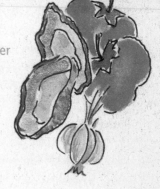

Louisiana Oyster Jubilee, http://oyster jubilee.com. This daylong event, held in the 300 block of Bourbon Street in the French Quarter, features live music and food with a special emphasis on the state's favorite bivalve. Several French Quarter restaurants come together to create the Longest Oyster Po-boy.

Treme Creole Gumbo Festival, Treme, www.jazzandheritage .org/treme-gumbo. Beginning in 2012 this two-day festival moves to March but will still celebrate what is widely believed to be the oldest neighborhood of free people of color in the United States, with live music and food, including some of the best gumbo to be found anywhere.

April

French Quarter Festival, various French Quarter locations, www .fqfi.org. One of the city's biggest festivals, this weekend-long event showcases the city's proud heritage with live music and food from some of the best restaurants in New Orleans.

New Orleans Jazz & Heritage Festival, New Orleans Fair Grounds Race Course and various locations, www.nojazzfest.com. Spread out over two consecutive weekends, the city's premier festival celebrates the food and musical heritage of New Orleans and Louisiana with a tour de force of nonstop live music on numerous stages, a plethora of food booths serving up local delicacies, and one-of-a-kind handmade arts and crafts.

May

Greek Fest, www.greekfestnola.com. If you can say "Opa!" you'll fit right in at this weekend-long celebration at Holy Trinity Greek Orthodox Cathedral of all things Greek including the music, food, and art of the Mediterranean country.

Mid-City Bayou Boogaloo, Bayou St. John, www .thebayouboogaloo.com. This weekend-long community-building event celebrates the unique and historic neighborhood of St. John with music, food, and creative art. Music runs the gamut from blues, jazz, funk, and Cajun to zydeco, Latin, and brass bands.

New Orleans Wine and Food Experience, various locations, www.nowfe.com. Among the most popular annual fetes in town is this prestigious five-day event that sees food and wine lovers from all over the region gather to celebrate and enjoy some of the city's legendary restaurants—not to mention their fine wines as well as vintners from around the world—with a packed roster of indoor and outdoor activities.

June

Oyster Festival, www.neworleansoysterfestival.org. Shuck, slurp, and enjoy is the pastime enjoyed most by festival-goers attending this weekend-long celebration of music and, of course, Louisiana's most popular (and tasty!) bivalve, held in a spot between the Hard Rock Cafe and Jackson Brewery Building.

Vieux-To-Do, various French Quarter locations. Only a city like New Orleans could pull off combining three festivals into a single weekend of music, food, cooking demonstrations, parades, arts and crafts, book signings, and other fun. But such is the case when three organizations got together: the **French Markets Creole Tomato Festival,** www.frenchmarket.org; the **Cajun-Zydeco Festival,** www.jazzandheritage.org/Cajun-zydeco; and the **Louisiana Seafood Festival,** www.louisianaseafood.com.

New Orleans Food Glossary

New Orleans has a tendency to have its own name for lots of things. The following "translation" of terms you may not be familiar with on local menus is designed to help you get the most out of every meal while you're in New Orleans. That's certainly what locals always try to do.

Andouille—A smoked Cajun sausage made primarily with pork and traditionally used as an ingredient in red beans and rice. Today, this flavorful and slightly spicy sausage can be found everywhere—even on fine dining menus.

Beignet—A square, hole-less donut, usually drenched in powdered sugar and the perfect complement to a steaming cup of cafe au lait.

Bisque—A traditional thick Cajun soup served over rice and usually containing seafood, primarily crawfish.

Boudin—Like andouille, this spicy Cajun sausage, generally made of pork and cooked rice, is (rightly) experiencing a renaissance. Look for and enjoy it in all kinds of dishes.

Cafe au lait—In New Orleans, chicory coffee and steamed milk, traditionally mixed in equal measures.

Cafe brûlot—An after-dinner hot coffee drink mixed with spices, orange peel, and liqueurs, mixed in a chafing dish, flamed, and served in special cups.

Chicory—A dried, ground, and roasted herb root used to flavor coffee.

Crawfish—Like a tiny lobster, but more flavorful.

En papillote—A fish baked in a paper bag to seal in the natural flavors. But you only need to know this to win a really weird bar bet. It's not even on Antoine's menu anymore.

Étouffée (ay-too-FAY)—Depending on who you ask, a roux-based or roux-less sauce used to smother Cajun seafood dishes. Good examples include crawfish or shrimp étouffée.

Filé (FEE-lay)—Powdered dried root bark of the sassafras tree used mostly to flavor and/or thicken gumbo, as in filé gumbo.

Grillades (GREE-yads)—A tomato-and gravy-based dish of thinly cut and browned veal or beef round. Grillades and grits is a popular New Orleans breakfast dish.

Gumbo—A roux-thickened soup prepared any number of ways but typically with one or more of the following: seafood (oysters, shrimp, and/or crab), sausage (such as andouille), chicken, okra, and z'herbes (mustard greens).

Jambalaya—A seasoned rice-and-tomato-based "sweep-up-the-kitchen" dish prepared with virtually endless combinations of beef, chicken, crawfish, pork, sausage, and shrimp.

Meunière—A New Orleans seafood butter sauce framed by freshly ground black pepper, lemon juice, and finely minced fresh parsley—usually served with fish, traditionally trout.

Mirliton—A locally popular green squash, called chayote or vegetable pear elsewhere, used both as an accent vegetable and an edible container for stuffing with ham or shrimp.

Po-boy—The classic New Orleans fresh French bread sandwich, which can be found stuffed with virtually everything under the sun—from fried shrimp, oysters, soft-shell crabs, and catfish to roast beef, meatballs, deli meats, rib-eye, pork chops, and even french fries.

Red beans and rice—A New Orleans staple of slow-cooked until creamy, seasoned kidney beans served over rice, often with hot or smoked sausage, a pork chop, or a piece of chicken. Traditionally served on Monday.

Remoulade—A tangy, salmon-colored sauce with Creole mustard, horseradish, vinegar, and other flavorings, first served in New Orleans with shrimp.

Roux—A reddish-brown base of flour and fat (butter, lard, or oil), plus the so-called holy trinity of chopped onions, bell peppers, and celery, for many New Orleans sauces and food preparations.

July

Tales of the Cocktail, various French Quarter locations, www
.talesofthecocktail.com. It only made sense for a city like New
Orleans that is responsible for creating so many well-known and
beloved cocktails to host a five-day festival dedicated to imbibing
refreshing adult beverages as well as "Spirited Dinners," lectures,
demonstrations, and special cocktail luncheons and parties.

September

New Orleans Seafood Festival, Lafayette Square, www.new
orleansseafoodfestival.com. This popular event features live entertainment, celebrity chef cooking demonstrations, local arts and
crafts, and world-famous cuisine from top New Orleans restaurants
and caterers.

October

Crescent City Blues & BBQ Festival, Central Business District,
www.jazzandheritage.org/blues-fest. Live music, arts and crafts,
and, of course, great barbecue highlight this popular weekend-long
annual event.

November

Mirliton Festival, Markey Park, www.mirlitonfestival.com. The
spotlight turns on the beloved mirliton at this popular Bywater park

with daylong festivities that include live music, arts and crafts, and food prepared by some of the best restaurants in the community.

New Orleans Coffee Festival, Freret Market, http://neworleanscoffeefestival.com. This relatively new kid on the block flies its java freak flag with this daylong event featuring live music, food vendors, and opportunities to taste the beverage for which New Orleans is famous.

New Orleans Po-boy Preservation Festival, Oak Street, www.poboyfest.com. The popular Oak Street thoroughfare of restaurants, coffee shops, boutiques, and galleries turns the day over to the city's favorite sandwich with daylong events that see some of the city's best restaurants preparing their favorite versions of the French bread-based tour de force of yummy ingredients, plus a po-boy judging contest.

French Quarter

Perhaps no neighborhood so embodies the infinitely rich color and character of New Orleans' distinct personality as this one. As the city's original settlement and bordered by Canal Street and Esplanade Avenue, Rampart Street, and the Mississippi River, this storied enclave of rollicking Bourbon Street bars and noisy jazz joints, Royal Street art galleries, boutiques, museums, and, of course, legendary Jackson Square and historic St. Louis Cathedral in many ways embodies the essence of the City that Care Forgot. What this section of the city didn't forget, however, was how to wine and dine locals and international visitors alike with its mix of restaurants that at times boggles the imagination. From centuries-old Creole fine-dining dens and swank hotel chophouses to hole-in-the-wall burger joints, European-style bistros, and cutting-edge venues serving globally inspired cuisine, most anyone would be hard-pressed to find another part of town boasting such a kaleido-scopic, near-dizzying array of culinary favors.

Bennachin, 1212 Royal St., New Orleans, LA 70116; (504) 522-1230; African; $$. The city counts among its culinary blessings the presence of this purveyor of West African dishes born in Cameroon and Gambia, the native countries of co-owners Alyse Njenge and Fanta Tambajang, respectively. Meals are simple and usually accompanied by a combination of *makdowa* (fried ripe plantains), *mbondo cone* (coconut-rice), couscous, steamed *mandowa* (broccoli), *cassava*, and *jama-jama* (sautéed spinach), depending on the dish. Among the best ways to taste the significant culinary role the African diaspora has played in local cooking traditions is with the *nsouki ioppa*, the traditional (and original) West African version of gumbo (which arrives at your table with beef sausage and smoked turkey strips), *doh-doh* (fried ripe plantains), and *akara* (black-eyed pea fritters). Entrees featuring poultry, fish, and lamb are prepared as spicy as guests request. Try the *kembel-ioppa*, sautéed lamb strips and bell peppers in a curry-accented ginger sauce. Some dishes can be ordered vegetarian style.

The Bistro at Maison de Ville, 727 Toulouse St., New Orleans, LA 70130; (504) 528-9206; www.bistromaisondeville.com; Creole French; $$$. Any frequent traveler to Paris will attest that there is nothing quite like the setting and atmosphere of a bona fide bistro in which to enjoy a traditional rosemary-crusted chicken au jus. Fortunately for Francophiles there is this little oasis of ooh-la-la

whose Parisian-style bistro ambience, complete with red-leather banquettes, ceiling fans, and beveled-glass mirrors, sets the table for Chef Greg Picolo's succinct and thoughtfully crafted menu of French and nouvelle-Creole dishes served with a Louisiana twist. Among the best examples of his Paris-meets-New Orleans creations are the frog legs served with apple-smoked bacon and cheddar grits, escargot with Louisiana crawfish bordelaise gnocchi, and pan-seared jumbo scallops served with truffle-scented mashed potatoes, roasted corn, tarragon, and crawfish cream.

Cafe Amelie, 912 Royal St., New Orleans, LA 70116; (504) 412-8965; www.neworleansrestaurants.com/cafe_amelie; Contemporary Creole; $–$$$. The courtyard at Cafe Amelie is one of the most romantic places to spend time in New Orleans, attested to by the large number of weddings held here. But you don't have to wait for the big day to experience it. Cafe Amelie serves lunch, dinner, and Sunday brunch. And a perfect complement to the lush surroundings is the traditional Creole food brilliantly prepared with a very untraditional light touch. Try the Louisiana crab cake with citrus drizzle, pan fried over mixed greens; or the Amelie Muffaletta with layers of warm Genoa salami, mortadella, Black Forest ham, provolone, and cold olive salad on ciabatta. Interesting entrees include jumbo Gulf shrimp tossed in a mushroom brandy cream sauce with linguine and fresh grated Parmesan, as well as the blackened rack of lamb with mango scotch bonnet pepper jelly, creamy mashed potatoes, and *haricots verts*. There are also two air-conditioned indoor dining rooms. Reservations are recommended, but not required.

Camellia Grill, 540 Chartres St., New Orleans, LA 70130; (504) 522-1800; www.camelliagrill.net; Diner; $. What a great idea this is. It's always been fun to visit the Camellia Grill diner, where waiters in crisp white uniforms raise simple counter service to an art form and you get to watch your meal being adeptly prepared on a grill just a few feet away. But a lot of visitors had a hard time making it to the original location Uptown. And if they did, there was usually a long line to get in. But now there's a Camellia Grill in the French Quarter! So every day until 1 a.m. diners can easily enjoy juicy hamburgers or omelets stuffed with ham and oozing with cheese (and don't forget the fresh pie, heated up on the grill). And the new location has actually made a couple of improvements: It's bigger, so no long lines, and it's on a corner with two walls of windows that flood the room with lots of light. Don't miss it.

Clover Grill, 900 Bourbon St., New Orleans, LA 70130; (504) 598-1010; www.clovergrill.com; Sandwiches; $. On its website this diner, open 24/7, boasts one of the more welcoming phrases seen in quite a while: "Enjoy Clover Grill or else!" For as long as anyone can remember, this quirky den of campy fun has been serving up plenty of attitude alongside such popular late-night, post-party favorites as triple-egg omelets "first concocted in a trailer in Chalmette, Louisiana," prepared to order and served with hash browns, grits,

CREOLE CUISINE

Admittedly, one of the most confusing cuisine descriptions can be "Creole." Believe it or not, people have been fighting for literally hundreds of years over that word's exact definition, and the truth is it means a lot of different things. For our purposes, Creole refers to cooking associated with New Orleans. That can encompass cuisine, ingredients, techniques, or all of these. So, both an upscale, white tablecloth restaurant and a little hole-in-the-wall neighborhood cafe could call themselves Creole, and they'd both be right. The chef at the high-end restaurant may use the term to reflect his use of classical technique and the expert employment of local ingredients to create a truly sophisticated gastronomic experience. Likewise, the chef at the neighborhood cafe, who makes killer red beans and rice or a rich, flavorful gumbo, calls his food Creole because he does it exactly the way his mama, his mawmaw, and his great-granny all made it. The first chef creates fine art, the second folk art. The point is—they're both art.

And then again, things can get even more confusing when additional words are used in conjunction with Creole—which happens every day in New Orleans. So, it also happens in this book. Here's a quick rundown of the different versions of Creole, to help you understand:

Creole—As already stated, this could mean pretty much any level of restaurant serving any number of traditional New Orleans foods, from the city's oldest restaurant, Antoine's, and its pompano Pontchartrain with sautéed lump crabmeat to Fury's Monday red beans and rice. Look at the price point as well as the description of the dishes and atmosphere to figure out whether you'll be wearing shorts or a tie.

Creole French—This is always going to be an upscale restaurant serving such dishes as Broussard's Louisiana-style bouillabaisse with oysters, shrimp, and Gulf fish. (And yes, it's sometimes impossible to tell the difference between a Creole-French and an upscale Creole restaurant.)

Contemporary Creole—This would be a place where the chef puts a new twist on an old dish, like Brigtsen's shrimp remoulade with guacamole, deviled egg, and mirliton corn relish.

Creole Italian—This is an example of very early fusion. It's usually a traditional New Orleans restaurant with Italian influences, as seen in Mandina's breaded veal cutlet po-boy.

Creole Soul Food—Another fusion, like the Praline Connection's stuffed crab with greens and corn bread.

Of course, there are the Creoles' country cousins, the Cajuns, whose cuisine historically mirrored Acadiana's more rural lifestyle. Typical meals were hearty, one-pot dishes often made with rice, sausage, and/or wild game—and flavored with spices that created that now-famous Cajun heat. However, Creole and Cajun foods have been so intermingled over the years that K-Paul's Chef Paul Prudhomme, the man who brought Cajun cooking to America, has postulated that the two have melded into a hybrid "Louisiana food."

(Just remember, it doesn't matter what it's called. It only matters how it tastes.)

or fries. Transform your plain-jane Geaux Girl waffles into luscious vamps with the optional banana, pecans, and ice cream. Burgers made to order, club and deli sandwiches, as well as chicken-fried steak and grilled chicken breast platters are served. House rules include "Please keep your date seated to avoid accidents" and "We don't eat in your bed, so please don't sleep at our tables." Though fun 'round the clock, the witching hours at this venue, opened in 1950, are the best times to soak up the vibes of this colorful, off-beat, and marvelously funky venue.

Coop's Place, 1109 Decatur St., New Orleans, LA 70116; www .coopsplace.net; Creole & Cajun; $–$$. Coop's is known as the Cheers of the French Quarter, a fun bar where locals hang out and everybody knows each other. But what could be easy to miss is that it is also a terrific restaurant. If you want to experience real New Orleans food made the way it's supposed to be, including the best jambalaya in town, Coop's is the place. And the prices are really good, too. Coop's Taste Plate is an excellent introduction to traditional local fare. It includes a cup of seafood gumbo, shrimp Creole, Cajun fried chicken, red beans and rice with sausage, and rabbit and sausage jambalaya. The Bayou Appetizer is a good sampler of fried seafood—crawfish, oysters, shrimp, and crab claws. If you want to go local but a little lighter, try the shrimp remoulade salad with Creole mustard sauce. And have the smoked duck quesadilla, served with sour cream and Coop's own salsa, just because it's delicious.

Deanie's Seafood, 841 Iberville St., New Orleans, LA 70112; (504) 581-1316; Seafood; $–$$$. Nearly half a century ago, Deanie's was the first seafood market in the Lake Pontchartrain fishing village of Bucktown. The market and adjacent restaurant are still there, but now diners can enjoy that same fresh seafood in the French Quarter. The meal starts off on the right track with hot, steamy new potatoes, which are served instead of bread in this casual, bright, and airy family-friendly eatery. Try the barbecue shrimp, crawfish étouffée, crabmeat au gratin, stuffed flounder, and the stuffed shrimp dinner. A kid's menu is also available. Deanie's can get really busy for dinner, especially on weekends. Lunch is the least crowded time to go. The original location is at 1713 Lake Ave. in Bucktown, (504) 831-4141.

Dickie Brennan's Steakhouse, 716 Iberville St., New Orleans, LA 70130; (504) 522-2467; www.dickiebrennanssteakhouse.com; Steak; $$$$. Launched by Dickie Brennan of the city's legendary Brennan restaurant family, this fine-dining venue offers die-hard carnivores some of the most succulent filets, porterhouse, and prime rib, cooked to order, available anywhere in town. But for some of us the best steak on the menu is the 14-ounce barbecue rib eye, grilled over an open flame, that arrives at the table topped with Abita Beer barbecue shrimp and with roasted garlic mashed potatoes. All steaks come with a choice of optional homemade steak sauces—béarnaise, hollandaise, pepper-cream Bourbon, or Worcestershire. Also available are a few seafood entrees including Maine lobster. Don't miss the sautéed jumbo shrimp and jalapeño-and-cheddar grits appetizer.

El Gato Negro, 81 French Market Place, New Orleans, LA 70116; (504) 525-9752; http://elgatonegronola.com; Mexican; $$. El Gato Negro offers authentic Mexican food (with a few interesting twists) and exotic cocktails at a terrific location—overlooking the French Market. You could almost make a meal of chips and dip. There's a sampler with four types of home-made salsa, and guacamole doesn't get any fresher than this. It's made tableside. For lunch or dinner daily, you can choose to fill your tacos, quesa-dillas, or burritos with chicken breast, pulled pork, chorizo, shrimp, crawfish, or even lobster claw. Or try Coyito's Pan Seared Wild Salmon topped with sautéed jumbo shrimp in a wine, cilantro, tomato, onion, corn, and buttery garlic-lime salsa and accompanied with sautéed squash, zucchini, poblano peppers, Vidalia onions, and mushrooms. And don't forget the margaritas and mojitos, made to order with hand-squeezed juices and top-shelf tequila, lovely to drink while sitting at one of the outside tables. El Gato Negro also carries hard-to-find Mexican beers and spirits.

Frank's, 933 Decatur St., New Orleans, LA 70116; (504) 525-1602; Italian; $$. Locals know that when it comes to traditional Italian food, Frank's is the real deal. Walk into the main dining room and you'll feel like you're in *The Godfather*. Frank Gagliano opened here in 1965 selling muffulettas (the local Italian answer to the po-boy), which are still popular at the restaurant. But half a century later, there's so much more. For lunch or dinner daily, try the stuffed artichoke or crabmeat-stuffed mushrooms. The Capraci salad of tomatoes, mozzarella, olive oil, and basil is simple and delicious. For a main course, the fettuccine Alfredo or veal parmigiana are best bets. Or if you're up to it, the seafood platter is huge and satisfying. Along with the main dining room downstairs, there's a little more upscale dining room upstairs, which boasts a balcony with a view.

Gumbo Shop, 630 St. Peter St., New Orleans, LA 70116; (504) 525-1486; www.gumboshop.com; Creole; $$. Hearty portions of consistently well-prepared local staples are a hallmark of this immensely popular venue, housed in a building that dates to 1795. As the name suggests, the venue's (award-winning) gumbo should not be the least of any patron's dining considerations, especially since the kitchen prepares this local favorite in one of three classic styles: seafood okra gumbo; chicken-andouille gumbo; and filé gumbo with chicken and sausage. Best bet? Order all three if dining with a group and lazy Susan your bowls around the table so everyone gets a chance to savor the nuanced and subtle flavors unique to each dish. A tidy menu of Big Easy classics runs the gamut from shrimp Creole and crawfish étouffée to alligator sauce piquant and red beans and rice with smoked sausage. A pair of don't-miss starters includes the grilled boudin with Creole mustard and crawfish remoulade.

GW Fins, 808 Bienville St., New Orleans, LA 70112; (504) 581-3467; www.gwfins.com; Seafood; $$$. Making your way into *Esquire*'s list of "Top 20 best new restaurants in America" is no easy feat, but partner and Executive Chef Tenny Flynn's wonderfully imaginative menu has been winning over discerning palates nationwide ever since this sophisticated, New York-hip locale opened its doors in 2001. Good examples of the simple, unpretentious, and brilliantly prepared fare for which this seafood house has earned numerous accolades include wood-grilled sea scallops (with mushroom risotto and mushroom sauce), pumpkin seed-crusted redfish, and sautéed New Zealand John Dory (served with ricotta gnocchi and wild mushrooms). But many of us could make a meal out of several of the creative appetizers, such as the crispy-fried Maine lobster tail, blue crab pot stickers (with creamy pea-shoot butter), and the yellowfin tuna tartare that comes with avocado, radish, and wasabi.

Irene's Cuisine, 539 St. Philip St., New Orleans, LA 70116; (504) 529-8811; Italian; $$$. This is the kind of spot New Orleans ex-pats insist on going to when they come back to town after a lengthy absence. What makes this all the more noteworthy is the fact this establishment, opened in the early 1990s, specializes not in your status quo Big Easy fare like jambalaya, barbecue shrimp, and po-boys, but rather the cuisine of Northern Italy—and nobody does it better. Tourists should count on lengthy waits for this admittedly off-the-beaten-path, tavernesque hangout, but the time will be well rewarded. During recent visits the turtle soup, cioppino, lamb Provencal, ricotta-and-spinach ravioli, and soft-shell crab pasta (served with garlic, crawfish, and tomato) earned praise and raves from tablemates who swore they have never had a bad meal here— ever. A romantic atmosphere makes it ideal for special occasions.

Iris, 321 N. Peters St., New Orleans, LA 70130; (504) 299-3944; www.irisneworleans.com; Contemporary American; $$$. This elegant restaurant started out in the Carrollton neighborhood in the cozy cottage that **Boucherie** (see p. 146) now inhabits. But Carrollton's loss was the French Quarter's gain when Iris took up residence in more spacious digs at the Bienville House Hotel in 2008. What's interesting about Iris is that it doesn't serve any traditional New Orleans cuisine. Chef Ian Schnoebelen relies on fresh ingredients and his imagination to create his daily-changing menu and dishes such as perfectly cooked snapper with baby beets, baby turnips, lacinato kale, roasted tomato "chips," fennel and olive vinaigrette; or seared sushi-grade yellowfin tuna with green papaya salad, king oyster mushrooms, and blood orange-ginger vinaigrette. And it seems to be working. Schnoebelen and partner Laurie Casebonne were rewarded for their efforts when Iris was named Best New Restaurant of 2006 by *New Orleans Magazine*, and Schnoebelen was honored by *Food and Wine* magazine as one of the Top 10 Best New Chefs in America in 2007.

Jager Haus, 833 Conti St., New Orleans, LA 70112; (504) 525-9200; www.jager-haus.com; German, $$. This casual family-run eatery is the French Quarter's only restaurant serving authentic traditional German food. (The menu also features dishes inspired by French, Czech, Polish, and Hungarian cuisines.) Open for breakfast, lunch, and dinner daily, Jager Haus offers starters such as potato pancakes with applesauce or sour cream; or a knackwurst skewer with sliced knackwurst, bacon, and onion, served with a pretzel stick and mustard. For a main course, try the sauerbraten marinated roast sirloin of beef in a house-made sweet and sour gravy, served with spaetzles, or wiener schnitzel—traditional breaded veal cutlets, served with asparagus and mashed potatoes. Considering the fact that at least half the dishes have names that many New Orleanians couldn't pronounce, you know Jager Haus is good at what they do to have survived the city of gumbo and remoulade. Not surprisingly, there's also a good beer selection.

La Divina Gelateria, 621 St. Peter St., New Orleans, LA 70130; (504) 302-2692; www.ladivinagelateria.com; Ice Cream; $. For full description, please see the Uptown listing, p. 138.

Le Meritage, 1001 Rue Toulouse, New Orleans, LA 70112; (504) 522-8800; www.lemeritagerestaurant.com; Contemporary Creole; $$$–$$$$. This upscale restaurant, located inside the Maison Dupuy

Hotel, takes an interesting approach to dining. All food on the menu is paired with wines. The wines are divided into six categories, by characteristics rather than varietal. Then menu items are matched to the wines based on which dishes complement each wine's flavor profile. Each category has three wines and three dishes. All wines are available by the half or whole pour, and each menu item can be served as either a small or large plate to give the diner added flexibility as to how many pairings they want to do. For example, if you were to choose the herb-crusted rack of lamb with spring vegetables, then you would choose a wine from the Robust Reds category, knowing that you are getting a pairing that will enhance the enjoyment of both. It's like having a wine expert at your table.

M Bistro, 921 Canal St., New Orleans, LA 70112; (504) 670-2828; www.ritzcarlton.com/en/Properties/NewOrleans/Dining/MBistro; Contemporary Creole; $$$–$$$$. Located inside the Ritz-Carlton, New Orleans, M Bistro has been ranked as one of the top farm-to-table hotel restaurants by *Travel + Leisure*. Taking "an indigenous approach" to the preparation of the best ingredients the Gulf Region has to offer, Chef de Cuisine Bradley McGehee and staff create gourmet breakfast, lunch, and dinner offerings. Dinner highlights include Creole tomato bisque with Ryal's Farm goat cheese and fresh pesto; New Orleans BBQ Shrimp with Abita-cane syrup sauce and Papa Tom's smoked gouda grits; crispy pecan-crusted sweetbreads with green peas, leek and bacon hash, herbes de Provence, and vermouth cream; and braised rabbit cassoulet with applewood-smoked bacon, red and white beans, and herb bread crumbs. Meals are served in the elegant M Bistro dining room. Reservations are recommended for dinner. For those who wish privacy, special reservations can be made for one of three velvet-draped booths, the chef's table, or private dining for up to 10 in the wine room.

Maximo's Italian Grill, 1117 Decatur St., New Orleans, LA 70116; (504) 586-8883; www.maximosgrill.com; Italian; $$$. If this chic little venue buzzes on weekend nights, chalk it up in part to the excellent wine selection (it's one of the city's few recipients of *Wine Spectator*'s prestigious "Best of Award of Excellence") and the fact that this bistro-ish locale is probably one of the best places in town to sample vintages by the glass. Jazz music and a collection of Herman Leonard's black-and-white photographs of jazz legends help set the mood in this 1829 building for a modern menu of gourmet recipes that include fire-roasted shrimp and fish, pan-roasted veal T-bones, antipasto, and grilled portobello mushrooms, as well as lamb and steak dishes. It's hard to go wrong ordering the fire-roasted chicken and sausage prepared with prosciutto, Fontina cheese, mushrooms, and cream.

Meauxbar Bistro, 942 N. Rampart St., New Orleans, LA 70116; (504) 569-9979; http://meauxbar.com; French; $$–$$$. Like its menu, this delightful little restaurant on the edge of the French Quarter is both sophisticated and unassuming, upscale yet warm and welcoming. It is the brainchild of Chef Matthew Guidry and his partner James Conte. Guidry seems to have combined his Cajun heritage, formal French training, and world travels to create a menu that is a harmonious blending of regional, classic French, and Indo-chine influences. And the results are delicious. You could easily make a meal from the appetizer menu alone. Start with the caramelized onion tart with goat cheese and bacon lardons, then move to the ginger crawfish dumplings with cilantro, *sambal olek,* and a sesame-soy dipping sauce, or maybe you're in the mood for "mac and cheese"—baked ziti with mushroom duxelle, goat cheese, Gruyère, and truffle oil. But don't miss the Trout Grenobloise with lemon caper beurre noisette, parsleyed potatoes, and sautéed haricots verts; or the shrimp risotto with asparagus spears and wild mushrooms.

Mena's Palace, 200 Chartres St., New Orleans, LA 70130; (504) 525-0217; www.menaspalace.com; Neighborhood Cafe; $–$$. With a menu long enough for pretty much everybody to find something they like, this is an inexpensive place to have breakfast or lunch in the French Quarter. Since the 1950s, Mena's has been where locals go for the kind of hearty home-style meals that remind a lot of us of the kind of food we ate growing up. The menu features traditional breakfast, plus salads, sandwiches, seafood, and daily lunch specials—all at reasonable prices. Lighter lunch offerings include shrimp remoulade salad and tuna-stuffed tomato. Or go for the chicken parmigiana and spaghetti, or the fried shrimp platter with french fries. Specials include local comfort foods like red beans and rice with smoked sausage or chicken, baked lasagna, stuffed bell pepper with mashed potatoes and salad, or baked chicken with dirty rice and beet salad. Mena's opens at 7 every morning.

Mona Lisa, 1212 Royal St., New Orleans, LA 70116; (504) 522-6746; Italian; $–$$. Mona Lisa is a laid-back little Italian restaurant offering pizzas, pastas, salads—and the chance to discover your artistic talent. The walls are adorned with numerous takes on Da Vinci's famous painting, and there are crayons on hand in case you want to take a shot at it yourself. The food is reasonably good and reasonably priced. All the usual pizza fare is here, plus the Breakfast Pizza with scrambled eggs and bacon (although they're not open for breakfast), and if you dare, the Seafood Pizza with shrimp, tilapia, and clams. On the sandwich menu, you can create your own calzone with any three pizza ingredients or just go for the meatball sub with mozzarella and spaghetti sauce. Salads include a tomato-onion with lettuce, mozzarella, and olive salad, as well as traditional spinach with feta, black olives, tomatoes, red onions, mushrooms, and egg. Mona Lisa serves lunch and dinner. But the place can fill up fast. Go early. They also deliver.

Mr. B's Bistro, 201 Royal St., New Orleans, LA 70130; (504) 523-2078; www.mrbsbistro.com; Contemporary Creole; $$$. It's never a bad thing when the likes of Emeril Lagasse is quoted in *Travel +*

Leisure saying your restaurant does "the best gumbo ya-ya (made with chicken and andouille sausage)." But then, this chic dining oasis in the heart of the French Quarter is no stranger to accolades that have included raves from notable zines like *Gourmet*, *Food and Wine*, and the *Washington Post*. Of course, this establishment has also culled raves from patrons who have dined amid its softly lit, club-meets-bistro decor accented by a wall-long dark-wood bar that bustles with the after-work crowd. But the menu at this eatery, run by the Brennan family restaurant dynasty (hence the "B" in Mr. B's), is known for a lot more than just the dark-roux gumbo ya-ya. The barbecue shrimp (served with French bread for dipping into the peppery butter sauce), duck spring rolls, braised Mississippi rabbit, and wood-grilled seasonal fish have become hallmarks of this gourmet Creole den that opened its doors in 1979.

Muriel's, 801 Chartres St., New Orleans, LA 70116; (504) 568-1885; www.muriels.com; Contemporary Creole; $$$. Housed in a building that has been beautifully restored to its 19th-century Vieux Carre splendor, this romantic, two-story restaurant offers a truly sensual dining experience that has far more to do with its splendid Courtyard Bar, old brick walls, and second-floor balcony tables overlooking Jackson Square than it does the fact that a 19th-century Creole ghost reportedly lives here. Dripping with Old World atmosphere and consistently ranked as among the best (and most beautiful) restaurants in the city, this intimate venue offers a menu of largely Creole specialties often with a nouvelle twist. Dining adventures have included braised veal cheek and oxtail ragout,

crawfish and goat cheese crepes, jambalaya risotto cake, lobster/truffle couscous, and cassoulet with rabbit (as opposed to traditional duck). From the wood-grilled fish of the day and pan-seared scallops or duck breast to the yellowfin tuna carpaccio and roasted eggplant pasta, this beloved eatery is a hands-down must-eat for the sensualist gourmand in us all.

Napoleon House, 500 Chartres St., New Orleans, LA 70130; (504) 524-9752; www.napoleonhouse.com; $. No matter what your tour guide tells you, Napoleon never lived in this historic landmark that dates back to 1797. But that was the plan. In 1821 the owner of the house, former Mayor Nicholas Girod, hatched a scheme to rescue the emperor from exile and bring him to New Orleans. But Napoleon died before it could be carried out. Walk into this cafe and bar, and you'll feel like you've stepped out of time. The best bets on the menu include: the warm muffuletta; the bruschetta with basil, cheese, and tomatoes; or the boudin sausage with Louisiana Satsuma Creole mustard. The spinach and artichoke dip is good, as is the Greco panini with roasted eggplant, red pepper, and goat cheese. But mostly, you're eating just to spend a little time hanging out in this New Orleans treasure. Oh yeah, and before you leave, have a Pimm's Cup, the signature cocktail of the house.

NOLA, 534 St. Louis St., New Orleans, LA 70130; (504) 522-6652; www.emerils.com; Contemporary Creole; $$$. The second of superstar chef Emeril Lagasse's present-day 10-restaurant empire, opened in 1992, is a funky-chic, Soho-ish habitat for the largely hip, upscale clientele of movers and shakers who frequent these digs for the eclectic menu that generates consistently good praise. Lagasse understands as well as any chef of his caliber the near fetish internationalist gourmands have for mixed-ethnic cuisine, and no better example of this is the pan-roasted rib eye served with Spanish *patatas bravas* and chimichurri from Latin America. But the menu also leans heavily on Louisiana's acclaimed cooking roots as found in the Louisiana crab cake with smoky eggplant puree, feta cheese, calamata olives, crispy spinach, and citrus butter. For the main course Lagasse kicks out the culinary jams with his slow-roasted duck au jus (prepared in a sweet and spicy glaze and served with buttermilk–corn bread pudding and fire-roasted corn salad).

The Old Coffee Pot Restaurant, 714 St. Peter St., New Orleans, LA 70116; (504) 524-3500; Creole; $$. No matter the plethora of breakfast-to-late-night dining spots there are in the French Quarter, many of us always find ourselves gravitating to this century-old French Quarter gem to satisfy both the palate and stomach's desire for hearty Creole recipes cooked with soul and always served with a smile. While seafood platters, po-boys, jambalaya, and other local staples grace the menu, it's the tour de force of outstanding break-fast dishes that never fails to win the hearts of early-morning and late-night diners alike at this venue, opened in 1894 and among the oldest restaurants in New Orleans. Whether it's Lost Bread

HELPFUL TIPS

There are a few other tips that may help you better acclimate to the local dining scene. A large percentage of restaurants in New Orleans are small family-run businesses in which it is common to see a chef-owner who routinely puts in 70 to 80 hours a week. This kind of situation tends to make a person rather independent-minded. We locals understand how hard these people work to make us such consistently good food, so we show them a lot of respect.

Here's how it could affect you: A lot of these small restaurants close at least one day a week, often, but not always, on Monday. Additionally, these types of family operations are likely to close down completely for a week or so to take a summer vacation. All of the restaurants in this book have their phone numbers listed. Rather than showing up hungry and walking away disappointed, just call ahead and make sure somebody's home.

(New Orleans' Creole version of French toast), blintzes, Creole-style poached egg dishes, or a well-herbed omelet Rockefeller (served with fresh creamed spinach, oysters, cheese, and topped with cream sauce), the kitchen turns out consistently excellent versions of the kind of food that makes any New Orleanian feel at home.

Palace Cafe, 605 Canal St., New Orleans, LA 70130; (504) 523-1661; www.palacecafe.com; Contemporary Creole; $$$.

Also, many New Orleans restaurants only accept cash. We've tried to be diligent about pointing out which restaurants those are, but we could have missed a few. It's probably best to just go ahead and scope out ATM locations when you arrive.

Independent and overworked restaurant owners are also more likely to set up their operation the way it works best for them. In a lot of places, this could mean, for example, that you order at the bar or counter, then find a seat. I've noticed that a number of complaints on food blog sites start with, "I was confused about what to do when I walked in . . . " If this happens to you, don't blow it out of proportion. Just take a moment to see if you can figure it out. (Make it an exercise in going with the flow.) If you can't, that's OK, too. New Orleanians are generally very friendly people and happy to help. Look around for a local (we're the, uh, full-bodied ones) and say, "How does it work?" Odds are really good that, within a couple of minutes, you'll be on your way to having a great meal.

It's always fun to take out-of-state guests to this establishment, housed in the historic Werlein's building, just to show off the decor of this beautifully grand Parisian-style cafe and its sweeping, Art Nouveau-style staircase. But this popular locals spot is more than just architectural eye candy—among the national awards this cafe has racked up over the years include *Wine Spectator*'s Award of Excellence, thanks in no small part to the stewardship by owner Dickie Brennan of the city's Brennan family restaurant dynasty and

Executive Chef Darin Nesbit. A largely nouvelle Creole menu consists of more than a handful of consistently noteworthy winners. Favorites include a signature crabmeat cheesecake (baked in a pecan crust with a wild mushroom sauté and Creole meuniere), *cochon de lait boudin*, pan-roasted oysters, pepper-crusted duck breast with seared *foie gras*, and andouille-crusted seasonal fish served with beurre-blanc and chive aioli.

Palm Court Jazz Cafe, 1204 Decatur St., New Orleans, LA 70116; (504) 525-0200; www.palmcourtjazzcafe.com; Creole; $$–$$$. The Palm Court brings together New Orleans' two great influences: food and music. Housed in an early-19th-century storefront featuring high ceilings, mosaic tile floors, and an imposing mahogany bar, the cafe offers diners the opportunity to enjoy classic Creole cuisine while listening to traditional jazz music. The Palm Court looks, sounds, and tastes like old New Orleans. Bands rotate, but there's live music every night. There is also a collection of GHB jazz recordings that can be played on request. You can start your meal very traditionally with shrimp remoulade or Creole gumbo, or change it up a little with flash-fried crispy crawfish tails and lemon tartar sauce. Then move on to crawfish pie or jambalaya. Finish the meal properly with either bread pudding and whiskey sauce, or pecan pie a la mode. Certainly, an evening to remember.

The Pelican Club, 312 Exchange Place, New Orleans, LA 70130; (504) 523-1504; www.pelicanclub.com; Contemporary Creole; $$$. Unrepentant globe-stompers who yearn for the unmistakable sophistication and elan of upscale yet unpretentious European restaurants find nothing short of a home away from home at this ambience-rich oasis of refined dining. From the imported hand-painted Italian tile floor to the bright and airy white walls, leather banquettes, and slowly spinning ceiling fans, this venue embodies why New Orleans has often been called "America's most European city." Popular with both the blue-jeans and dress-up crowds, the East-meets-West-meets-South menu mixes Louisiana, European, and Asian culinary traditions for memorable meals. Executive Chef Richard Hughes Jr. has concocted some gratifying palate pleasers including such starters as the Louisiana blue crab with wild mushroom ravioli, escargot casserole, and lump crabmeat and shrimp cakes. But the Pelican Club really takes flight when it comes to this venue's trio of duckling—pan-seared breast, leg confit, and barbecue. During another visit the seared yellowfin tuna arrived at the table topped with crawfish etouffee and a jalapeño hollandaise, while the Louisiana-style cioppino proved a simmering, delicious example of what happens when a chef pushes the envelope of even the most simple of classic recipes.

Red Fish Grill, 115 Bourbon St., New Orleans, LA 70130; (504) 598-1200; www.redfishgrill.com; Seafood; $$$. The whimsical and colorful decor of this French Quarter mainstay includes sculpted metal branches that transform the wooden columns in the main dining room into encircling palms, and the half-dozen yard-high oyster half shells with mirrors inside that hang from the exposed-brick back wall. The menu is divided into such categories as Bait (appetizers, soups, and salads), Fin Fish, Shell Fish, Go Fish (meat, pasta, vegetarian), and Overboard (dessert). Leave it to longtime restaurateur and proprietor Ralph Brennan of the Brennan restaurant family to create a comfortable bistro as whimsical to the eye as the Asian-Cajun tapas plate and the wood-grilled Gulf fish taco are pleasing to the palate. What Brennan has concocted inside this renovated 1800s building, once home to D.H. Holmes department store, is a parade of heavenly delights using earthy crawfish, oysters, and pasta. Other must-tries include the Creole-style sweet potato catfish, sesame-crusted salmon, and spring rolls filled with grilled chicken, shrimp, and andouille sausage.

Remoulade, 309 Bourbon St., New Orleans, LA 70130; (504) 523-0377; www.remoulade.com; Creole; $$. Visitors strolling Bourbon Street who are looking for an affordable grazing menu of local flavors and a fun vibe, courtesy of the late Archie Casbarian (the restaurateur who put the famed Arnaud's next door back on the map), should look no farther. Local staples include café au lait, beignets, red beans and rice, half-size po-boys dubbed "po-babies," boiled and fried seafood, and oysters on the half shell. Arnaud's famous remoulade sauce (the same kind found atop the celebrated restaurant's filet mignon Charlemond) tops the burgers and franks. Other offerings include smoked boudin, thin-crust 8-inch gourmet pizzas, Nachitoches meat pies, and baskets of spare ribs. Mixed drinks, shooters, and a selection of "bayou potions guaranteed to ward off alligators" are served from behind the restored 1870s mahogany bar.

Sekisui Samurai, 239 Decatur St., New Orleans, LA 70130; (504) 525-9595; www.sekisuiusa.com/web/sekisui-neworleans; Japanese; $$. This classically decorated restaurant is part of a popular chain with locations across the South and the only place to get sushi in the French Quarter. The menu offers more than 50 rolls to choose from, as well as tempura and teriyaki selections. Best bets include the gyoza, udon bowls, and lunch specials, which include a trio of rolls, a salad, and miso soup. Popular specialty rolls include the Hurricane featuring tempura-battered and deep-fried salmon and cream cheese; and the MiMi with crab, shrimp, apple, and avocado. There's also a good selection of sake and Japanese beer. Sekisui Samurai is open for lunch and dinner every day, and take-out orders are welcome.

Stanley!, 547 St. Ann St., New Orleans, LA 70116; (504) 587-0093; http://stanleyrestaurant.com; Diner; $$. This snazzy diner with its marbletop tables, soda fountain, and enviable location on Jackson Square was established by Chef Scott Boswell as a complement to his fine dining restaurant Stella!. (Stanley and Stella are main characters in the Tennessee Williams play *A Streetcar Named Desire*.) Boswell's concept for Stanley! was to serve classic comfort foods with a twist, plus homemade ice cream. And it seems to have caught on. The short breakfast menu, which includes pancakes with cane syrup and vanilla ice cream, as well as Eggs Stella—cornmeal-crusted soft-shell crab, poached eggs, Canadian bacon and Creole hollandaise on a toasted English muffin—is served all day. The best bet for lunch is the "World Famous Stanley Burger"—a grilled 7-ounce Certified Angus burger with American cheese, mustard, mayonnaise, ketchup, lettuce, tomato, and onions. And save room for ice cream. You can get Stanley!'s ice cream by the scoop or in a shake, a float, a soda, or a sundae.

Stella!, 1032 Chartres St., New Orleans, LA 70116; (504) 587-0091; www.restaurantstella.com; Eclectic; $$$$. This recently renovated, intimate French Quarter restaurant is Chef Scott Boswell's fine dining counterpoint to his Stanley! diner, serving an eclectic menu that Boswell describes as "global-modern cuisine." Starters include local cherry tomato gazpacho with Louisiana jumbo lump crab and virgin olive oil as well as roasted potato puree with applewood-smoked bacon, fingerling potatoes, and caviar crème fraiche. Also look for the Composition of Heirloom Carrots salad featuring confit of baby carrots, carrot sorbets, carrot spheres, carrot cake crumbles, traditional carrot salad, petite carrot greens, and sweet carrot cloud. As a main course, try kabayaki-glazed prime beef tenderloin with seared sweet potato, steamed baby vegetables, wilted bok choy, and sweet soy-sake butter; or miso- and sake-glazed Japanese mero sea bass with udon, green tea and soba noodles, buna shimeji mushrooms, Canadian lobster, blue crab, and shrimp broth.

Verti Marte, 1201 Royal St., New Orleans, LA 70116; (504) 525-4767; www.vertimarte.com; Deli; $–$$. When this beloved French Quarter corner grocery and deli reopened in January 2011, after being closed for eight months due to fire damage, customers were already waiting in line for sandwiches when the doors were unlocked at 8 a.m. Verti Marte doesn't have the best food in town or a huge stock of groceries. But like Shelba Hatfield, who's run the kitchen since 1968, it's there—open 24 hours a day. Local residents know that if they run out of dog food or just need a bite to eat, they can count on this corner shop to be open and ready to serve. Plus, Verti Marte delivers! And there are tasty treats on the surprisingly extensive menu. One of the most popular items is the All That Jazz Po-Boy featuring a medley of grilled ham, turkey, and shrimp, with Swiss and American cheeses, grilled mushrooms, and tomatoes, with the deli's original "wow sauce," served on French bread—all for $11.25.

Landmarks

Acme Oyster House, 724 Iberville St., New Orleans, LA 70130; (504) 522-5973; www.acmeoyster.com; Seafood; $$. It took 86 years for this French Quarter landmark to open a second location, but that is about the only thing this venue doesn't do fast. Just check out the speed of its oyster shuckers at the bar, which is the No. 1 reason visitors from all over the world eventually wind up at this restaurant. This relaxed, classic oyster bar is the kind of place where you're just as likely to run into locals, foreign visitors, or celebrities such as Matt Dillon, Deion Sanders, and Ellen DeGeneres. At the bar or at a table, the raw oysters are always a best bet and are routinely ranked as the city's most popular in local surveys. However, for those who insist on having their food cooked, the oysters are just as good deep-fried in a po-boy or as part of a seafood platter. And there's a good stock of local beers to wash it all down. There are also locations at 3000 Veterans Blvd., Metairie, LA 70005; (504) 309-4056; and 1202 N. Highway 190, Mandeville, LA 70433; (985) 246-6155.

Antoine's, 713 St. Louis St., New Orleans, LA 70112; (504) 581-4422; www.antoines.com; Creole; $$$$. This is the city's first restaurant and the sign hanging outside announces modestly SINCE 1840. Inside, the guest list of notables who have dined at this venerable haute Creole dining institution reads like a who's who. Mark Twain, Groucho Marx, Enrico Caruso, Tennessee Williams, five US presidents (including both Roosevelts), Pope John Paul II—the list goes on. And this venue's 14 legendary dining rooms are as steeped in history as the guest list. Ditto for the library—yes, you heard right—that contains more than 400 volumes on cooking and wine, some of which are more than 250 years old. Many menu items such as oysters Rockefeller and eggs Sardou were born here while others come with a history every bit as rich as the sauces prepared under the watchful eye of fifth-generation proprietor Bernard Guste. The exhaustive menu in French may be overwhelming to the uninitiated, but that's what the gentle waitstaff is for (many of whom have worked here for decades). While the kitchen rarely ventures far from its time-honored Creole staples like pompano Pontchartrain (grilled pompano filet with sautéed lump crabmeat) and *cotelettes d'agneau grilles* (grilled prime center-cut lamb chops served with mint jelly), it's difficult indeed to find many places in town that do them better. If your wallet is fat and your appetite grand, splurge on the Chateaubriand-for-two, which arrives at your table replete with sautéed mushrooms and a duo of Antoine's famously delicious tasty sauces (marchand de vin and béarnaise).

Arnaud's, 813 Bienville St., New Orleans, LA 70112; (504) 523-5433; www.arnaudsrestaurant.com; Creole French; $$$$. This grand purveyor of haute-Creole cuisine and truly one of the country's fine-dining legends was opened in 1918 by "Count" Leon Bertrand Arnaud Cazenave, a French-born wine salesman, raconteur, and gastronome. Over the years a who's who of guests has included US presidents, princes, movie stars, and other celebs. The good news for the less luminary is that the international award-winning menu still includes favorite dishes created by the founder, such as shrimp Arnaud (chilled, boiled shrimp marinated in the restaurant's famous homemade remoulade sauce), oysters Bienville (baked with shrimp, mushrooms, and bread crumbs and topped with *glacage*), and smoked pompano Bourgeás. Not to be missed is the New Orleans tradition that is café brûlot (coffee flamed with cinnamon sticks, cloves, orange, and lemon rind with brandy and Grand Marnier). This massive restaurant is composed of six public and 10 private dining rooms in a block-long rambling structure of restored 18th- and 19th-century French Quarter buildings connected by hallways.

Bayona, 430 Dauphine St., New Orleans, LA; 70112; (504) 525-4455; www.bayona.com; Eclectic; $$$. In a food city like New Orleans, it's not uncommon for the chef-owner of an establishment to be as warmly cherished as the restaurant's menu and dining experience itself. Such is the case with the trademark bandana-wearing Susan Spicer, one of a handful of Next Generation kitchen maestros that have been surprising and delighting local palates with her "New World cuisine" ever since she opened this venue in 1990 in a beautiful 200-year-old cottage. The three-room main dining area downstairs offers a warm, European-style ambience, with terra-cotta-colored walls, dark green faux-marble accents, and huge hand-colored photographs of Italian gardens and trompe l'oeil Mediterranean landscapes. While a short roster of dinner specials changes nightly, the house staples that consistently win praise include the sautéed salmon with Choueroute and Gewürtzraminer sauce and boudin-stuffed rabbit loin with Creole mustard cream sauce. Slightly more adventurous diners should try Spicer's take on the classic veal sweetbreads, which arrive at your table with sherry mustard or lemon-caper sauce.

Brennan's, 417 Royal St., New Orleans, LA 70130; (504) 525-9711; www.brennansneworleans.com; Creole French; $$$$. Too often even locals forget that this Creole dining den best known for its "breakfast at Brennan's" eye-opening brunch cocktails and menu is by no means asleep at the wheel when it comes to dinner. Whether opting for a traditional trout amandine (topped with lemon-butter sauce and slivered almonds) or grilled salmon served with a tangy mix of Creole mustard and hollandaise, the entrees here reflect the culinary customs and high standards established early on when founder Owen E. Brennan Sr. opened this landmark at its original location back in 1946. Dinner is also the best excuse for oenophiles to take advantage of this venue's 50,000-bottle wine cellar (rated by *Wine Spectator* as one of the best in the world), especially since wine-pairing suggestions can be found alongside entrees on the menu. Be that as it may, there are probably few places in town that can give such a tasty spin to Big Easy brunch legends like this establishment's hearty turtle soup, eggs Benedict or Sardou, and, of course, the flaming bananas Foster invented at Brennan's.

Broussard's, 819 Rue Conti, New Orleans, LA 70112; (504) 581-3866; www.broussards.com; Creole French; $$$. Whether dining inside one of its smartly appointed dining rooms of gilt mirrors and bent-wood chairs or amid the romantic, candlelit ambience of its tree-dotted fountain courtyard, there is no escaping the grande-dame allure of this Creole-French mainstay. After diving into an appetizer sampler of crabmeat ravigote (with lemon, onions, capers, and avocado slices), shrimp with two remoulades, and house-cured salmon, or a plate of oysters flash-fried or prepared New Orleans-style a la Bienville or Rockefeller, smart diners will want to move smartly to this establishment's time-tested entrees that include pompano Napoleon (with shrimp and scallops in a puff pastry daubed in mustard-caper cream), roasted duck (with roasted shallots, tasso, potato-gnocchi hash, and hoison-balsamic cherry sauce), or the Louisiana-style bouillabaisse (with oysters, shrimp, and Gulf fish in a saffron-flavored tomato broth topped with crab-meat and rouille croutons). Not to be missed is the grilled wild game, a tour de force of quail breast, boar sausage, and venison chop on apple red cabbage.

Cafe du Monde, 1039 Decatur St., New Orleans, LA 70116; (504) 525-4544; www.cafedumonde.com; Dessert and Coffee; $. Worldwide only a handful of cosmopolitan European cities like Vienna can boast of coffee-shop landmarks that are (1) still open, and (2) pre-date lava lamps. So imagine the pride and high regard with which New Orleanians fondly embrace this cherished java purveyor that opened in 1862. In fact, no trip to New Orleans would be complete without a stop at this French Market coffee shop where locals routinely indulge in hot, creamy café au lait (coffee and chicory with steamed milk) and the sweet perfection of beignets (square hole-less donuts topped with powdered sugar) at all hours of the day or night (this spot is open 24/7). On the way out, walk around the back of the cafe, where a picture window allows visitors to watch the beignets being made.

Cafe Maspero, 601 Decatur St., New Orleans, LA 70130; (504) 523-6250; Creole; $$. For many newcomers to the city, this spot is where longtime locals take them to experience what some insist is the most mouth-watering pastrami sandwich this side of Manhattan. Not only will there invariably be a line of people outside the restaurant waiting to get in, the line will be long during peak tourist season. Not to worry, though. According to restaurant staff, your best bet for beating the sidewalk blues is to come after 2 p.m. weekdays and 3 p.m. weekends. The sandwich includes a generous portion of thinly sliced New York-style peppery pastrami, oven-warmed and served (with melted cheese if you're smart) on freshly baked French bread with fries. A quick check of nearby tables reveals the popularity of the seafood plates and sandwiches (with oysters, shrimp, or catfish) as well as the chicken sandwich served with two grilled chicken breasts sautéed in Greek spices.

Central Grocery, 923 Decatur St., New Orleans, LA 70116; (504) 523-1620; Sandwiches; $$. Sitting elbow-to-elbow with locals and tourists alike at one of the two narrow counters in the back of this Tusa family–owned Italian market while munching on a muffuletta sandwich has been a tradition almost from the day this place opened in 1906. Several establishments (including this one) lay claim to being the originator of the popular Italian-bread feast overstuffed with provolone cheese and deli meats and topped with tangy olive salad. Sidestepping the controversy, it's safe to say the mighty muffuletta certainly helped put this enterprise on the map as well as in the hearts of New Orleanians. Don't stop at the sandwiches, though. Floor-to-ceiling shelves are stocked with gallon-sized containers of imported extra-virgin olive oil, balsamic vinegars, anchovy fillets, tins of mackerel and codfish, grape leaves, and other cooking essentials from the Mediterranean.

The Court of Two Sisters, 613 Royal St., New Orleans, LA 70130; (504) 522-7261; www.courtoftwosisters.com; Creole French; $$$. Best loosen your belts and girdles because this perennially popular brunch spot boasts a buffet with more than 60 freshly prepared items that include eggs Benedict, waffles, and omelets (all made while you wait), hot boiled shrimp and crawfish, roast beef, grillades and grits, shrimp and oyster pasta, quiches, ceviche, jambalaya, gumbo, steaming Creole seafood creations, imported cheeses, and desserts—not the least of which are the crepes Suzette and bread pudding in whiskey sauce. A regular a la carte menu is available. Equally as good as the buffet is the ambience of dining in what is hands-down one of the city's most beautiful (and, at night, romantic) courtyards, featuring white-linen tables, quietly flowing fountains, flowering plants, and flickering gaslights, all set under a canopy of wisteria and sycamores. When Charlie Fradella's Sensational Jazz Band strolls by your table, ask them to play "St. James Infirmary"—you won't be disappointed.

Felix's Restaurant and Oyster Bar, 739 Iberville St., New Orleans, LA 70130; (504) 522-4440; www.felixs.com; Seafood; $$.

Although the eating is good, the wait can be long in this 220-seat restaurant that, especially when big conventions are in town, often has lines coming out both the Iberville and Bourbon Street entrances. But don't let that deter you from the chance to savor the freshly shucked bivalves that have made this always-buzzing, half-century-old oyster bar a near-institution among locals and visitors alike. Oyster offerings include raw, Bienville, Rockefeller, en brochette, stewed, fried, broiled, or in an omelette. Other good choices include gumbo, crawfish po-boy, seafood platter, and fried or grilled fish of the day. A full bar features more than a dozen types of beer with which to wash down your "ersters."

Galatoire's, 209 Bourbon St., New Orleans, LA 70130; (504) 525-2021; www.galatoires.com; Creole French; $$$$. If you come for your first time on a Friday afternoon with a local who has his own personal waiter, prepare for a kaleidoscope of New Orleans food and culture the likes of which are rarely duplicated elsewhere in town. For it is during this time when a veritable who's who of fresh-scrubbed debutantes, lawyers in Brooks Brothers suits, politicians, dowagers sporting broad-brimmed hats, and the like, can be seen holding court at various tables. Meantime, waiters pass to and fro with dishes that have made this venue an institution—trout meunière or amandine, escargot bordelaise, Crabmeat Maison, grilled pompano, oysters en brochette, crabmeat canape Lorenzo, and filet béarnaise. Founded in 1905 by French Pyrennes-born Jean Gala-toire, this place has the kind of if-only-the-walls-could-talk cachet that imbues the restaurant with the kind of Old Guard cool best enjoyed with a dining companion who can give you the inside track.

Green Goddess, 307 Exchange Place, New Orleans, LA 70130; (504) 301-3347; www.greengoddessnola.com; Eclectic; $$. We thought we had died and gone to heaven the first time we tasted the pan-fried boudin patty, served with cane syrup and pepper jelly, and the corn-jalapeño pancake topped with smoky pulled pork and barbecue gravy. Ditto for the *muhammara* (a traditional Syrian-Turkish dip of roasted red peppers, walnuts, garlic, and pomegranate sauce served with cooked veggies) and *banh xeo* (a tumeric-flavored Vietnamese rice flour crepe stuffed with crabmeat and avocado and topped with sweet chili garlic sauce). Since opening in 2009, Chefs Paul Artigues and Chris DeBarr have cobbled together a progressive menu seemingly designed for globe-trotters at heart whose palates are open to new twists on earthy, multicultural pleasures executed with aplomb. Grab an outdoor table on the pedestrian thoroughfare of Exchange Place and sink your imagination into the shrimp and grits that come with a side of sweet potato biscuits and pepper jelly, the brilliantly paired seared tuna and water-melon, or the savory Indian lentil pancake with shrimp, bison, and bacon meat loaf—you won't be disappointed. If you're feeling a twinge of wanderlust, you can wash it all down with a glass of Brazilian cashew fruit juice, Thai young-coconut juice, or African coffee berry juice.

Johnny's Po-Boys, 511 St. Louis St., New Orleans, LA 70130; (504) 524-8129; http://johnnyspoboy.com; Sandwiches; $–$$. A French Quarter institution since 1950, Johnny's is the oldest family-owned po-boy restaurant in the city and, without a doubt, the best place to get po-boys in the Vieux Carre. Rated by *Good House-keeping* magazine as one of the "100 great values for your money" restaurants in the country, Johnny's serves more than 45 varieties of po-boys as well as breakfast (till noon), home-style hot lunches, seafood, gumbo, and salads. Try the hot roast beef po-boy, a specialty of the house, which is always delicious (and don't forget to ask for lots of gravy). The seafood platter is also a winner. Johnny's serves breakfast and lunch every day, and only accepts cash.

K-Paul's Louisiana Kitchen, 416 Chartres St., New Orleans, LA 70130; (504) 596-2530; www.chefpaul.com; Cajun; $$$. As the man credited with inventing blackened redfish and spreading the culture of Cajun food throughout the United States beginning back in the 1980s, Chef Paul Prudhomme over the decades has become not only a beloved icon of the local dining scene but also an ambassador of the centuries-old culinary traditions for which southeast Louisiana is deservedly famous. Typically crowded with tourists but always well worth the wait, this 200-seat venue, housed in an extensively renovated and restored 1834 building, is a daily showcase for excellent preparations of many now-familiar dishes that only years ago were literally unheard of outside Louisiana. Prime examples include classic Cajun-style jambalaya, crawfish étouffée, and blackened Louisiana drum. An especially good nouvelle-Cajun dish is the blackened stuffed pork chops, which are stuffed with ricotta, asiago, mozzarella, and caciocavello cheese and fresh basil, and served with a marchand de vin sauce of prosciutto ham, red wine, and mushrooms. Save room for the sumptuous sweet potato pecan pie served with Chantilly cream.

Port of Call, 838 Esplanade Ave., New Orleans, LA 70116; (504) 523-0120; www.portofcallneworleans.com; Sandwiches; $$. For as long as anyone can remember, this lively, dimly lit corner restaurant has been the place to drop anchor for one of the biggest and juiciest hamburgers in town. These plump, half-pound treasures, ground fresh daily, arrive hot on a toasted sesame seed bun. By the time you've added the lettuce, pickles, and thick slices of onion and tomato served on the side, using a knife and fork makes pretty good sense. The baked potato that comes with the burgers is almost a meal in itself, especially if you order it with the works. Steaks and specialty house drinks such as the Windjammer, a blend of tropical juices mixed with two kinds of rum, and the Bahamian-style Goombay Punch round out the menu. During weekends the bar near the front door is usually crowded with people waiting for tables. The rope fishing nets hanging from the ceiling and an oldies-playing jukebox add to the entertaining atmosphere of this popular eatery.

The Rib Room, 621 St. Louis St., New Orleans, LA 70130; (504) 529-7046; www.ribroomneworleans.com; American; $$$. The heady aromas wafting from the French rotisserie that dominates the back of the dining room are proof you have arrived at a *palais du boeuf* nonpareil. For generations the city's politicians, lawyers, and art dealers have made this French Quarter dining den on the ground floor of the Omni Royal Orleans Hotel a lunchtime favorite. And Chef Anthony Spizale's prime rib and selection of rotisserie classics such as the chateaubriand, roti-assorti (English-cut prime rib, loin pork chop, and grilled lamb sausage), filet mignon, and lamb T-bone steaks seasoned with fresh herbs will tell you why. Elegant 20-foot ceilings, exposed brick, gracious arches, and cypress barge-board walls from 19th-century keel boats set the stage for fine dining. At night when the lights are turned down, the ambience changes from power-lunch buzz to pure hushed-tone romance. (Tip: reserve a table overlooking Royal Street.) The menu stays the same with the addition of a few noteworthy seafood creations such as the blackened Atlantic salmon.

Tujague's, 823 Decatur St., New Orleans, LA 70116; (504) 525-8676; www.tujaguesrestaurant.com; Creole; $$$. Politicians, artists, and travelers still rub elbows around the 1849 cypress bar—the oldest standing bar in the city and a classic in every sense of the word. In 1982 the Latter family bought the restaurant, which opened in 1856, making it the second oldest in the city, but the six-course-only, table d'hote menu for which the establishment is known is still built around such longtime staples as shrimp remoulade, beef brisket, filet mignon, and fresh seafood. While Tujague's can never be accused of impulsive innovation, patrons today have their choice of several desserts including bread pudding and pecan pie. Lunch at this landmark is a far less fussy way to experience the ambience. Order the chicken and andouille pasta.

Learn to Cook

The New Orleans Cooking Experience, 2275 Bayou Road, New Orleans, LA 70119; (504) 945-9104; www.neworleanscookingexperience.com. The New Orleans Cooking Experience offers a wide variety of classes in its kitchen at the House on Bayou Road, a restored 18th-century home located in the Esplanade Ridge neighborhood. Half-day classes, which include the preparation of and dining on a four-course meal, are limited to 10 students and start at $150/ per person (all-inclusive). Also in the offing are immersion classes, given over two, three, or four days, as well as short- and long-weekend programs. Private classes are also offered, and group discounts are available.

The New Orleans School of Cooking, 524 St. Louis St., New Orleans, LA 70130; (504) 525-2665; www.neworleansschoolof cooking.com. The New Orleans School of Cooking, housed in a renovated early-19th-century molasses warehouse in the French Quarter, offers a variety of classes to teach the preparation of such Creole and Cajun specialties as gumbo, jambalaya, shrimp Creole, and pralines. There are two-and-a-half-hour classes most mornings, open to individual registration, which include preparation and "generous sampling" of four items. Private demonstrations, hands-on classes, and off-site programs are also available.

Ruby Slippers Nola: A Culinary Journey, 1129 St. Philip St., New Orleans, LA 70116; (504) 616-4089; www.rubyslippersnola .com. The focus of the customized cooking classes conducted by New Orleans cookbook author Amy Sins is the creation of more sophisticated New Orleans and regional meals "perfect for wowing guests at your next dinner party." Sample dishes include andouille-crusted Gulf fish, crabmeat or crawfish cheesecake, and caramelized garlic soup with lump crabmeat and andouille. Group classes are conducted at Sins' French Quarter B&B, the New Orleans Jazz Quarters, or off-site. Both demonstration and hands-on classes are available and can include grocery shopping with Sins to learn how to choose the best ingredients. Two- to three-hour classes start at $45 per person, plus the cost of ingredients.

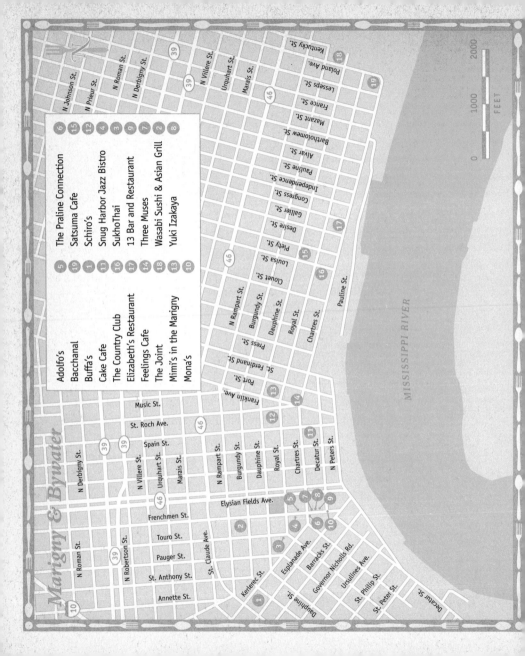

Marigny & Bywater

MISSISSIPPI RIVER

N

FEET
0   1000   2000

Legend

5 Adolfo's
19 Bacchanal
1 Buffa's
11 Cake Cafe
16 The Country Club
17 Elizabeth's Restaurant
14 Feelings Cafe
18 The Joint
13 Mimi's in the Marigny
10 Mona's
6 The Praline Connection
15 Satsuma Cafe
12 Schiro's
4 Snug Harbor Jazz Bistro
3 SukhoThai
9 13 Bar and Restaurant
7 Three Muses
2 Wasabi Sushi & Asian Grill
8 Yuki Izakaya

Streets

N Johnson St.
N Prieur St.
N Roman St.
N Derbigny St.
N Villere St.
Urquhart St.
Marais St.
France St.
Lesseps St.
Mazant St.
Bartholomew St.
Alvar St.
Pauline St.
Independence St.
Congress St.
Gallier St.
Desire St.
Piety St.
Louisa St.
Clouet St.
N Rampart St.
Burgundy St.
Dauphine St.
Royal St.
Chartres St.
Press St.
St. Ferdinand St.
Port St.
Franklin Ave.
Pauline St.
Kentucky St.
Poland Ave.

Music St.
St. Roch Ave.
Spain St.
N Roman St.
N Derbigny St.
N Villere St.
Urquhart St.
Marais St.
N Rampart St.
Burgundy St.
Dauphine St.
Royal St.
Chartres St.
Decatur St.
N Peters St.
N Robertson St.
Frenchmen St.
Touro St.
Pauger St.
St. Anthony St.
Annette St.
St. Claude Ave.
Elysian Fields Ave.
Kerlerec St.
Esplanade Ave.
Barracks St.
Governor Nicholls Rd.
Dauphine St.
Ursulines Ave.
St. Philip St.
St. Peter St.
Decatur St.

Marigny & Bywater

Faubourg Marigny is the French Quarter's next-door neighbor, just downriver. Founded in 1805, the Marigny was the city's first suburb. It's not quite as old as the Quarter, but not quite as expensive either. In fact, the Marigny renaissance, which has resulted in a community full of beautifully restored homes, was started about 30 years ago by folks who found themselves priced out of the Vieux Carre. Today, the Marigny triangle (the part immediately adjacent to the French Quarter) is home to the city's premier live music district, Frenchmen Street. Most of the Marigny restaurants are on or near Frenchmen. A few others are found on corners a little farther in, tucked between the neighborhood's many bed-and-breakfast inns. Continuing downriver, we come to Bywater. It's a little more funky, a little less gentrified. The Marigny and Bywater are both home to many artists and musicians, and, as you'll find, some pretty terrific restaurants.

Adolfo's, 611 Frenchmen St., New Orleans, LA 70116; (504) 948-3800; Creole Italian; $$. It may be a little hard to find this intimate Creole Italian restaurant, but it's worth the effort. Look for a small sign outside the Apple Barrel bar. Upstairs, you'll find a funky little place to coat your stomach with an early dinner before hitting the Frenchmen Street music clubs in Faubourg Marigny. This Creole Italian restaurant serves dinner only and doesn't take reservations, so show up early (around 6 p.m. is recommended) for the best service. The atmosphere is casual and friendly; the food is satisfying. Try the escargot, the signature rack of lamb, or any of the fish dishes with ocean sauce. Note that Adolfo's is located in an old building at the top of a pretty steep set of stairs and is not wheelchair accessible. They are also cash only, but there's an ATM.

Bacchanal, 600 Poland Ave., New Orleans, LA 70117; (504) 948-9111; www.bacchanalwine.com; Deli & More; $$. Actually, calling Bacchanal a deli is like calling Allen Toussaint a piano player. If you're willing to go way off the beaten tourist path, Bacchanal is a place where you can really relax into the local groove. But take a cab, because unless the sandwich board announcing lunch is out, it's easy to miss the unadorned brick and what's-left-of-the-plaster building. Inside, there's an excellent wine shop and a gourmet deli. But out back, there's an old New Orleans-style courtyard where there's live music every night and a local chef cooking on the grill almost every night. Sit and sip your wine, feel the balmy breeze on your skin, smell the heady aroma coming from the grill, and listen to the live local music. You may never go home.

Buffa's, 1001 Esplanade Ave., New Orleans, LA 70116; (504) 949-0038; http://buffaslounge.com; Neighborhood Cafe; $. This is basically a neighborhood corner bar on the Faubourg Marigny side of Esplanade Avenue (a block before Rampart). But it comes into play when someone sends you to Port of Call for great burgers and you arrive to find a line out the door (which there always is). Cross the street and walk down a block to Buffa's, where you'll find a welcoming attitude and burgers just as good. The spicy black bean vegan burger is also good, and order the fries with either one. You'll be glad you did. Breakfast is served from 2 a.m. to noon. Ask to be seated in the back room if the smokiness of the bar bothers you while you're eating. Buffa's is now open 24 hours and has started accepting credit cards.

Cake Cafe, 2440 Chartres St., New Orleans, LA 70117; (504) 943-0010; www.nolacakes.com; Neighborhood Cafe; $. Officially known as the New Orleans Cake Cafe and Bakery, this cozy little restaurant can be found 3 blocks on the downriver side of Elysian Fields Avenue in the Marigny. A breakfast and lunch spot as well as a full bakery, Cake Cafe serves, hands down, the best bagels in New Orleans. Everything is made fresh here by the friendly staff and owner Steve Himelfarb, who is known locally as The Cake Man. Try the shrimp and grits with a big homemade biscuit, the plump fried oysters and eggs on a bed of organic grits, or the crab sandwich with fresh locally caught crab, bacon, and brie. And don't forget dessert. There's always a variety of pastries (such as pear and goat cheese Danish) or try a red velvet cupcake with cream cheese icing, which is only a buck with a meal. Outdoor dining is available. See Chef Himelfarb's recipe for **Roasted Tomato & Watermelon Gazpacho** on p. 258.

The Country Club, 634 Louisa St., New Orleans, LA 70117; (504) 945-0742; www.thecountryclubneworleans.com; Eclectic; $$. The name of this Bywater facility can be misleading, as can be its façade, which looks like a well-preserved historic home with its traditional yellow paint and colonnaded front porch. It's actually a terrific restaurant with a pool area out back. The casually elegant eatery is gay-friendly, but all are welcome to enjoy its eclectic menu influenced by Creole, Cajun, and Southern culinary traditions. Try the andouille/cornbread-stuffed pork loin, glazed with cane syrup and Creole mustard, or a grilled fennel and beet salad with arugula, spiced pecans, Stilton bleu cheese, and a warm tasso vinaigrette. The mac and cheese made with smoked Gouda is a popular side. Diners can also eat alfresco either on the wide front porch or out back by the pool. Be forewarned, though, the pool area is clothing optional.

Elizabeth's Restaurant, 601 Gallier St., New Orleans, LA 70117; (504) 944-9272; www.elizabeths-restaurant.com; Breakfast; $. Breakfast, lunch, and dinner draw a loyal fan base from throughout the New Orleans area, but it's during weekend brunches when customers likely have to wait for a table inside this cozy bohemian haunt. And it's time well spent. Halfway into one of the house specialty eye-openers like the Bywater Crutch (gin, Cointreau, B&B, orange juice, and dash of grenadine), deciding on your appetizer and entree becomes a little easier. Among the best starters are the fried grit cakes with tasso gravy, fried chicken livers with pepper jelly, and seafood-stuffed mirliton with green onion sauce. A couple of near-genius if not always satisfying entrees include the duck waffle (sweet potato and duck hash on a corn bread waffle with pepper jelly), French toast stuffed with strawberry cream cheese, and smoked salmon with grilled Brie. No meal is complete without a side of maple bacon.

Feelings Cafe, 2600 Chartres St., New Orleans, LA 70117; (504) 945-2222; www.feelingscafe.com; Creole; $$–$$$. The tropically lush, romantic courtyard, crumbling with history and serving as the restaurant's bar, has been a favorite among locals for years. For an untouristed spot in which to unwind with pre-dinner cocktails, it has few equals. The restaurant is located in the former D'Aunoy Plantation. Dating to 1795, it is one of the oldest buildings in the

Faubourg Marigny. Guests can dine downstairs in the main dining room adjacent to the bar. Or, for an extra touch of romance, when making reservations request one of the candlelit tables on the second-floor balcony that overlooks the courtyard. Try the Gulf Fish Nicholas, a fresh grilled fillet, brushed with Dijon mustard, topped with grilled shrimp, and served on a bed of creamed spinach, or the Seafood Baked Eggplant featuring shrimp, crab, and crawfish blended with sausage and dirty rice over fried eggplant and topped with hollandaise. Feelings is only open for Sunday brunch and dinner Thu through Sun. So, reservations are recommended.

The Joint, 801 Poland Ave., New Orleans, LA 70117; (504) 949-3232; www.alwayssmokin.com; Barbecue; $–$$. If you're in the mood for meat, barbecue just doesn't get much better than it is at this funky Bywater eatery. And locals aren't the only ones who've noticed. The Joint was listed among the Top 10 New Barbecue Restaurants by *Bon Appetit* magazine. There's nothing fancy here—just happy diners sitting on benches and enjoying the juiciest slow-

cooked ribs, beef brisket, pulled pork, and chicken—all to be finished with either of two types of barbecue sauce or both, if you like. Or try the sausage sandwich made with Chaurice, a local Cajun sausage, smoked on-site. Down-home sides include potato salad, baked beans, coleslaw, and green salad with smoked tomato and onion dressing. The Joint is now open for lunch and dinner Mon through Sat.

Mimi's in the Marigny, 2601 Royal St., New Orleans, LA 70117; (504) 872-9868; myspace.com/mimisinthemarigny; Tapas; $–$$. If you're heading out for the night and you're not sure if you want to just have drinks, eat, or go dancing, try this slightly off-the-beaten-path Marigny haunt where you can do all three. Mimi's in the Marigny is one of those cool New Orleans kinds of places where you can hang out with locals and nobody's worried about heading home early. Downstairs is a laid-back pool-table-and-couches neighborhood bar that stays open till the wee hours and features quite respectable wine and beer lists. Upstairs is the place to dance the night away and eat some unexpectedly good tapas, which are served late into the night. The tapas are reasonably priced, especially for the quality. Try the scallops, the beef-filled empanadas, or the calamari with chorizo. For a really good time, enjoy the tapas on Saturday and Sunday nights when DJ Soul Sister spins vinyl and the party really gets going.

Mona's Cafe, 504 Frenchmen St., New Orleans, LA 70116; (504) 949-4115; www.faubourgmarigny.org; Mediterranean; $–$$. If it's traditional Mediterranean fare you're hankering for, the no-hassle Faubourg Marigny location of this popular local chain, which started in Mid-City, is the place to go. The restaurant is open every day for lunch and dinner. Especially good are the falafel, chicken kabob, gyros, and the vegetarian plate. The staff is friendly and the restaurant is easily wheelchair accessible. There's no need for reservations, and while there, visitors can shop the small store for good prices on jars of capers, bags of chickpeas, and even a hookah.

Snowballs in the Big Easy

Some historians believe the first-ever snowballs were created by the Romans, who added syrup to snow hauled to town from mountains. But most agree that it wasn't until the early 1930s, when New Orleanian Ernest Hansen invented and patented the first motorized ice-block shaver, that high-volume production of the frozen treat really took off—and into the eager mouths of locals hungry for a cool treat during summertime months. In New Orleans more often than not the thinly shaved-ice delicacy is spelled "sno-ball" or "snoball," without the "w," or sometimes "snowball," both of which distinguish the local version from its crudely chipped-ice cousin best known as the snowcone. Either way, it's been a staple of this city since the early 1930s and today, generations later, is still beloved by old and young alike.

There are literally dozens of snowball stands located throughout the metropolitan area from which to choose. Many locations boast "specialties" like homemade chocolate syrup flavoring or a condensed milk topping. Expect lines on busy summer days, but it's always worth the wait.

Following are but a few locals' faves:

In the suburb of Metairie is a pair of popular longtime establishments—**Sal's Sno-Balls,** 1823 Metairie Rd., Metairie, LA 70005; (504) 566-1823; and **Casey's Snowballs,** 4608 W. Esplanade Ave., Metairie, LA 70006; (504) 888-3920. A late-night joint open until 10:30, Sal's, opened in 1960, is popular among residents of Old Metairie who bring their kids to enjoy snowballs while sitting on logs—a family tradition for decades. Casey's, meantime, is a blue-brick structure tucked near a busy corner intersection, which boasts a nice list of sundaes, yogurt, and shakes in addition to the customary lengthy roster of snowball flavors.

Pandora's Snowballs, 901 N. Carrollton Ave., New Orleans, LA 70119; (504) 486-8644; caters mostly to New Orleans' Mid-City community of Bayou St. John, but like many snowball stands this one, opened in the 1970s, draws loyal customers from all over town.

Tucked amid a tree-shaded residential street in New Orleans' Carrollton neighborhood is beloved **Williams Plum Street Snoballs,** opened in 1931 and located at 1300 Burdette St., New Orleans, LA 70118; (504) 866-7996; www.plumstreetsnoball.com. This spot is known for serving the shaved-ice treat in Chinese food take-out boxes (wrapped in small plastic bags to avoid dripping), which presumably makes it easy to use larger spoons for larger mouthfuls of the snowball. A relative new kid on the block, opened in 1987, is **SnoWizard SnoBall Shoppe,** 4001 Magazine St., New Orleans, LA 70115; (504) 899-8758. The corner take-out stand offers a few sitting areas for customers to enjoy their snowballs outside.

If **Hansen's Sno-Bliz,** founded in 1939, has a special claim to fame, it's that it has on display the first snowball machine Sno-Bliz inventor Ernest Hansen ever created back in the early 1930s. Located at 4801 Tchoupitoulas St., New Orleans, LA 70115; (504) 891-9788; www.snobliz.com; this perennially popular spot is always abuzz with customers eager to sample the traditional treat from one of the two oldest snowball stands in town (the other being Williams Plum Street Snoballs).

Other locations include the original Mona's at 3901 Banks St. in Mid-City, (504) 482-7743; 1120 S. Carrollton Ave. in Carrollton, (504) 861-8175; and 4126 Magazine St., Uptown, (504) 894-9800.

The Praline Connection, 542 Frenchmen St., New Orleans, LA 70116; (504) 943-3934; www.pralineconnection.com; Creole Soul Food; $$. Walk into this intimate Faubourg Marigny restaurant with its stainless-steel ceiling fans, black-and-white tile floor, and a waitstaff adorned in flashy ties and fedoras, and one word comes to mind: slick. No doubt, this Creole soul food restaurant is one of the coolest places you'll ever eat in. And will you be glad you did. The fried chicken is crispy and delicious, and the filé gumbo is hearty and satisfying. Most meals include melt-in-your-mouth corn bread. Other best bets include barbecued ribs, hot chicken wings, and soft-shell crabs in this casual yet bustling setting populated with a mix of locals and tourists. No reservations are accepted; lunch and dinner served daily. To avoid the biggest crowds in this small dining room, take in a late lunch or early dinner. On your way out, stop in the adjacent candy shop to stock up on pralines and other goodies for the trip home.

Satsuma Cafe, 3218 Dauphine St., New Orleans, LA 70117; (504) 304-5962; http://satsumacafe.com; Breakfast & Lunch; $. With its high ceilings, exposed brick walls, and artsy-clutter decor, Satsuma is basically a coffee shop that serves simple breakfasts, sandwiches, and salads. But Peter and Cassi Dymond, owners of this Bywater spot, go to the trouble of using fresh ingredients from local farmers. Because of the seasonal ingredients, the menu changes, but the beet and strawberry salad with roasted beets, sliced strawberries, crumbled goat cheese, arugula, and toasted walnuts with walnut vinaigrette dressing is a good example of the offerings. A good breakfast menu bet is the One-Eyed Jack—a fried egg in toast, topped with avocado and hot sauce. Open for breakfast and lunch every day, Satsuma also offers fresh-squeezed organic juices with various combinations of orange, grapefruit, fennel, apple, carrot, celery, kale, and cucumber. And there's free Wi-Fi.

Schiro's, 2483 Royal St., New Orleans, LA 70117; (504) 945-4425; www.schiroscafe.com; Creole/Indian; $–$$. Schiro's is sort of the food and beverage version of a one-man band. It's a cafe serving New Orleans and Indian food, plus breakfast on the weekends. It's a neighborhood corner bar. It's a small grocery featuring, but not limited to, a good selection of beer and alcohol. It's also a Laundromat. And that's just the first floor. Upstairs is a bed-and-breakfast inn with five guest rooms. (Imagine what their business card must look like.) The cafe features po-boy sandwiches and fried seafood, as well as vindaloo and traditional chicken curry. There are also daily specials, such as red beans and rice, and spaghetti and meatballs. The weekend breakfast menu ranges from oatmeal and fruit to a rib eye and eggs. What can I say? Eventually, everybody needs something at Schiro's.

Snug Harbor Jazz Bistro, 626 Frenchmen St., New Orleans, LA 70116; (504) 949-0696; www.snugjazz.com; Creole/Steakhouse; $–$$$. Snug Harbor is first and foremost a contemporary jazz club. In fact, it was the first one that started the whole Frenchmen Street as the center of the local music scene 30 years ago. But if you're lucky enough to be going to a show there (and if you can, you should), you can also get a bite first. The menu features traditional New Orleans favorites, such as shrimp remoulade, gumbo, and a fried oyster platter. If you want to go all out, there's an aged Angus New York strip or filet mignon. On the other end, there are sandwiches and burgers in the $10 range. The dining room opens nightly at 5. And if you have show tickets, it's better to make reservations for dinner, just to be sure you don't miss anything.

SukhoThai, 1913 Royal St., New Orleans, LA 70116; (504) 948-9309; www.sukhothai-nola.com; Thai; $$. If the local Cajun food isn't hot enough for you, step into SukhoThai. Patrons can order the spice level of their food as mild, medium, hot, or Thai hot at this elegant restaurant featuring authentic Thai cuisine. Try the shrimp with plum dipping sauce or the seafood clay pot, as well as a number of vegetarian dishes. Portions are generous. One appetizer and an entree can easily feed two people. The restaurant, open for lunch and dinner Tues through Sun, is perfect for a romantic date-night dinner before going to listen to music on Frenchmen Street. And if you're staying in the Marigny or the French Quarter and feel like eating in, they deliver. A second location is at 4519 Magazine St., Uptown, (504) 373-6471.

13 Bar and Restaurant, 517 Frenchmen St., New Orleans, LA 70116; (504) 942-1345; Neighborhood Cafe; $. Open every night until 4 a.m., this is a good spot to find late-night food when club-hopping on Frenchmen Street. The menu is full of good "drinking" food—the three-egg frittata, pizza, sandwiches, and lots of vegetarian-friendly choices—all very well priced. Try the pulled pork sandwich or the turkey, bacon, and provolone on po-boy bread. On the vegetarian side, best bets include the barbecue tofu sandwich and the portobello mushroom sandwich with roasted red pepper sauce. Especially popular with the late-night crowd is the crispy baked Tater Tots covered in melted cheese, jalapeños, salsa, black beans, and sour cream, referred to by locals as "tachos."

Three Muses, 536 Frenchmen St., New Orleans, LA 70116; (504) 298-8746; www.thethreemuses.com; Eclectic; $$. Three Muses is a music club, bar, and restaurant—all in the same small room. The atmosphere is casual and the crowd is very friendly, partly because they have to be. There's not much sense of personal space once the diners, the drinkers, and those who just came to hear music all show up. But if you relax into it, it just all kind of works. Everybody orders at the bar, and the menu, which regularly changes, is made up of a variety of mostly tapas-size dishes (which is good, because there's really no room for big meals in here). Best bets include the lamb sliders (we ordered seconds last time) and the duck confit spring rolls with hoisin plum sauce. If you're not into crowds, go when they start serving dinner at 5 nightly (closed Tues, though). Or go for happy hour at 4, and maybe by the time the crowds get there, you won't mind.

Wasabi Sushi & Asian Grill, 900 Frenchmen St., New Orleans, LA 70116; (504) 943-9433; http://wasabinola.com; Sushi; $$. Wasabi Sushi & Asian Grill serves expertly prepared authentic Japanese food. The service is always cordial, the decor tasteful, and the dining room a peaceful place to enjoy good food and quiet conversation. The extensive menu features a number of traditional, popular American and vegetarian dishes. Try the shrimp tempura, beef and asparagus maki, or fried tofu from the appetizer menu. The sushi and sashimi are consistently fresh and beautifully presented. A favorite is the baby soft-shell crab sushi. And don't forget the perfect complement to your meal—either a cold Japanese beer or nice warm sake. The restaurant is open for lunch and dinner daily and there's a second location at 8550 Pontchartrain Blvd. at West End, near the New Orleans lakefront (504-267-3263).

Yuki Izakaya, 525 Frenchmen St., New Orleans, LA 70116; (504) 943-1122; www.myspace.com/yukiizakaya; Japanese tapas; $$.

This modern Japanese izakaya (tavern) is a relative newcomer to the Frenchmen Street scene, but certainly an interesting addition. Here visitors will find a different vibe than most of what surrounds it. Yuki has its own take on the music club scene. The walls of the cozy and mellow tavern are adorned with old Japanese posters, and Japanese movies are sometimes silently projected on the wall. A variety of live music can be heard. Open dinner hours only, Yuki doesn't serve sushi, but there's an excellent sake menu, complemented by elegantly prepared Japanese tapas, including *shumai* crab dumplings, *shichimi* peppered french fries with wasabi mayonnaise, and, if you're brave enough, *maguro natto*, which is a very traditionally prepared tuna with fermented soybeans. The menu warns that "due to its powerful smell and spider's web consistency it can be an acquired taste."

Downtown & Central Business District

Bambu Asian Grille & Sushi Bar	14	Liborio Cuban Restaurant	8
Besh Steak	15	Lüke	7
Bon Ton Cafe	11	MiLa	2
Cafe Adelaide	17	Morton's the Steakhouse	6
Domenica	1	Mother's	16
Drago's	20	Rambla	5
The Grill Room	13	Restaurant August	12
Herbsaint	18	Ruby Slipper Cafe	9
Horinoya	10	Ruth's Chris Steakhouse	19
Le Foret	4	The Store	3

MISSISSIPPI RIVER

Bienville St.
Canal St.
Basin St.
Iberville St.
Cleveland Ave.
N Rampart St.
Burgundy St.
Dauphine St.
Loyola Ave.
Common St.
Gravier St.
Clay St.
N Front Blvd.
Union St.
Canal St.
S Rampart St.
Perdido St.
Picayune Pl.
Iberville St.
Penn St.
Canal St.
Poydras St.
Natchez St.
N Maestri St.
Lafayette St.
Constance St.
S Maestri St.
O'Keefe Ave
Girod St.
Baronne St.
Lafayette St.
St. Charles Ave.
Church St.
Julia St.
Carondelet St.
Notre Dame St.
Howard Ave.
Camp St.
Convention Center Blvd.
Baronne St.
St Joseph St.
Magazine St.
Constance St.
Tchoupitoulas St.
Commerce St.
Peters St.
Fulton St.

0   500   1000

FEET

90

N

Downtown & Central Business District

Petula Clark's 1960's song "Downtown" implores us to "listen to the music of the traffic in the city." And what sweet music it is indeed for those of us urban animals for whom the bright lights of tall buildings tucked between Canal and Poydras Streets, Loyola Avenue, and Convention Center Boulevard are a veritable big-city playground for romance and the promise of nighttime dining adventures still to be discovered. Whether your palate leads you to the CBD for a lunchtime repast of redfish courtbouillon at a French bistro or a sizzling-in-butter rib eye at a cherished chophouse, chances are it will be your after-dark heart that guides you—and, hopefully, someone you know really well—to some of this enclave's best-known dinner retreats. What could be better than exchanging glances with your inamorata over shrimp and tasso "corndogs" at one of the city's newest (and hippest) dining dens? Like the song says, "You're gonna be all right now."

Foodie Faves

Bambu Asian Grille & Sushi Bar, Harrah's Casino, 8 Canal St., New Orleans, LA 70130; (504) 525-3689; www.harrahsnew orleans.com; Pan-Asian; $$–$$$. Veteran Chef Philip Chan's latest restaurant, located inside Harrah's Casino (near the Canal Street entrance), serves Japanese, Chinese, Vietnamese, and Thai dishes in a casually elegant dining room featuring lots of backlighting and displays of Asian pottery. Look for Cantonese barbecue roast duck, traditional Pad Thai, Vietnamese clay pot fish, and the teriyaki rib eye steak. But start with the excellent chicken with pine nuts appetizer or the pan-fried oysters. Bambu is open every day for lunch and dinner, and sitting within its cocoon of water features and bamboo is a great way to find a little respite from the casino floor's bells and blinking lights.

Besh Steak, 8 Canal St., New Orleans, LA 70130; (504) 533-6111; www.harrahsneworleans.com; Steak house; $$$$. This venue tucked inside Harrah's New Orleans casino will rock your world with appetizers alone. Your first bite of Crabmeat Maison with caviar (part of a dish called Louisiana Seafood 3 Ways that also includes shrimp remoulade and fried oysters with blue cheese dressing) will make you realize that, yes, there are still new and exciting ways of turning out traditional Louisiana seafood. Jump to the equally creative pork belly spring rolls with sweet chili dipping sauce. Such imaginative cuisine seems to always be springing from the culinary mind of local superstar Chef John Besh. With an airy dining room dripping with a clubby, cosmopolitan vibe, this is no run-of-the-mill steak house. In fact, since it opened in 1993, this spot has helped make Harrah's a destination for non-gamblers who enjoy the special spin Besh gives this venue's best bet—steak. Even if you're not hungry enough—nor ever will be—for the 48-ounce beef porterhouse, there are plenty of other options such as the cast-iron roast rib eye, bacon-wrapped wild boar (with sweet and spicy fig sauce over grits), and prime New York strip.

Bon Ton Cafe, 401 Magazine St., New Orleans, LA 70130; (504) 524-3386; www.thebontoncafe.com; Cajun; $$$. Local dining connoisseurs first discovered this casual restaurant when it originally opened in the early 1900s. It closed for a spell only to be reopened in the 1950s by Al and Alzine Pierce when they arrived in New Orleans from their bayou home in south Louisiana. Like many Acadian restaurateurs who have set up shop in the Big Easy over the decades, they brought their family recipes with them. Today the Pierces' nephew, Wayne, and his wife,

Debbie, continue the family tradition of authentic Cajun cookery in the historic 1840s Natchez building. Amid a decor of red-and-white checkered tablecloths, wrought-iron chandeliers, shuttered window blinds, and exposed brick walls, guests will find many time-honed Bon Ton creations: crawfish étouffée, shrimp and crab okra gumbo, turtle soup, pan-fried oysters, shrimp étouffée, shrimp jambalaya, and fresh Gulf fish fillet topped with grilled Louisiana oysters. Truth be told, locals have a soft spot in their hearts for this don't-miss dining destination.

Cafe Adelaide, 300 Poydras St., New Orleans, LA 70130; (504) 595-3305; www.cafeadelaide.com; Contemporary Creole; $$. This newest member of the city's acclaimed Brennan family restaurant empire was named in honor of Adelaide Brennan, who is remembered by younger Brennans as glamorous and who "squeezed more fun out of life" than virtually anyone around. This venue, located in the Lowe's New Orleans Hotel, lives up to the name and the legend with the Adelaide Swizzle, a cocktail of New Orleans rum, lime juice, bitters, a splash of soda, and "a secret ingredient." Don't-miss dishes include the shrimp and tasso "corndogs" served with pepper jelly and hot sauce, mushroom and arugula flatbread with shaved Manchego cheese and marjoram, and the *foie gras* pontine that arrives with potato-crusted onion rings and black pepper *foie gras* gravy. Chef Chris Lusk doesn't drop the ball with entrees either as measured by his commanding versions of Muscovy duck (cured in Parmesan and served with balsamic-smoked duck bacon), and shrimp and grits that combines dried shrimp–crusted shrimp and grilled oregano red grits with absinthe-basil *beurre vert*.

Domenica, 123 Baronne St., New Orleans, LA 70112; (504) 648-6020; www.domenicarestaurant.com; Italian; $$$. Imagine an Italian restaurant that serves what many claim is the best pizza in town and whose Jewish Chef Alon Shaya offers guests Passover-, Rosh Hashana- and Chanukah-inspired menus during those times of the year. Now you can begin to understand why this most atypical venue, located inside the renovated and historic Roosevelt Hotel, has been winning over locals' palates almost from day one. This particular John Besh restaurant (see also **Besh Steak** [see p. 76], **American Sector** [see p. 92], **La Provence** [see p. 231], **Lüke** [see p. 83], and **Restaurant August** [see p. 86]) offers patrons a large selection of gourmet pizzas (try either that spicy lamb meatball with ricotta or the roast pork shoulder with fennel, apples, and bacon to see what all the fuss is about), as well as a large selection of antipasti, cured meats and hams, and heartier dishes including short ribs and grilled redfish. Colorful art-work hanging on the walls pops like crazy in this venue decorated in heavy dark colors.

Drago's, 2 Poydras St., New Orleans, LA 70130; (504) 584-3911; www.dragosrestaurant.com; Seafood; $$. For a full description, please see the Metairie, Kenner, Harahan & River Ridge listing, p. 201.

Herbsaint, 701 St. Charles Ave., New Orleans, LA 70130; (504) 524-4114; www.herbsaint.com; Creole French; $$$. It came as little surprise for most New Orleanians when rising superstar Chef Donald Link brought home the 2007 James Beard Winner for Best Chef, South. This considering his growing restaurant empire includes not only this venue but also **Cochon** (see p. 93) and its 'round-the-corner, kissing-cousin deli **Cochon Butcher** (see p. 94). Maybe it's all the time he spent working in West Coast kitchens as well as this city's **Bayona** (see Bayona, French Quarter, p. 46), but the distinctly intuitive, cosmopolitan touch he lends to classic and contemporary dishes like Muscovy duck leg confit, steak and frites, and slow-cooked lamb neck with bacon-braised borlotti beans and onion confit, is nothing short of masterful. Dinner isn't the only good excuse to come here. Sitting at one of the white-linen sidewalk tables on a blissful spring or autumn afternoon for a lunch of tapas-size, cornmeal-fried Louisiana oysters, shrimp and grits, mussels and french fries, or a roasted duck sandwich on wheat toast with Seville-style orange mustard, is simply not to be missed.

Horinoya, 920 Poydras St., New Orleans, LA 70112; (504) 561-8914; Japanese; $$. Among the best things about this Japanese restaurant is its location: Poydras Street, which means it's within easy walking distance for downtown lunchtime workers who need to satisfy their barbecue eel craving—and fast. What many of us also like is the authenticity of the dishes and no-compromise philosophy when it comes to freshness, especially as it pertains to fish. This means diners are in for that melt-in-your-mouth, near-buttery texture of their favorite salmon and Toro tuna sashimi, sushi, and sushi rolls, as well as virtually anything else raw they order. Even the cucumber-seaweed salad is so fresh it tastes like it came straight from the garden (and sea) to the table. Hard-to-find items like *mochi* (Japanese rice cakes made of glutinous rice pounded into paste and molded into shape) and monkfish liver make this venue a hands-down favorite among those who have traveled in or lived in Japan and are looking for the real deal.

Le Foret, 129 Camp St., New Orleans, LA 70130; (504) 553-6738; www.leforetneworleans.com; French; $$$. A spectacularly elegant corner dining room with floor-to-ceiling windows offers views of the Central Business District during lunch and at night is transformed into a romantic candlelit venue (right down to the Italian china) perfect for the French dishes that comprise the majority of the truly noteworthy menu. Located in a 170-year-old building, the restaurant received a top-to-bottom renovation prior to its opening in 2009 and today shines brightly with starters like crispy veal sweetbreads. Although the list of seasonal entrees rarely exceeds eight to 10 dishes, patrons can expect nothing short of culinary magnificence on their plates if they ordered the roasted raisin-stuffed rabbit loin and herbed rack, the roasted saddle of prime lamb, or the Moulard duckling with duck frickadelles. A recent meal found the wild mushroom and goat cheese ravioli (served with porcini cream, oysters, and Japanese *maitake* and *shimeji* mushrooms) simply delicious and a virtually perfect dish.

Liborio Cuban Restaurant, 321 Magazine St., New Orleans, LA 70130; (504) 581-9680; www.liboriocuban.com; Cuban; $$. It's the simple, consistently prepared Cuban mainstays, served in a dining room that buzzes with Latin music and a lively crowd (especially during lunch), that has helped this downtown spot earn its foodie destination stripes. Indeed, the unique Spanish- and African-influenced cooking traditions of the Caribbean's largest island have found a fitting home in a city that enjoys centuries-old ties to the region. Order a Honduran Port Royal beer served ice cold (or the nonalcoholic tamarind- and ginger-flavored Tamarindo) and dive into a traditional Cubano fried sandwich (pork, ham, and Swiss cheese on pressed grilled French bread) or the garlic-roasted pork. Many dishes come with rice and peas (the Latin-Caribbean's answer to New Orleans' red beans and rice) and either sweet or green fried plantains, always tender to the fork. If your meal doesn't include the boiled yucca with garlic sauce, do yourself a favor and ask for it as a side order.

Lüke, 333 St. Charles Ave., New Orleans, LA 70130; (504) 378-2840; www.lukeneworleans.com; French; $$$. It's nearly impossible not to find large crowds day or night enjoying the Franco-German brasserie atmosphere—right down to the old-fashioned wooden newspaper racks and pulley-and-belt ceiling fans—that help make this venue another feather in the toque of local superstar Chef John Besh (see **Besh Steak** [p. 76], **Domenica** [p. 79], and **Restaurant August** [p. 86], CBD; **The American Sector** [p. 92], Warehouse District; **La Provence** [p. 231], North Shore). But this is no mere restaurant eye candy. Since opening in 2007, Besh and Executive Chef Steven McHugh have fashioned a cool cosmopolitan enclave for the palate without so much as a hint of stuffy pretentiousness. Rotating daily lunch and dinner specials often feature whole-roast *cochon de lait* (with cherry mustard), smoked beef brisket with horseradish ravigote sauce, and redfish courtbouillon. But those eager to feast on a mouth-watering Provencal take on a local favorite should arrive on a night when the menu features slow-cooked lamb daube.

MiLa, 817 Common St., New Orleans, LA 70112; (504) 412-2580; www.milaneworleans.com; Eclectic; $$$. Not near enough praise is heaped upon those truly dedicated chefs who most likely lie awake nights pondering how to make a dish flavorful and exciting rather than complicated and self-conscious. Such is the case with the husband-and-wife co-chef team of Slade Rushing and Allison

Vines-Rushing, whose shared culinary vision can be discovered within the walls of this stylish establishment inside the Renaissance Pere Marquette Hotel. The dining room's sleek, post-modern-meets-deco decor, whimsical by day and romantic at night, doesn't get in the way of the imaginatively delicious pan-roasted sweetbreads paired with creamy black truffle grits in sherry-bacon jus. Yet this appetizer is just the tip of the iceberg. Equally creative kitchen creations include sweet potato pepperadelle, roasted rack of lamb (with black-eye pea puree, roasted okra, and tomato jam), and pan-roasted grouper. But it was the sweet tea-brined rotisserie duck with wilted spinach and roasted beets that quickly shot to the top of one regular's favorites.

Morton's the Steakhouse, 363 Canal St., New Orleans LA 70130; (504) 566-0221; www.mortons.com; Steak house; $$$$. Although its corporate headquarters are in Chicago and can boast of 77 locations worldwide, there is no denying the big splash this chophouse made when it opened its doors here in the Canal Place Mall—mostly because this venue knocks out consistently good steaks. This we discovered with the first bite of the double-cut filet mignon, cooked rare, that might have been one of the best (and certainly most tender) steaks ever savored. That is until we passed around the bone-in rib eye, cooked medium, that tasted so flavorful we didn't want to pass it back to its rightful diner. In restaurant clichés where "cooked to perfection" seems near the top of the list, it's refreshing to note a restaurant like this that doesn't lean on hackneyed promises but prefers rather to simply deliver what each and every patron has a right to expect of their steak. Don't skip the tuna tartare—it's among the best in the city.

Mother's, 401 Poydras St., New Orleans, LA 70130; (504) 523-9656; www.mothersrestaurant.net; Sandwiches; $$–$$$. An unobtrusive little brick corner building sits in the shadow of towering office buildings and hotels, just a few blocks from the convention center. Hanging over the door is a small white sign reading, MOTHER'S WORLD'S BEST BAKED HAM, EST. 1938. Inside, the dining room, with brick walls and concrete floors, is usually overflowing with diners as well as those standing in line, especially at lunchtime. The most popular item on the menu is the tender and crispy caramelized ham created with a time-honored secret family recipe. The signature po-boy is the Ferdi Special—a combination of baked ham, roast beef, "debris" (the part of the roast that falls into the gravy in the oven), shredded cabbage, and Creole mustard. Mother's serves breakfast, lunch, and dinner daily, but the place gets crowded fast. Go early. See Mother's recipe for **Jerry's Jambalaya** on p. 264.

Rambla, 221 Camp St., New Orleans, LA 70130; (504) 587-7720; Spanish; $$. This hip, European-style enclave of Spanish- and French-inspired small-portion dishes puts its best foot consistently forward when combining unusual ingredients, offering seasoned tapas fans tired of the status quo something new and exciting for the palate. A trio of shining examples includes the Medjool dates with smoked bacon, the pecan- and andouille-filled calamari with olive-tomato concassee, and the Serrano ham and fig served on Cabrales blue-cheese flatbread. Extra-large 12-top tables big enough for separate parties to sit around without ever feeling too close for comfort add a decidedly bohemian flavor to this artsy and atmospheric establishment, tucked inside the International House hotel. Patrons new to the tapas game should try some of the more traditional dishes like *patatas bravas*, roast duck cassoulet, Catalan pork sausage, grilled octopus, and, of course, the *paella Andalucia*, the original version of Spain's national dish, which features mixed seafood, chorizo, and chicken in saffron-flavored rice.

Restaurant August, 301 Tchoupitoulas St., New Orleans, LA 70130; (504) 299-9777; www.restaurantaugust.com; Eclectic; $$$$. A regularly changing menu of admirable entrees, a tip-off that award-winning Executive Chef-Owner John Besh prides himself on using only the freshest seasonal ingredients available, is underscored by the whole-roast rabbit cassoulet (with white beans and andouille) and the crispy-seared scallops that arrive at the table with picholine olives, shaved garlic, and rouille. Personal past favorites include the crispy veal sweetbreads with grilled lobster and French lentils, and porcini-crusted sea bass with orzo and Crowder pea risotto. Among the best ways to start off your meal in one of the city's consistently top-ranked restaurants and gastronomic Vahallas is with Besh's three-way *foie gras*—simply to die for. If you're lucky to see the hand-made potato gnocchi or crispy-seared sable fish on the menu, order it. You won't be disappointed.

The Ruby Slipper Cafe, 200 Magazine St., New Orleans, LA 70130; (504) 525-9355; www.therubyslippercafe.net; Neighborhood Cafe; $. Among the best aspects of dining out in this city is finding one of those rare and charming venues (often times by word of mouth) that serves tasty and soulful, New Orleans-style Southern breakfasts that are consistently delicious. You just won't find in many parts of the country a guy like Chef Nate Hilderbrand, who can turn barbecue shrimp over creamy slow-cooked grits into pure, start-your-morning-off-right magic. Ditto for his thyme-accented European omelet prepared with portobello mushrooms and Brie. A roster of more traditional egg, omelet, and pancake dishes is available, but it would be a shame to miss the chef's bananas Foster *pain perdu* (lost bread), a distinctly New Orleans-style, French bread-based French toast served

with applewood-smoked bacon under a bananas Foster topping. There's also a location at 139 S. Cortez St., New Orleans, LA 70119; (504) 309-5531.

Ruth's Chris Steakhouse, 525 Fulton St., New Orleans, LA 70130; (504) 587-7099; www.ruthschris.com; Steak house; $$$$. The late founder Ruth Fertel, a beloved culinary fixture in this city, bought her first restaurant from Chris Matulich (hence Ruth's Chris) in 1965 after seeing a classified ad in *The Times-Picayune*. Although the next few decades would see dozens of franchises open in 33 states, people in this town still think of Fertel—and her restaurant—as their own. And for good reason. Even if you've dined here only once in your life, you'll always remember the first time this venue's signature filet, rib eye, New York strip, porterhouse or T-bone arrives at your table cooked to order and literally sizzling in butter. Sure, there's a selection of soups and salads, appetizers, sides, and other entrees (the barbecue shrimp and lamb chops are quite good), but let's face it: The reason you should visit this USDA Prime Beef repository, located in Harrah's Hotel, is for the glorious steaks that honor a woman and entrepreneur who gave this city something they truly will never forget. There's also a location at 3633 Veterans Blvd. in Metairie, LA 70002; (504) 888-3600.

The Store, 814 Gravier St., New Orleans, LA 70112; (504) 322-2446; thestoreneworleans.com; Breakfast & Lunch; $. When Chef and owner Reuben Laws was a child, every Thanksgiving vacation, he would work on his uncle's sugar cane farm in St. Mary Parish. His fondest memory was the daily trips to the country store, a gathering place where farm workers could get a bite to eat, along with a little break from the sun. It was that setting, full of colorful conversation and good food, he had in mind when he opened his breakfast and lunch spot in the Central Business District. The menu is a cut above the usual diner fare, thanks to Chef Reuben's culinary education and training at some of the city's fine dining restaurants. Breakfast offerings range from muffins to shrimp and grits. Best bets at lunch include the pulled pork sandwich on pressed jalapeño cheddar bread or Chef's own version of the Reuben with pulled short rib meat, caramelized onions, sun-dried tomato spread, and Swiss cheese on pressed rye bread. See The Store's recipe for **Collard Greens** on p. 261.

Landmarks

The Grill Room, 300 Gravier St., New Orleans, LA 70130; (504) 522-1994; www.grillroomneworleans.com; American; $$$$. Seamless *savoir faire* imbues this elegant fine-dining venue with a worldliness that would make it as at home in Istanbul and Paris as Vienna and Hong Kong. Fortunately for New Orleanians this cosmopolitan den is tucked close to home inside the posh, Euro-swank digs of the city's acclaimed and internationally recognized Windsor Court Hotel. Among the best (and prettiest) restaurants not only in the city but also the country, this sophisticated continental venue is a showcase for the refreshingly succinct menu of globally inspired recipes Executive Chef Drew Dzejak has refined over the years. In the hands of a lesser chef, for instance, the crispy-skin, wild-striped bass might not arrive at the table replete with risotto, spinach, and leeks. Nor might the seared Maine scallops share the same dinner plate as *foie gras*, lentils, and shiitake mushrooms with warm bacon vinaigrette. Those with smallish appetites might be best served by ordering the side of duck fat-roasted fingerling potatoes—yes, it's really as good as it sounds.

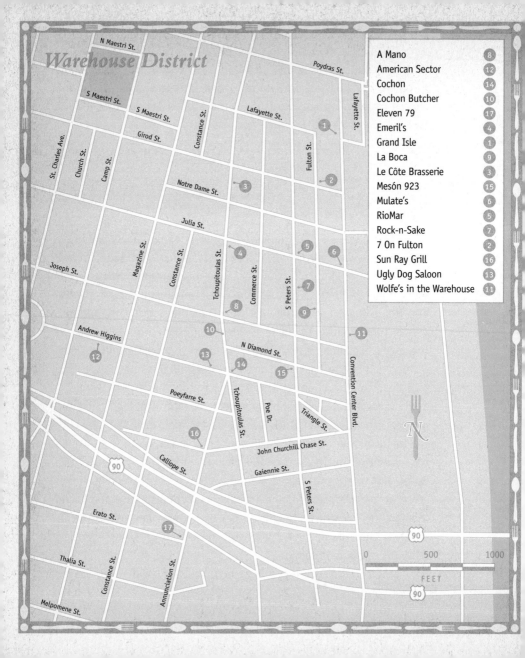

Warehouse District

Restaurant	#
A Mano	8
American Sector	12
Cochon	14
Cochon Butcher	10
Eleven 79	17
Emeril's	4
Grand Isle	1
La Boca	9
Le Côte Brasserie	3
Mesón 923	15
Mulate's	6
RioMar	5
Rock-n-Sake	7
7 On Fulton	2
Sun Ray Grill	16
Ugly Dog Saloon	13
Wolfe's in the Warehouse	11

Warehouse District

A Soho-cool amalgam of art galleries, converted warehouse condos, wine bars, design studios, auction houses, and no fewer than three museums sets the stage for hands-down one of the most hip and eclectic dining districts in town. Tucked in between the CBD/French Quarter to the north and Uptown to the south, this neighborhood offers an escape from the madding crowds of both and a mix of dining dens second to none in the metropolitan area. From Argentine chophouses and trendy nouvelle Cajun dens that can turn ham hocks into forkfuls of pure heaven, to sushi joints, paella venues, and the first-ever restaurant opened by superstar Chef Emeril Lagasse, this enclave is a perennially popular destination among the city's trend-setting culinary set.

Foodie Faves

A Mano, 870 Tchoupitoulas St., New Orleans, LA 70130; (504) 208-9280; www.amanonola.com; Italian; $$. **"A mano" means "by**

hand" and so much at this upscale Italian restaurant is created that way—from the delicious handmade pasta to the savory house-cured salumi (Italian cured meats). Chef Joshua Smith begins with the freshest ingredients from local farmers and purveyors. He then uses artisanal culinary techniques and sometimes centuries-old methods to create the art of Italian dining. The salumi and array of antipasti offerings make for a very satisfying meal in A Mano's warm and romantic dining room featuring exposed brick, muted Mediterranean colors, and a glass-front aging room full of hanging meats and sausages. Don't miss the Fegatini Bruschetta with chicken liver pâté, saba, and sea salt (so simple and so perfect) and from the antipasti list, the *Affettati Misti* plate of assorted house-cured meats or the *Coppa di Testa*—fried hogshead cheese, poached yard egg, and pickled peppers. Pasta is a must. The *Spaghetti alla Carbonara* is a good choice. Reservations are recommended.

American Sector, 945 Magazine St., New Orleans, LA 70130; (504) 528-1940; www.nationalww2museum.org/american-sector; American; $$. Many foodies turn up their nose at the thought of dining at a museum restaurant because quite honestly most of them are not worth the price of admission. All of which is why this establishment, attached to the city's acclaimed National World War II Museum, is a pure delight of discovery and another notch in the belt of acclaimed local superstar Chef John Besh, who designed both the restaurant and its menu. From the World War II-era black-and-white photographs of Hollywood legends to the waitstaff dressed in restaurant uniforms of the day, the canteen-like vibe sets the stage for a menu filled with Beshian twists on classic favorites. During a recent visit the delicious pork cheeks entree arrived at the table in a deep bowl over fresh corn bread as the waitperson topped it all with steamy black-eyed peas poured from a reproduction WWII-era rations can. The shrimp salad sandwich, served between two slices of rustic bread and presented on a mini butcher block, proved a yummy variation of a popular standard.

Cochon, 930 Tchoupitoulas St., New Orleans LA 70130; (504) 588-2123; www.cochonrestaurant.com; Cajun; $$$. The fashionable wooden booths with indirect lighting in this casually hip, Soho-ish dining den might be sufficient for small groups, but our coterie of highly opinionated diners required the restaurant's only 10-top from which to hold court while exploring the highly touted Cajun-meets-soul-food dishes cobbled together by Chef-Owner Donald Link (see **Herbsaint**, p. 80), winner of the James Beard Foundation's 2007 award for Best Chef, South. Where this venue rocks the menu is with dishes that were once almost exclusively the domain of bayou Cajuns (with a healthy nod to the city's Creole and modern-day continental cooking traditions tossed in for good measure). Examples include the fried alligator with chili-garlic aioli, poached yard egg with roasted mushrooms and grits, pickled pork tongue with radish and turnips, and grilled pork ribs with watermelon pickle. When Link pulls out the stops with entrees like his mustard-crusted ham hock, catfish courtbouillon, and rabbit and dumplings is when our forks began intruding on our tablemates' plates, eager to taste what everyone's oohs-and-ahhs were all about.

Cochon Butcher, 930 Tchoupitoulas St., New Orleans, LA 70130; (504) 588-7675; www.cochonbutcher.com; Cajun; $. This has become a favorite dine-in and take-out "sandwich shop" for a lot of foodies who brave the oft-times long lunch lines for the chance to savor the specialty preparations that go into making this spot such a bona fide winner. Opened as a culinary annex to Chef-Owner Donald Link's main pork-centric restaurant **Cochon** just around the corner, Butcher, as many regulars refer to it, has a rotating daily specials board as well a set menu of temptations that can include a boudin-and-pepper-jelly sandwich that takes the traditional Cajun pork-and-rice dish to a whole new taste level. Ditto for the pressed pastrami on rye, pork belly on white bread with mint and cucumber, and Carolina-style barbecue pork ("The best I've ever had," gushed a first-time patron). If you arrive on a day when the duck pastrami and Gruyère slider is on the specials board, don't think twice—order it!

Eleven 79, 1179 Annunciation St., New Orleans, LA 70130; (504) 299-1179; www.eleven79.com; Italian; $$$. It takes a lot to impress someone who's not a huge fan of Italian food, but Chef Anthony DiPiazza did precisely that during a recent visit by turning out one of the truly best versions of *osso bucco* the patron had ever enjoyed. Further proof that traditional Italian food doesn't have to be fancy or fussy to woo hard-to-please diners arrived in the form of fettuccine Alfredo, Milanese-style veal shank, and roasted pepper shrimp bisque, all of which were not only excellent but brilliantly paired with wine thanks to the waitperson. While some say this spot reminds them of an old-fashioned goodfellas-style restaurant and the kind of place where Ol' Blue Eyes would have felt right at home, others quite like the European-ish, cozy and elegantly upscale atmosphere of this former merchant's cottage that still features exposed brick-between-posts walls.

Emeril's, 800 Tchoupitoulas St., New Orleans, LA 70130; (504) 528-9393; www.emerils.com; Contemporary Creole; $$$$. Emeril Lagasse, the James Beard award-winning celebrity chef whose 12-restaurant empire today stretches from Orlando to Las Vegas, opened this, his first restaurant, in 1990. While regular restaurant-goers will likely not be swayed by the pretty dining room's hard-wood floors, exposed wine racks, and artsy bar, what will set the imagination afire are menu favorites that include grilled homemade andouille and boudin sausage, sweet barbecue-glazed rainbow trout, Mississippi rabbit remoulade, grilled pork chop with caramelized sweet potatoes, and Lagasse's homage to the irretrievably rib-sticking soul-food staple of chicken and waffles. (If all else fails try the andouille-crusted Texas redfish.) As much as some food boffins like Anthony Bourdain have at times tried to poke a hole or three in Lagasse's larger-than-life culinary stature, truth is there are few who do it better than the Bam! Man.

Grand Isle, 575 Convention Center Blvd., New Orleans, LA 70130; (504) 520-8530; www.grandislerestaurant.com; Seafood; $$. Walking into this seafood den is in some ways like stepping back to the WPA days of the heavily Cajun waterfront community in Southern Louisiana from which the restaurant derives its name. This is thanks to the 1930s- and '40s-era black-and-white photographs of weathered and hardscrabble residents who breathed life into the Grand Isle community, today a popular fishing spot. When a member of the waitstaff brags that the only thing they keep in the freezer is ice cream, you know the bounty of seafood dishes on the menu is going to reflect a philosophy that demands unwavering freshness. The proof was in the tasting when a group of hungry diners sampled the fresh shucked oysters on the half-shell, smoked fried oysters with tarragon aioli, boiled crawfish, and a sautéed catch of the day. Po-boys and salads round off the lunch menu while dinner entrees branch into familiar territory in the form of shrimp and stone-ground grits smothered in andouille gravy, crawfish étouffée, and fried seafood plates and platters.

La Boca, 857 Fulton St., New Orleans, LA 70130; (504) 525-8205; www.labocasteaks.com; Steak; $$$. Fans of Argentine steak houses will find kindred spirits in this delightful venue dedicated to the rich cooking traditions of the South American country best known for its grilled meat wizardry. Opened by locally acclaimed chef Adolfo Garcia (see **RioMar** [p. 99] and **A Mano** [p. 91]), Warehouse

District), this rustic-hewn establishment celebrates co-proprietor Nicolas Bazan's Argentine heritage with a tour de force of 10 steak entrees expertly prepared using some of the best beef in the world including Certified Angus beef and American Kobe. Whether your inner-gaucho is craving a 24-ounce bife ancho (cowboy-cut bone-in rib eye), a slow-cooked 14-ounce "outside skirt," 20-ounce Angus T-bone, or a 12-ounce lean-and-tender "bistro" tenderloin, no one ever leaves the table hungry. Arrive extra hungry unless you plan to skip the impressive roster of Latin America-inspired appetizers that range from Argentine-style empanadas and homemade chorizo to the grilled Argentine cheese prepared with olive oil and oregano.

Le Côte Brasserie, 700 Tchoupitoulas St., New Orleans, LA 70130; (504) 613-2350; www.lecotebrasserie.com; French-Creole; $$. It doesn't hurt that this aesthetically rendered casual dining venue, with its stainless steel exposed kitchen and 50-foot-long serpentine bar counter, is tucked on the ground floor of the Renaissance Arts Hotel and its perennially eye-pleasing and artistically appointed lobby, originally part of a 1910 warehouse. But it's Executive Chef Chuck Subra who deserves all the credit for cobbling together a menu that reflects his native Louisiana upbringing and zeal for adding exciting spins to classic and contemporary recipes. Proof comes in the form of Subra's char-grilled lobster on the half-shell served with lobster beignets and his cedar-smoked barbecue shrimp with goat cheese stone-ground hominy grits. If Subra sounds like one of those young creative chefs who understand that food at its best is like consumable art, you're spot on. This becomes all the more evident when you've ventured into his scallop strawberry-Satsuma gazpacho and Bloody Mary shrimp and mirliton ceviche.

Mesón 923, 923 S. Peters St., New Orleans, LA 70130; (504) 523-9200; www.meson923.com; American; $$$. Many people opt for the special-occasion elegance of the upstairs dining room, but others prefer the chic ambience of the downstairs dining room with its high-top bistro-style tables and textured concrete floors. But wherever you choose to hunker down, you can expect precision and brilliance from the kitchen under the direction of Executive Chef Baruch Rabasa at this chic new hot spot that has been hailed as "the best thing to happen to New Orleans recently." When Rabasa turns loose his Catalan roots and classical European culinary repertoire on virtually anything on the menu—for instance, the carpaccio, pork shoulder, pork belly, veal cheeks, tuna tartare, or Jamaican-style grilled quail—even the most discerning self-styled food critic can't help but take note of the nuance he brings to each dish. Guests are going to want to lazy Susan their dishes so everyone can have a bite of the duck confit (with port-braised shallots) and diver scallops.

Mulate's, 201 Julia St., New Orleans, LA 70130; (504) 522-1492; www.mulates.com; Cajun; $$. Most nights this spot is packed to the rafters—and seemingly not just with tourists. Drop in for a bite to eat and discover what all the fuss was about—namely, a wonderful exploration of Cajun food and music. Mercy, this place is fun. Owner Kerry Boutte, who hails from Arnaudville in the heart of Cajun Country, opened this venue in 1990 and daily rolls out a tour de force of food he learned to cook as a youth that includes everything from blackened alligator and Cajun-style boudin sausage to meat pies, corn and shrimp bisque, fried crawfish tails, and seafood gumbo. House specialties not to be missed include catfish stuffed with crabmeat dressing, jumbo lump crabmeat au gratin, and a bust-a-gut seafood platter brimming with deep-fried oysters, shrimp, crawfish tails, and catfish, served with jambalaya and a twice-baked potato. The music is so toe-tapping good that even Paul Simon once shared the stage with the regular Cajun bands that perform nightly such as Bayou Deville and La Touche.

RioMar, 800 S. Peters St., New Orleans, LA 70130; (504) 525-3474; www.riomarseafood.com; Spanish; $$$. Rising superstar chef and Panamanian native Adolfo Garcia (see **La Boca** [p. 96], Warehouse District) crafted this corner eatery, adorned with metal wall sculpture of aquatic life, into a homage to the Latin flavors of Spain and Central and South America. A nice selection of well-prepared hot and cold tapas range from piquillo peppers stuffed with Louisiana shrimp to bacalaitos (Spanish-style cod fritters) and four different types of ceviche (all four can be enjoyed together in the ceviche sampler). Recommended entrees include yellowfin tuna steak wrapped in Serrano ham and topped with spicy romesco sauce, and *escabeche* (grilled fish with peppers, olives, and caper relish). What has won the heart and palate of more than one diner is Spain's answer to France's classic bouillabaisse: a hearty and flavorful seafood stew called *zarzuela*. *Zarzuela* means "operetta" or "variety show," a perfect way of describing the delicious mix of squid, clams, shrimp, sea bass fillets, mussels, and scallops all served swimming in a seasoned saffron broth. Not to be missed.

Rock-n-Sake, 823 Fulton St., New Orleans, LA 70130; (504) 581-7253; www.rocknsake.com; Japanese; $$. This lively, casual dining den specializing in Japanese cuisine and sushi "so fresh it practically swims to your plate!" While the music can get a bit loud at times, there is no mistaking the fact this venue is designed to appeal to the fun-spirited eel lover in us all. A lengthy list of traditional "rolls" runs the gamut from those filled with a mix of tuna, crabstick, and avocado to slightly more adventurous snow crab concoctions prepared with chili sauce and green onions. Also available are sashimi, two-piece sushi, and a large selection of "small plates" ranging from salmon cakes and beef *tataki* to sizzling squid steak and *yaki tori* (skewered chicken and onions smothered in teriyaki sauce). Hungry patrons will want to check out the full entrees like the pan-seared salmon fillet and barbecue eel served over seasoned sushi rice.

7 On Fulton, 700 Fulton St., New Orleans, LA 70130; (504) 525-7555; www.7onfulton.com; Contemporary Creole; $$$. At night, cushy banquettes and candlelit white-linen tables with Chinese bamboo cane-back Chippendale chairs set a romantic stage for Executive Chef Matthew Fultz's menu of imaginatively presented and unpretentious contemporary Creole–New Orleans dishes. Recipes that have helped put this venue on the radar include the seared scallops (served with smoked tomatoes, almonds, and hollandaise), pan-seared duck breast (served with potato 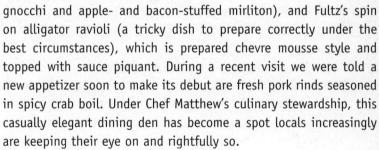 gnocchi and apple- and bacon-stuffed mirliton), and Fultz's spin on alligator ravioli (a tricky dish to prepare correctly under the best circumstances), which is prepared chevre mousse style and topped with sauce piquant. During a recent visit we were told a new appetizer soon to make its debut are fresh pork rinds seasoned in spicy crab boil. Under Chef Matthew's culinary stewardship, this casually elegant dining den has become a spot locals increasingly are keeping their eye on and rightfully so.

Sun Ray Grill, 1051 Annunciation St., New Orleans, LA 70130; (504) 566-0021; www.sunraygrill.com; Eclectic; $$. A Southern California ex-pat yearning for the ubiquitous fish tacos of his "ancestral homeland" had heard through the grapevine of the version prepared at this hip Warehouse District eatery. Sure, the venue's globally eclectic menu runs an intriguing gamut from combo ginger, pork, and shrimp spring rolls and goat cheese fritters to crimini mushroom and basil quesadillas and snow crab-stuffed baked salmon served over grilled pineapple. But could it possibly have mastered  what in San Diego is regarded as the singular defining dish of an entire surfer/beach culture? Totally, dude. Turns out the lightly battered and deep-fried redfish (grilled is available) used in Sun Ray's recipe is so delicate, tender, and flavorful that the soft taco wrap and accompanying fresh-made guacamole and oh-so-creamy black beans not only proved a winner worthy of SoCal fish-taco cred but also made a believer out of a skeptic. There are also locations at 619 Pink St., Metairie LA 70005; (504) 837-0055; and 2600 Belle Chasse Highway, Gretna (West Bank), LA 70056; (504) 391-0053.

Ugly Dog Saloon, 401 Andrew Higgins Dr., New Orleans, LA 70130; (504) 569-8459; www.uglydogsaloon.net; Barbecue; $. On a recent Saturday afternoon patrons were gathered inside this most un-froufrou venue watching sports on the three large-screen TVs while eating lunch or sitting outside at one of the umbrella-shaded tables that offer a view of Warehouse District passersby. In an area of town known for its chic and upscale dining dens, it's refreshing to have a retreat such as this that is so unpretentious as to make virtually anyone feel right at home. Equally good news is this establishment keeps it simple by serving up some of the tastiest barbecue in town. Whether you like yours with chicken, beef brisket, pork, or pulled pork, the reasonably priced barbecue platters for which this place is known always seems to hit the spot. Sandwich versions are available as well as a small selection of salads and sides.

Wolfe's in the Warehouse, 859 Convention Center Blvd., New Orleans, LA 70130; (504) 613-2882; www.wolfesinthewarehouse .com; Contemporary Creole; $$. This airy, well-lit venue tucked off the lobby of the New Orleans Marriott at the Convention Center might not always be on the tip of every local gastronome's tongue, but its crab cakes with chutney and herbs and pressed chicken sandwich have lured more than one hard-to-please diner through the doors of this lively establishment. Lunch is probably the best time to sample the hard-won labors of Executive Chef Tom Wolfe and his staff. While the duck roulade (stuffed with roasted sweet pepper) and Italian duck sausage never fail to garner rave reviews, a recent visit found the Parmesan-crusted oysters as good as ever.

Uptown

At night the rumbling streetcars and pantheon of oak trees lining St. Charles Avenue compete for attention with the beautifully columned Italianate and Greek Revival mansions, Audubon Park, and Tulane and Loyola Universities, for which this stretch of town is well known. But what truly makes this sublimely romantic neighborhood a destination for many locals is the veritable Valhalla of restaurants, from po-boy shops to fine-dining dens, serving up a little bit of everything under the sun. When it comes to food, if you can't find it Uptown, chances are you won't find it anywhere in town.

Foodie Faves

Atchafalaya, 901 Louisiana Ave., New Orleans LA 70115; (504) 891-9626; www.cafeatchafalaya.com; Contemporary Creole; $$$. Tucked in the quiet Irish Channel neighborhood about as far as you can get from the Uptown bustle is this artistic and romantic, candlelit retreat for those whose discerning eye for artistically artic- ulated "restaurantscapes" (in this case, exposed original cypress woodwork) is equaled only by a palate wise to the ways of sophis- ticated yet wholly unpretentious Southern cuisine. Among the best examples are the classic shrimp and grits. "We own it," a staff member said matter-of-factly. And he wasn't off course when the dish arrived served with bacon, smoked tomatoes, and spicy butter sauce on a crispy grit cake. If, as a rule, a relatively brief entree list signals the kitchen relies on only the freshest available ingredients, this can be best tasted here by ordering the pasta Atchafalaya (a fettuccine feast of Louisiana crawfish, duck, shrimp, and tasso) and the applewood-smoked bacon-wrapped quail that is stuffed with boudin and served alongside collard greens and mashed potatoes. Whatever you do, don't miss brunch—especially the duck hash with duck confit, blackberries, mangos, poached eggs, and hollandaise.

Bistro Daisy, 5831 Magazine St., New Orleans, LA 70115; (504) 899-6987; www.bistrodaisy.com; Creole French; $$$. One of the nicest aspects of dining on Magazine Street is the chance to drop into one of the little Creole cottages that have been renovated and pressed into service as a splendidly romantic restaurant whose ambience typically begins with the flickering gas lantern hanging outside by the front door. But when you're waiting to be seated and the middle-aged couple just leaving takes time to tell you how much you'll enjoy your meal if you order the sweetbreads and pan- roasted duck breast in reduction sauce, you just sense you've hit the proverbial culinary jackpot. In 2007 husband-and-wife team Anton

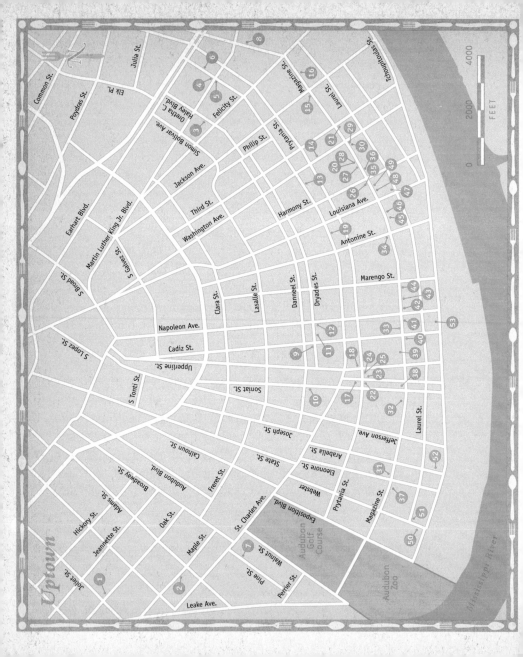

and Diane Schulte opened this venue, named for their daughter, and since then have been wooing loyal patrons with a menu that blends American, French, and Creole cooking traditions. This is best explored with not only the sweetbreads and duck but also the braised lamb shank, grilled pork loin medallions, and pan-roasted and porcini-dusted chicken over mushroom, Parmesan, and roasted shallot risotto.

The Bulldog, 3236 Magazine St., New Orleans, LA 70115; (504) 891-1516; http://bulldog.draftfreak.com; Burgers; $. The Bulldog is a tavern with 50 beers on tap and 100 bottled varieties. (See more in the Cocktail Culture chapter.) But it also serves up some pretty good bar food, including excellent burgers—all of which are named for types of beer and made from a half-pound of fresh ground chuck, grilled to order and served on a sesame, wheat, or the house cheddar jalapeño bun. The Dunkel is topped with applewood-smoked bacon, cheddar, and Sweet Baby Ray's barbecue sauce; the Delirium Mushroom Jack features sautéed mushrooms and Monterey Jack cheese; and the Dead Guy is loaded with jalapeños, guacamole, ranch dressing, bacon, cheddar, and Jack cheese. Enjoy your burger and ale on the Bulldog's patio, featuring a cascading fountain created by water flowing from a line of open beer taps. The Bulldog is open every day from lunch-'till, and there's a second location on the edge of Mid-City at 5135 Canal Blvd., New Orleans, LA; (504) 488-4191; www .bulldog-midcity.draftfreak.com.

Cafe Reconcile, 1631 Oretha Castle Haley Blvd., New Orleans, LA 70113; (504) 568-1157; http://reconcileneworleans.org; Lunch; $. Dining at Cafe Reconcile is not only enjoyable, it's inspiring. This Central City restaurant works to end generational poverty by training young people, who come from some of the direst of social and economic situations, to work in the food-service industry. Since the cafe's opening in 2000, more than 500 young people have completed the program and obtained industry jobs. Every weekday, 120 to 150 guests dine on local comfort foods such as baked chicken and garlic mashed potatoes, or smothered pork chops with string beans and jalapeño corn bread. And don't forget the bananas Foster bread pudding for dessert. Cafe Reconcile is open for lunch only. Visitors unfamiliar with the area should take a taxi.

Casamento's, 4330 Magazine St., New Orleans LA 70115; (504) 895-9761; www.casamentosrestaurant.com; Seafood; $$. At night the shiny-white tile walls and floors of this brightly lighted, venerable oyster den might be a little hard on the eyes. Some say it reminds them of a swimming pool, but founder and Italian immigrant Joseph Casamento wanted tile in order to make his restaurant, opened in 1919, easier to clean (even though it reportedly took four tile companies coast to coast to fulfill his wishes). Either way, generations of New Orleanians have walked past the door under the old neon sign to enjoy what many claim is the best gumbo in town, soft-shell crab dinners, seafood platters, and po-boy loaves made not with traditional French bread but rather the family's signature "pan bread." The menu isn't long or fancy, but locals like it that way. Besides, they know the best thing to put on their plates—and in their mouths—are the fresh oysters for which this venue is famous, which are shucked just behind the oyster bar where people in the front dining room can watch. Traditions like this are not to be trifled with.

Charlie's Steak House, 4510 Dryades St., New Orleans, LA 70115; (504) 895-9323; http://charliessteakhousenola.com; Steak house; $$$. The folks at Charlie's Steak House have perfected the art of keeping it simple. There are four steaks from a 10-ounce fillet to a 32-ounce rib eye, called "The Charlie." With that, you can get either Charlie's famous potatoes au gratin or hand-cut steak fries. There are a few other incidentals, like salad and steamed vegetables—but that's it. And the system's worked for this popular local restaurant since 1932. The running joke is: if you ask for a menu, everybody knows it's your first time. This casual restaurant was opened by Charles Petrossi in the midst of the Great Depression and was run by his family until Hurricane Katrina closed it in 2005. Two years later, neighbor Matthew Dwyer, who had unofficially worked at the restaurant (when they got busy, someone would knock on his door and ask him to come tend bar), decided to buy the place. And a New Orleans tradition was reborn.

Coquette, 2800 Magazine St., New Orleans, LA 70115; (504) 265-0421; www.coquette-nola.com; American; $$$. Chef-Owner Michael Stoltzfus trained at **Restaurant August** (see p. 86) before opening this posh bistro on a busy Uptown corner in 2008 with partner Lillian Hubbard. The menu changes daily and generally offers half a dozen or so appetizers and as many entrees, including such dishes as sea scallops, hanger steak, or fried quail. The best deal is the $20 three-course lunch special including such choices as roast oysters or white asparagus soup to start; followed by Gulf shrimp with cherry tomatoes and English peas, or crawfish tails with green asparagus and brown butter; and finished with a dessert of beignets (local square donuts) or goat cheese mousse. Nighttime diners have an option of a four-course tasting menu, which is available with wine pairings.

Courtyard Grill, 4430 Magazine St., New Orleans, LA 70115; (504) 875-4164; www.courtyardgrillnola.com; Mediterranean; $$. It's such a pleasure during nice afternoons and evenings to sit at one of the outdoor tables on the deck overlooking Magazine Street while enjoying some of the culinary surprises found on the menu. By "surprises" we're referring to the Turkish specialties that help set this new kid on the block, opened in 2010, apart from the pack in a city brimming with excellent Middle Eastern and Mediterranean restaurants. Certainly diners will find the usual suspects like *dolma* (stuffed grape leaves), hummus, *baba ghanoush*, *tabouli*, and falafel. But to taste the real forte this promising young venue brings to the culinary scene requires venturing into less familiar Turkish territory. A best bet includes the Iskandar kabob, which mixes beef and lamb, slow-cooked on a vertical rotisserie and served over the restaurant's spongy, homemade rustic bread under a warm tomato sauce with yogurt and rice. Ditto for the Adana kabob, a hearty dish of char-broiled beef and lamb mixed with red pepper, onion, and parsley, served with grilled tomatoes and rice. Save room for the *kayisi*, a Turkish dessert of sweet apricots filled with light cream and walnuts and drizzled with light syrup.

Delachaise, 3442 St. Charles Ave., New Orleans, LA 70115; (504) 895-0858; www.thedelachaise.com; Eclectic; $$–$$$. Housed in a long narrow building that fronts picturesque St. Charles Avenue, Delachaise is a place to find high-quality food for a late-night dinner (with doors generally staying open until midnight or later). It's also an excellent spot to relax and enjoy a glass of the grape chosen from their long wine list, while you watch the streetcars go by on the avenue. Daily wine specials start at $5 a glass in this casually elegant restaurant. A satisfying meal could be made from the appetizer menu, which includes a European cheese plate, Mediterranean olives, and house-made pates. And there's a reason you'll hear almost everybody order the *pommes frites*. These gourmet french fries, cooked in goose fat, are worth the trip. From the entree menu, try the Cuban twice-cooked pork (stewed in aromatic broth, then crisped in duck fat and served with orange mojo and fried yucca) or the spicy frog's legs, which are fried and glazed with house remoulade sauce.

Dick & Jenny's, 4501 Tchoupitoulas St., New Orleans, LA 70115; (504) 894-9880; http://dickandjennys.com; Contemporary Creole; $$$. Expect a wait because this perennially popular joint doesn't take reservations. But you won't regret the time—even if it's an hour—spent in the lovely courtyard enjoying a carafe of house wine while waiting for your table in this establishment, housed in a 19th-century barge-board cottage in a largely working-class neighborhood. Fans of fine dining in funky atmospheres adore this place. And it's likely you will too once you get a taste of eclectic Euro-American-Creole starters like the to-die-for crawfish and alligator sausage cheesecake topped with chipotle aioli; the *pain perdu* of duck confit with apples, Brie, and peach chutney; or the garlicky escargot that arrives in a bread bowl with a creamy bacon demi-glace. While the a la carte menu changes to reflect seasonally available ingredients, count yourself lucky if the menu features the seared duck breast with Louisiana alligator sausage or the roasted pork tenderloin stuffed with goat cheese and pine nuts and topped with a red pepper balsamic vinaigrette. Good eats like these are the stuff of memories.

Dominique's on Magazine, 4729 Magazine St., New Orleans, LA 70115; (504) 894-8869; www.dominiquesonmag.com; American gourmet; $$$. Just approaching this lovely, converted Creole cottage at night and seeing the small grouping of alfresco tables in front and the tiny white lights twined around the wooden rails and banisters leading to the front door imbues the first-time visitor with a sense of having arrived at a special place. And then you open the front door and feel as though you've stepped into the Europe of your dreams. The romantic, hushed ambience and bistro-like vibe of banquettes, mirrors, exposed wood, and original artwork set the stage for the imaginative European-American fare-with-a-twist that arrives at your table in the form of duck leg confit and poached pear, sautéed sweetbreads (with chimichurri!), and beef tartare with ginger and avocado crème fraiche. And those are just appetizers. The best is still to come when you dive fork-first into entrees like the maple leaf duck breast with porcini and parsnip puree, the chimichurri-rubbed grilled pork chop, and the pan-seared local flounder that arrives with corn-mirliton risotto with lime, grapefruit, and scotch bonnet mojo. It's love at first bite.

Dunbar's Creole Cooking, 501 Pine St., New Orleans, LA 70118; (504) 861-5451; Neighborhood Cafe; $. Laugh all you want, but The Travel Channel didn't mince words when raving about the Southern soul-food specialties served during breakfast and lunch at this hard-to-find dining den, which, in so many words, is the Loyola Law School cafeteria. Neither will you once you get a taste of co-Chefs Celestine Dunbar and Peggy Ratliff's creamy red beans and rice, mustard greens, fried chicken, and pork chops with grits. The two high-spirited women ran their successful business from a freestanding Uptown restaurant before Hurricane Katrina begged to differ, but since then have found their new digs a blessing. Ditto for loyal patrons who can't get enough of the time-honored recipes with which Dunbar and Ratliff prepare dishes like shrimp and okra, turkey necks with greens, and fried catfish. So what if you have to press the front-door buzzer for security to let you inside the Loyola University Broadway Activities Center? Trust us—it's well worth the effort.

Emeril's Delmonico, 1300 St. Charles Ave., New Orleans, LA 70130; (504) 525-4937; www.emerils.com; Contemporary Creole; $$$–$$$$$. This iconic St. Charles Avenue restaurant has been part of the New Orleans dining scene since 1895. Locals were understandably dismayed when it closed its doors in 1997. But a year later, celebrity chef Emeril Lagasse bought the place, freshened it up with a clean contemporary interior design, and elegant dining on the Avenue was back. Emeril's menu at this, his most New Orleans-style restaurant, finds its foundation in local tradition. There's Emeril's barbecued shrimp and baked grit cake, as well as green onion sausage-stuffed bell pepper with Creole tomato sauce, and don't miss the slow-cooked crispy pork cheek with Creole dirty rice. But there are also more exotic offerings, such as spicy octopus served with anise crostini. Dinner is served nightly and reservations are recommended.

Franky & Johnny's, 321 Arabella St., New Orleans, LA 70115; (504) 899-9146; www.frankyandjohnnys.com; Seafood; $–$$. They just don't make 'em like this anymore—an old-fashioned, family-owned neighborhood eatery, opened in 1942, housed in a former Mission-style home today filled with red-checkered tablecloths, original tile floors, and a decor that looks like it hasn't changed since the 1960s (OK, maybe the '70s). Doesn't matter because it's the award-winning menu that continues to draw a fiercely loyal clientele for New Orleans-style comfort foods like roast beef po-boys, Italian muffalettas, stuffed artichokes, boiled and fried seafood platters, and, of course, sweet potato pie. Try the pork chop platter, which arrives with your choice of fries or potato salad, for a taste of the kind of mama's cooking most mamas just don't cook anymore.

Gautreau's, 1728 Soniat St., New Orleans, LA 70115; (504) 899-7397; www.gautreausrestaurant.com; American; $$$–$$$$. Tucked like a secret in a lush Uptown neighborhood is this seamlessly elegant yet unpretentious French bistro-style retreat boasting *trompe l'oeil* hand-painted walls and which often buzzes with a trendy, well-heeled crowd. Despite the city's penchant for casual dress even in fine-dining dens, it's best to ditch your jeans, logo T-shirts, and girls-gone-wild attire if you wish to feel at home in this classy establishment. If for no other reason, consider the fact *Food and Wine* magazine throughout the years has bestowed upon three of this restaurant's chefs America's Top 10 Best New Chefs awards, while five have been nominated for James Beard awards. Always at home in the kitchen is Chef Sue Zemanick, a James Beard Rising Star Chef finalist three years in a row and in 2011 a contestant on Bravo Network's *Top Chef Masters* competition. You'll understand why when you taste your first forkful of her crispy sweetbreads with crawfish tails, bacon-wrapped pork tenderloin, or Black Angus filet mignon, which arrives in a balsamic demi-glace with crispy polenta and rapini. The French-inspired New Orleans-style menu consistently draws rave reviews for repasts like Chef Sue's melt-in-your-mouth wild mushroom pierogies with asparagus, caramelized onions, and crème fraiche.

Gott Gourmet Cafe, 3100 Magazine St., New Orleans, LA 70115; (504) 373-6579; www.gottgourmetcafe.com; Neighborhood Cafe; $$. Chef David Gotter and wife Christy Parker opened this "casual gourmet" restaurant in 2008 to provide an upscale flair to the informal dining experience. The most interesting menu item here from the perspective of the overall New Orleans dining experience is one that is hard to find elsewhere—a great hot dog. Fortunately for local diners Gotter is a Windy City native and he brought his Chicago-style hot dog expertise with him. The all-beef Vienna dog comes with "Chicago" relish, diced onions, tomato, celery salt, and yellow mustard, served on a steamed poppy seed bun. Gott Gourmet also serves burgers, sandwiches, salads, and, on the weekends, breakfast.

The Grocery, 2854 St. Charles Ave., New Orleans, LA 70115; (504) 895-9524; http://thegroceryneworleans.com; Sandwiches; $. Don't let the name confuse you. The Grocery is actually a sandwich shop, housed in a late-19th-century corner storefront that was originally a pharmacy. Along with traditional po-boys, the Grocery also serves terrific pressed sandwiches, including Creole-ized versions of a turkey melt, corned beef on rye, and a Cuban, as well as the popular sausage melt with pork and alligator sausage, sautéed onions, roasted peppers, provolone, and horseradish mayo. And if you like, they'll press your po-boy sandwich, too. The Grocery also serves salads and soup, including a fine dark-roux chicken and smoked sausage gumbo. And save room for dessert—a triple chocolate pecan brownie. The Grocery is open for lunch only Mon through Sat.

Il Posto Cafe, 4607 Dryades St., New Orleans, LA 70115; (504) 895-2620; www.ilpostocafe-nola.com; Breakfast/Italian; $. Stepping into this charming take-out and dine-in spot is like walking into one of those old-fashioned cafes one finds in an Umbrian village. While there might be a short line at the counter, it's always worth the wait (plus it gives you time to decide what to order from the large hand-scrawled chalkboards on the wall). From antipasto platters and pressed paninis (try the proscuitto with roasted red peppers, basil pesto, and fresh mozzarella) to bruschetta, traditional fontina and rocchetta cheeses, and cured pork sausages, this establishment hits all the high notes when it comes to freshly prepared "fast food"—Old World Italian-style.

Jamila's Cafe, 7808 Maple St., New Orleans, LA 70118; (504) 866-4366; Middle Eastern; $$. Just when you were beginning to wonder if all Mediterranean restaurants served more or less the same fare, along comes this cozy Maple Street retreat of mouthwatering Tunisian surprises. The appetizers alone will be enough to make even seasoned lovers of traditional Greek, Turkish, and Lebanese fare sit up and take note. Best bets include the appetizers *ojja merguez* (sautéed homemade seasoned lamb sausage, caraway seeds, tomatoes, and bell peppers mixed with eggs), grilled *merguez* (with lentils), and leg of lamb. A succinct mix of traditional Mediterranean meat, fish, and vegetarian dishes served with couscous (steamed whole-wheat semolina) is available.

Joey K's, 3001 Magazine St., New Orleans, LA 70115; (504) 891-0997; www.joeyksrestaurant.com; Neighborhood Cafe; $$. Joey K's is a traditional casual dining restaurant serving home-style New Orleans food, as locals would say, "like ya' mama used to make." This is a good place to try red beans and rice, as well as fried seafood and fried chicken that's made to order. Standout specialties include Shrimp Magazine, made with large butterfly shrimp lightly floured and pan fried, then sautéed in olive oil, garlic, artichoke hearts, ham, and green onions, served over pasta; and Trout Tchoupitoulas (named for the downtown street) featuring seasonal fish lightly floured and pan fried, topped with shrimp and crabmeat, served with mixed vegetables and new potatoes. Joey K's is open Mon through Sat for lunch and dinner, but is closed in the late afternoon, so call ahead for hours.

Juan's Flying Burrito, 2018 Magazine St., New Orleans, LA 70130; (504) 569-0000; www.juansflyingburrito.com; Mexican; $. Since 1997 this cheap-eats Tex-Mex gem has been serving up some of the best nachos and quesadillas in town. This always crowded venue bustles with not only the collegiate bohemian crowd but also virtually anyone else who yearns for brilliantly prepared down-home specialties like chicken and chorizo tacos, pizza-style crawfish Pizzadilla, or Jamaican-style braised jerk alligator burrito stuffed with avocado, mango salsa, Jack cheese, sour cream, yellow rice, and black beans (not to be missed!). The open kitchen's regular menu features 10 different types of burritos and enough enchiladas, quesadillas, tacos, and fajita plates to satisfy even the pickiest fan of food from south of the border. A new alfresco dining option was created with the restaurant's recent addition of a roofed backyard with ceiling fans, adorned with a mural by local artist Clayton Nepveux. There's also a location at 4727 S. Carrollton Ave., New Orleans, LA 70119; (504) 486-9950.

Kyoto, 4920 Prytania St., New Orleans, LA 70115; (504) 891-3644; www.kyotonola.com; Japanese; $$. At this Japanese restaurant, everything from the salmon and yellowtail to the mackerel and eel consistently wins high praise. Lovers of local seafood should try the soft-shell crab and crawfish rolls. Another a la carte favorite is the giant clam, fresh and succulent to the taste. But where this bastion of fresh raw fish really earns its stripes is with the small but delicious roster of special rolls seemingly designed with the connoisseur in mind. Among the best examples is the Funky Margarita Roll—crawfish mixed with crunchy tempura flakes, topped with slices of fresh tuna and fresh salmon, and finished with a spicy avocado sauce. Another don't-miss is the Desiree Roll, in which "dynamite," crawfish and crabstick are rolled together, tempura fried, and served with a creamy wasabi sauce. The kitchen menu features a large appetizer section as well as numerous traditional Japanese noodle soups and grilled and fried dinners.

La Crepe Nanou, 1410 Robert St., New Orleans, LA 70115; (504) 899-2670; www.lacrepenanou.com; French; $$–$$$. French restaurants come and go, but this little gem has been treating locals to classic bistro cuisine for nearly 20 years—and isn't likely to be going anywhere anytime soon. Romantic and (typically) crowded as are all truly good French dining dens, this establishment offers a twin nod to art nouveau and contemporary design along with a menu that leans heavily on time-tested Francophile favorites like garlic-steamed mussels *mariniere* in white wine sauce, a wonderfully herbed whole grilled fish, and crepes stuffed or topped with a variety of tasty options ranging from crabmeat and creamed spinach to Swiss cheese and caramelized onions, braised chicken, sautéed shrimp in lobster sauce, and beef tip filets. Rounding off the menu are pates, cheeses, fondues, and meat dishes including lamb chops and roasted leg of lamb (both served with cognac sauce) and sweetbreads with lemon butter and capers. Grab a sidewalk table for a bona fide taste of French-style alfresco dining.

La Petite Grocery, 4238 Magazine St., New Orleans, LA 70115; (504) 891-3377; www.lapetitegrocery.com; French; $$–$$$. Don't let the name throw you off—this establishment, opened in 2004, is nothing resembling a grocery (although it was at one time back in the day) but has everything to do with French-style fine dining thanks in no small part to Executive Chef Justin Devillier, who pulled duty working at some of the city's best restaurants including Bacco, **Stella!** (see p. 42), and Peristyle before joining the staff here. Push past the green double doors and the first thing you'll notice is the mostly smart-dressed groups of patrons sitting at white-linen tables and feasting on dishes like blue-crab beignets with remoulade sauce, steak tartare, roasted veal sweetbreads, and grilled beef tenderloin. What really earned kudos from diners during a recent visit, however, was the paneed rabbit (which arrives with wilted spinach and a lemon-caper brown butter), the courtboullion with blue crab and "popcorn" rice, and the handmade saffron fettuccine, which was augmented instead of overpowered by the lemon and arbequina olives.

La Thai Cuisine, 4938 Prytania St., New Orleans, LA 70115; (504) 899-8886; www.lathaiuptown.com; Thai; $$–$$$. Diana Chauvin seemed destined to open her own restaurant, having grown up learning about Thai cooking at her mother's two local restaurants, Mai Tai and Bangkok Cuisine. Today she and her brother, Merlin Chauvin, are owners and co-executive chefs at this venue that a local weekly newsmagazine has voted Best Thai Restaurant two years in a row. Best bets include Chef Diana's signature panko-crusted sea bass with spicy coconut green curry sauce, and Chef Merlin's jumbo lump crab cake topped with a lightly battered soft-shell crab and seasoned with Thai chili glaze. A nice array of excellent starters, salads, noodle and rice dishes, and curries include the crispy coconut shrimp in a sweet chili soy glaze and the pecan-crusted oyster salad with jumbo lump crabmeat. Don't miss the green curry with coconut milk, bamboo shoots, bell peppers, onions, and basil.

Lilette, 3637 Magazine St., New Orleans, LA 70115; (504) 895-1636; www.liletterestaurant.com; French; $$$. Dark-wood chairs and white-linen tables set against rich maroon walls set the stage for meals in what *Travel + Leisure* calls the "sexiest dining room in New Orleans." But you can thank Chef John Harris, a 2009 James Beard Best Chef South nominee and onetime sous chef under Susan Spicer (see **Bayona**, p. 46), if your palate experiences taste-bud lust at your first spoonful of his brilliantly rendered bouillabaisse. Swimming in a richly flavorful saffron broth equal to if not better than anything enjoyed in Marseilles (the Mediterranean French city where the classic fish stew originated and is still held to the highest standards) are lobster, scallop, cod, shrimp, clams, mussels, and Alaskan king crab claw. Since opening in 2001, this cozy and romantic retreat has garnered not just great reviews but also a loyal clientele who nightly indulge in the French gastronomy Harris creates in the form of fried Japanese Kurobuta pork belly, roasted Muscovy duck, and paneed black drum served with Israeli couscous. Do yourself a favor and save room for dessert—the quenelles of goat-cheese crème fraiche with poached pears, pistachios, and lavender honey are not to be missed. (FYI: If you want a quiet spot for dinner, reserve one of the tables outside around the side of the building.)

Mahony's Po-Boy Shop, 3454 Magazine St., New Orleans, LA 70115; (504) 899-3374; http://mahonyspoboys.com; Neighborhood Cafe; $. Every one in the city has their favorite po-boy den, and for many people this humble spot serves some of the best in town. (It's hard to argue with the fact this establishment won the 2009 New Orleans Po-Boy Preservation Festival's award for Best Specialty Po-boy—a chicken liver version topped with coleslaw.) Other signature po-boys include those made with cochon and Creole-slaw; fried oysters, bacon, and cheddar; root beer–glazed ham and cheese; and grilled pork with tomatoes and remoulade sauce. Don't expect any surprises with the fairly traditional daily-plate specials that can include red beans and rice, seafood gumbo, and meatballs and spaghetti. But what you can count on are generous portions of homemade classics prepared with fresh local ingredients.

Mona's Cafe, 4126 Magazine St., New Orleans, LA; 70115; (504) 894-9800; Mediterranean; $-$$. For a complete description, see Marigny & Bywater chapter, p. 65.

Ninja, 8433 Oak St., New Orleans, LA 70118; (504) 866-1119; www .ninjasushineworleans.com; Japanese; $$. The day has come and gone when fresh fish used in the preparation of sushi and sushi rolls was almost all that was needed to guarantee a modern-day Japanese restaurant a spot on the local culinary map. While this family-owned and -operated establishment, which opened in 1993 and relocated to its current location in 2001, can be counted on for fresh fish, the venue earns even higher praise from some locals for its lengthy vegetarian and wheat-free menus. The vegetarian side of the menu offers tasty versions of soba rolls, tofu steak dinners, vegetable tempura, vegetarian sushi and rolls (the radish sprout and sweet potato tempura rolls are excellent), and cold noodle salads. Meantime the wheat-free side treats customers to a full roster of sushi, sushi rolls, and dinners such as the melt-in-your-mouth tuna served over sushi rice, and *yosenabe*—a traditional Japanese "steamboat dish" and flavorful combination of seafood, tofu, noodles, and vegetables that arrives in a large pot (with vinegar sauce), perfect for sharing with tablemates.

Pascal's Manale, 1838 Napoleon Ave., New Orleans, LA 70115; (504) 895-4877; Creole Italian; $$$. The photographs hanging on the wall of guests who have dined here attest to the lure of this timeless restaurant owned and operated by the same family since 1913. The old-fashioned oyster and cocktail bar is lively and draws a spirited after-work crowd. But one look around the linen-covered tables reveals that this joint remains the uncontested and legendary home of one of the city's most delicious comfort foods: barbecue shrimp. Newcomers are astonished to learn the dish has nothing whatsoever to do with barbecue, but rather involves large, pan-cooked fresh Gulf shrimp served still in the shell (with the heads on, too!) in a peppery butter sauce alongside freshly baked French bread for dunking into the warm, buttery nirvana that only seems to taste better the longer the meal lasts. Daily specials as well as traditional Italian, Creole, seafood, and steaks are served nightly.

Patois, 6078 Laurel St., New Orleans, LA 70118; (504) 895-9441; www.patoisnola.com; Creole French; $$$. The ego of any chef understandably might be expected to swell beyond architectural safety standards after he earns slots as a James Beard semifinalist for Best Chef South three years in a row, or when *USA Today* opines that his cooking "deftly accentuates the French-Mediterranean roots of modern Louisiana cuisine." But that hasn't happened with New Orleans native and Executive Chef Aaron Burgau, whose resume includes a stint with renowned culinary maestro Susan Spicer (see **Bayona**, p. 46). He hasn't allowed the accolades that routinely fall his way to encroach on his recipes that succinctly blend French country flavors with a decidedly Southern twist. Inside this cozy and intimate neighborhood oasis are brilliantly rendered dishes like crispy pork belly with seared scallops (served with Cane's syrup and spicy mustard drizzle), charred baby octopus with roasted chickpeas, roasted pheasant breast with duck confit leg, Japanese Kurobuta pork chop, and paneed rabbit served with a pork confit cake. White-linen tables with window views of Webster Street add to the neighborhood ambience of this consistently well-received establishment opened in 2007.

Rocky's Pizza, 3222 Magazine St., New Orleans, LA 70115; (504) 891-5152; www.facebook.com/RockysPizza; Pizza; $$. Rocky's is a fun and funky pizza joint where the walls are adorned with life-size cutouts of Marilyn Monroe, Scarlett O'Hara, and Rhett Butler—making you feel like you're dining with celebrities. And the pizza's pretty good, too, featuring lots of local flavors. Try the muffaletta pizza (based on the Italian sandwich) with olive salad, sliced genoa salami, sautéed red peppers, pepperoni, mozzarella, and provolone—all on Rocky's crisp thin crust (regular or whole wheat). Or choose Rocky's crawfish étouffée pizza with sautéed crawfish, onions, spices, and andouille sausage. If you want to go a little lighter, consider the Toulouse Street salad with Roma tomatoes, artichoke hearts, feta, toasted pecans, and hard-boiled egg. Rocky's, open for lunch and dinner daily, also serves pasta dishes and paninis.

Sake Cafe, 2830 Magazine St., New Orleans, LA 70115; (504) 894-0033; Japanese; $$. The food here is as fresh and finely crafted as the spacious dining room is beautiful and sophisticated. Routinely voted best sushi in New Orleans by various publications and surveys, Sake Cafe offers a wider range of sushi and sashimi than most other Japanese restaurants in New Orleans, as well as good renditions of cooked classics, such as chicken teriyaki and shrimp tempura. The bento box lunch specials (served daily until 3 p.m.) are filling and value-priced. This is also a great place for date night, as well as an after-work meet-up spot with friends for happy hour. Sake Cafe is open for lunch and dinner every day and offers off-street parking, which is a real plus on busy Magazine Street.

Salú, 3226 Magazine St., New Orleans, LA 70115; (504) 371-5958; www.salurestaurant.com; Tapas; $$–$$$. This wine and small-plate restaurant offers tapas-size portions of Mediterranean-inspired dishes. Executive Chef Ryan Gall and much of his staff trained at various restaurants in the Emeril Lagasse empire and have concen-

trated their culinary skills to create more than two dozen tapas offerings, as well as soups and salads. Start with a salad of sliced duck breast over baby greens with dried cranberries, walnuts, crumbled blue cheese, and shaved apples. Then dive into the tapas with roasted red pepper and fava bean hummus, served with grilled flatbread; or the empanadas two ways: chorizo-manchego and wild mushroom-goat cheese. The upscale dining room features at its center an eye-catching hand-painted circular skylight. But diners can also opt to enjoy their wild mushrooms with sherry cream at one of the many outdoor tables. Salú is open daily for lunch and dinner. Reservations are recommended.

Slice, 1513 St. Charles Ave., New Orleans, LA 70130; (504) 525-7437; http://slicepizzeria.com; Pizza; $–$$. There's nothing fancy here—just good traditional, hand-tossed, thin-crust pizza, served by a friendly staff. For toppings, try the prosciutto di parma, the fresh house-made mozzarella, and the percorino romano. Also good are the tomato and fresh basil bruschetta, the four-cheese ravioli, and the mesclun salad with petite greens, chevre goat cheese, toasted walnuts, and fresh local berries. Pasta dishes and salads are served in either half or whole portions. And don't forget to check out the chef's daily specials. Odds are you'll end up ordering one. There's a full bar, which serves wine by the glass or bottle, as well as a variety of specialty drinks. Slice has a second location farther Uptown at 5538 Magazine St.; (504) 897-4800.

Slim Goodies, 3322 Magazine St., New Orleans, LA 70115; (504) 891-3447; Diner; $. If you're looking for breakfast, slide into one of the upholstered red booths or grab a stool at the counter (where you can watch the short-order cooks do their thing) at this popular diner. The walls are adorned with funny posters, retro diner memorabilia, and Polaroids of customers. The entertaining menu features traditional diner fare of eggs, burgers, and sandwiches, most of which have been given amusing names. There's the Orleans Slammer featuring a small hurricane of hash browns, Slim's famous slim-made chili, two strips of extra thick hickory-smoked bacon, two eggs, and melted cheddar cheese, served with toast or a biscuit. This meal will not only fill you up, but the menu also touts it as "a hangover chaser extraordinaire." There's a burger named for the Delta Blues singer Robert Johnson, who recorded "Cross Road Blues." The beef patty is crossed with two pieces of bacon and topped with blue cheese. Slim's is open for breakfast and lunch daily. See Slim Goodies' recipe for **Jewish Coonass** on p. 262.

St. Charles Tavern, 1433 St. Charles Ave., New Orleans, LA 70130; (504) 523-9823; http://stcharlestavern.com; Neighborhood Cafe; $–$$. It's fair to say that traditionally a good percentage of customers have never seen the inside of the St. Charles Tavern during the day. That's because for decades this 24-hour cafe near Lee Circle has been the place to go for late-night food after a long evening of partying. The menu features hearty down-home fare like oversize omelets, corned beef hash, half-pound burgers, and po-boys. Specialties include chicken-fried steak with mashed potatoes and country gravy, rib eye steak with a loaded baked potato,

Crawfish Monica made with rotini pasta tossed in a crawfish cream sauce, and spaghetti and meatballs. The small dining room had always been rather dive-y, but things have begun to change. Renovations by new owners in 2009 have spruced up the place. Also, the addition of nightly food and/or drink specials, along with live music (Charmaine Neville on Wednesday nights!) has started bringing in more than the ravenous 2 a.m. crowd.

SukhoThai, 4519 Magazine St., New Orleans, LA 70115; (504) 373-6471; www.sukhothai-nola.com; Thai; $$. For a complete description, see the Marigny & Bywater chapter, p. 70.

Surrey's Cafe & Juice Bar, 1418 Magazine St., New Orleans, LA 70130; (504) 524-3828; www.surreyscafeandjuicebar.com; Breakfast; $. This casual breakfast and lunch den of artsy, handmade collage tables and walls decorated with original local artwork really hit the spot during a recent visit when the kitchen was turning out succinctly tasty versions of huevos rancheros (order the optional capers) and Caribbean-style grilled chicken sandwich on focaccia, dressed with melted cheddar and Muenster cheese with sautéed spinach, basil pesto, and tomato. This funky venue is especially popular among the bohemian crowd and anyone else who doesn't have the budget for a fancy breakfast yet enjoys meals that taste like it. Whether your breakfast yearnings lean toward bananas Foster French toast or a crabmeat omelet, or your lunch palate is hankering for a whole-wheat flatbread topped with eggplant spread, goat cheese, roasted red pepper, and sun-dried tomatoes, this establishment rarely disappoints.

Taqueria Corona, 5932 Magazine St., New Orleans, LA 70115; (504) 897-3974; www.taqueriacorona.com; Mexican; $. Restaurateur and El Salvador native Roberto Mendez studied cooking in Japan and worked as a chef for Benihana prior to opening his first restaurant on Magazine Street in 1983 (at a time when he was the only employee) with the simple goal of using only the freshest ingredients to create the unpretentious, home-spun Mexican food version of a New Orleans po-boy shop. It wasn't just a hit with locals; the success that followed was nothing short of, well, amazing. Those old enough to remember will recall with relish their first-ever taste of those to-die-for beef tongue tacos Mendez introduced to New Orleans along with his uniquely flavorful spins on *cebollitas* (charbroiled and seasoned green onions), homemade-from-scratch *pico de gallo*, *queso fundido con chorizo*, and black bean soup. No matter your preference, this always bustling and buzzing, budget-friendly den, which features murals of Central American scenes, can be counted on to deliver excellent Latin-American fare ranging from fish tacos and shrimp *flautas* to combo platters, gazpacho, and rice pudding. Ole! There are also locations at 3535 Severn Ave., Metairie, LA 70002; (504) 885-5088; and 1827 Hickory Ave., Harahan, LA 70123; (504) 738-6722.

Tracey's, 2604 Magazine St., New Orleans, LA 70130; (504) 899-2054; http://traceysnola.com; Sandwiches; $–$$. Tracey's is an interesting story. Jeff and Jamie Carreras had run the wildly popular po-boy shop Parasol's for a dozen years, but the owner of the building (and the Parasol's name) sold it to someone else in 2010. So the Carrerases moved 1 block over to reopen Tracey's, purported to have been the original Irish Channel bar. The new place is bigger and has lots of shady outdoor seating as well. There are 18 TVs, and apparently the business subscribes to every sports channel there is. On a recent Saturday, Major League Baseball, soccer, and women's fast-pitch softball were all on at the same time. But most importantly, the excellent po-boys (including the legendary roast beef), fried seafood, and other pub food are all here. And the priorities are still the same. On the Tracey's website, you can always see exactly how many days are left until St. Patrick's Day, when the green beer flows and Tracey's is the place to be.

Upperline, 1413 Upperline St., New Orleans, LA 70115; (504) 891-9822; www.upperline.com; Contemporary Creole; $$$. Proprietor and longtime restaurateur JoAnn Clevenger is one of the indefatigably charming and beloved figures of the local fine-dining scene. She encourages patrons to ask questions and explore her 45-year rotating collection of artwork, which includes paintings, sculpture, and pottery. Some regulars have referred to the establishment as a fun after-hours museum. Most nights a largely local clientele is found inside this 1877 town house, which offers a classy, warm mood framed by fresh-cut flowers, an Art Deco bar, high ceilings, and lace curtains. The sophisticated, award-winning menu is exciting but never stuffy thanks to Executive Chef Ken Smith. Winners abound: fried green tomatoes in a zesty shrimp remoulade; spicy shrimp with jalapeño corn bread and aioli; duck and andouille gumbo; seared salmon with crawfish bouillabaisse and aioli; and braised lamb shank in Burgundy with saffron risotto. Clevenger hosts her restaurant's famous garlic "festival" Jun through Aug.

Vizard's, 5015 Magazine St., New Orleans, LA 70115; (504) 895-2246; www.vizards.net; Contemporary Creole; $$. It's not uncommon for some Big Easy chefs to spend nearly half their lives honing their craft at well-known restaurants prior to opening their own establishments and gracing patrons' palates with a tour de force of recipes that are as surprising as they are surprisingly good. Such is the case with dyed-in-the-toque Executive Chef Kevin Vizard, who recently replaced his beautiful fine-dining bistro's entrees with a small-plate menu tailor-made for the city's hip culinary set of contemporary diners who prefer diversity of flavor to gargantuan, high-caloric meals. Best bets include Vizard's commanding version of (porcini-dusted) grilled lamb, pan-seared Gulf fish with Caribbean-style crawfish johnnycakes, and seared scallops with

orange vinaigrette. That said, Vizard, wise to the ways of a diverse New Orleans dining demographic, offers entree-size versions of his small-plate dishes.

Landmarks

Clancy's, 6100 Annunciation St., New Orleans, LA 70118; (504) 895-1111; www.clancysneworleans.com; Contemporary Creole; $$. Oprah had the roasted garlic chicken when she ate here. Michael Jordan, Larry Hagman, and Alec Baldwin have also dined on some of Executive Chef Brian Larson's tasty creations. Truth be told, this bastion of modern Creole cooking is the kind of tucked-back-in-a-neighborhood place that concierges recommend to savvy hotel guests when they ask for a locals' spot that oozes with elegant simplicity but most of all character. Today this street-corner restaurant draws a stylish crowd; on the far wall of the main dining room, amid the ceiling fans, candles, white linens, and mirrors, are sketches of neighborhood regulars. Elsewhere upstairs are framed Jazzfest posters and paintings by local artist Peter Bryant of the surrounding Uptown neighborhood. But you don't have to be famous to enjoy Chef Brian's veal liver Lyonnaise, smoked pork loin (with a Creole mustard and green peppercorn sauce), grilled baby drum with smoked salmon, or filet mignon (with Stilton and a red wine demi-glace).

Commander's Palace, 1403 Washington Ave., New Orleans, LA 70130; (504) 899-8221; www.commanderspalace.com; Contemporary; $$$$. A generation of chefs who have gone on to make their own culinary marks in the city have worked in the Commander's kitchen—even the short list is impressive: Emeril Lagasse, Paul Prudhomme, and Frank Brigtsen. Now helmed by Executive Chef Tory McPhail, the restaurant offers a menu that still woos even the most hard-to-please palate with starters such as the restaurant's acclaimed turtle soup, bacon and artichoke-poached oysters with absinthe and double cream under a flaky French pastry, and Hudson Valley *foie gras* served with spring berry beignets, crushed pecan brittle and *foie gras* ganaché, and blackberry jam. Just wait until you try the entree of Tabasco and garlic shrimp, marinated with lemon and blackening spice and cast iron-seared with cognac and roasted mushrooms, and served with cracked-corn jalapeño grits. Is it any wonder this culinary bastion was honored with a James Beard Foundation Lifetime Outstanding Restaurant Award? See Commander's Palace's recipe for **Crawfish Maque Choux** on p. 268.

Specialty Stores, Markets & Producers

Creole Creamery, 4924 Prytania St., New Orleans, LA 70115; (504) 894-8680; www.creolecreamery.com. Sit in this old-fashioned ice cream parlor, with its checkerboard floor and menu written in colored chalk on a blackboard, and you'll feel like you're on the set of *Happy Days*. The Fonz and Richie Cunningham could walk in any minute and order a double scoop. But they'd find a decidedly modern twist on this smooth, house-made ice cream. Along with traditional favorites, the creamery offers more than a hundred unique flavors on a rotating basis. Try Chocolate Chai, Creole Cream Cheese, or Sweet Potato Sassafras Praline. If you can't decide, there's the ice cream sampler with your choice of four or six different mini-scoops. No-sugar-added varieties are also available at this family-friendly spot. Creole Creamery has a second location in Lakeview at 6260 Vicksburg St., New Orleans; (504) 482-2924.

La Boulangerie, 4600 Magazine St., New Orleans, LA 70115; (504) 269-3777. Oft-voted the city's best bakery, this traditional French-style venue sticks to what it does best and offers no apologies. This, a recent visitor quickly learned when he expressed dismay that the establishment didn't sell espresso. "I'm sorry but this is a proper bakery," the counter person said in a decidedly French accent. "You'll find coffee shops down the street." Opened in 1999, this Franco-flavored venue offers a tour de force of flans, cheesecakes, sandwiches, fruit tarts, scones, and Danishes—but, most importantly, a variety of breads baked daily (beginning at 3 a.m.) that includes La Boulangerie's signature blue-cheese bread loaves. Patrons can take out or hunker down at one of the cheery establishment's handful of tables near the sidewalk window. Don't miss the raspberry croissants.

La Divina Gelateria, 3005 Magazine St., New Orleans, LA 70115; (504) 342-2634; www.ladivinagelateria.com. A lot of people say they use only the finest and freshest ingredients, but at La Divina it's really true. This is the only ice cream producer in the state to use no bases, powders, or pastes. And you can taste it in every bite of their creamy, delicious gelato that's made fresh daily. While living in Florence, owners Carmelo and Katrina Turillo came to appreciate the Italian affinity for life's simple pleasures, such as families taking evening strolls to visit with friends and enjoy a scoop of gelato. Wanting to take that experience back home to New Orleans, they studied the Italian art of making gelato and sorbetto from scratch. And now every day, you can experience what they learned. Flavors change seasonally, but some of the most popular are Crème Brulee, Sorbetto di Limone, and Chocolate Azteca (spiced with cayenne!). La Divina also serves paninis and espresso drinks. The French Quarter location is at 621 St. Peter St.; (504) 302-2692.

Martin Wine Cellar, 3500 Magazine St., New Orleans, LA 70115; (504) 899-7411; www.martin wine.com. For a full description, please see the Metairie, Kenner, Harahan & River Ridge listing, p. 215.

St. James Cheese Co., 5004 Prytania St., New Orleans, LA 70115; (504) 899-4737; www.stjamescheese.com. Travelers who had once bemoaned the absence of a true cheesemonger in this city did backflips when New Orleans natives and former London residents Danielle and Richard Sutton opened this formidable fortress of fromage in June 2006. With its clear focus on domestic and international artisanal cheeses, visitors will find everything from a French *Pont L'Eveque Failaisiens* and Italian *Pecorino Pienza* to a Spanish *Garrotxa* and Welsh *Gorwydd Caerphilly*. And that's saying a mouthful. Spanish and Italian specialty meats, French pates and *foie gras*, and local andouille and duck pastrami can also be found behind the counter, as well as a slew of gourmet sandwiches and specialty olives, spreads, sauces, and condiments. Visitors can opt for takeout or enjoy a meal in the shop's courtyard or street-front-porch.

Stein's Market & Deli, 2207 Magazine St., New Orleans, LA 70130; (504) 527-0771; www.steinsdeli.net. Most New Orleans sandwich spots are po-boy shops, which have very little in common with New York-style delis. But Stein's is a traditional Jewish and Italian deli. This is where you'll go if you're hungry for a Reuben (hot corned beef, Swiss, sauerkraut, and Russian dressing on rye) or an Italian hoagie (mortadella, Molinari genoa, Molinari hot coppa, aged provolone, lettuce, tomato, onion, and garlic vinaigrette on an amoroso hoagie). Stein's menu also includes more than 20 other sandwiches, salads, matzah ball soup, H&H bagels from New York, traditional deli meats, and a huge list of specialty cheeses. The market carries high-quality pastas and rices, oils and aged balsamic vinegars, salts and other seasonings, coffees and teas. Stein's is open Tues through Sun.

Sucre, 3025 Magazine St., New Orleans, LA 70115; (504) 520-8311; www.shopsucre.com. If you're in the market for fancy desserts, Sucre is the place. In fact, this business is so high style, the locations are called sweet boutiques rather than sweet shops. The boutique walls are adorned with Sucre's smart-looking signature boxes, which can be filled with premium chocolates, specialty macaroons, or other upscale treats. Walk along the counter and admire rows of desserts so perfectly put together, you'll wonder if Martha Stewart works there. At the back of the shop are the smaller chocolates and bonbons that you can mix and match to fill one of those decorative boxes. Sucre also offers gelato, espresso drinks, and gift sets, as well as making specialty cakes to order. Sucre also has a suburban location at Lakeside Shopping Center, 3301 Veterans Blvd. in Metairie; (504) 834-2277.

Tee-Eva's Famous Pies & Pralines, 5201 Magazine St., New Orleans, LA 70115; (504) 899-8350; www.tee-evapralines.com. Talk about a success story. Eva Louis Perry (aka Tee-Eva, which means Aunt Eva) was a well-known L.A. caterer whose celebrity clients included Governor Jerry Brown (the first time he was governor) before returning to her native Louisiana, where she opened up a string of locations in New Orleans beginning in the 1980s from which she shared her grandmother's recipes for pralines and pies. In 2000 she retired and passed on to her granddaughter her recipes for the same delicious Creole-style pies that can be found today at this newest

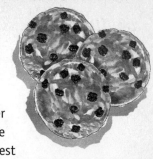

venue. For proof wait until your first bite of the deep-dish cream cheese pecan pie—it's out of this world! Other pastry confections for those with a sweet tooth include the sweet potato pecan pie, regular pecan pie, crawfish pie, and, of course, some of the best bite-size pecan pralines to be found anywhere in the metropolitan area.

Carrollton–Riverbend

Parker Park

Monticello Ave.
General Ogden St.
Eagle St.
Monroe St.
Leonidas St.
Panola St.
Spruce St.
Sycamore St.
Neron Pl.
Cohn St.
Hickory St.
Green St.
Birch St.
Jeannette St.
Joliet St.
Cambronne St.
Dante St.
Dublin St.
Freret St.
Burthe St.
Leake Ave.
Willow St.
Plum St.
Oak St.
S. Carrollton Ave.
Short St.
Zimple St.
Fern St.
Burdette St.
Adams St.
Hillary St.
Cherokee St.
Maple St.
Hampson St.
Huso St.
St. Charles Ave.
Dominican St.

FEET
0   500   1000

Carrollton-Riverbend

This finger-shaped neighborhood runs from where Carrollton Avenue meets the I-10 all the way down to where the river bends like a comma at St. Charles Avenue and River Road. Here diners discover a veritable UN of flavors ranging from Spanish and Thai to Old World French, Middle Eastern, Contemporary Creole, and even soul food. Unifying these cuisines is the distinctly casual and laid-back vibe of the neighborhood that invites people to come as they are, sit for a spell, and enjoy whatever makes their palate happy.

Foodie Faves

Bangkok Thai, 513 S. Carrollton Ave., New Orleans, LA 70118; (504) 861-3932; Thai; $$. **The city's evolving multicultural landscape**

saw the opening in the early 1990s of this establishment, which is today the oldest Thai restaurant in town. Despite the rather Spartan dining room, the menu reflects the kind of authenticity that keeps this venue near the top of the short list of many diners' favorite Thai establishments. Start off with the delicious coconut-milk soup (seasoned with lemongrass, onion, cilantro, mushrooms, and lime juice), to which chicken or prawns can be added depending on personal taste. While an abundance of sautéed, fried rice, and stir-fried noodle dishes are available, those in the know stick with the tried-and-true Thai specialty: curry. At this establishment, five main curries—red, green, yellow, panang, and mussaman—are used along with coconut milk in a variety of tasty vegetable, shrimp, chicken, pork, and beef recipes. Highly recommended is the roasted duck with spicy red curry, which is served mixed with pineapple, tomato, bell pepper, and spinach with outstanding results.

Barcelona Tapas, 720 Dublin St., New Orleans, LA 70118; (504) 861-9696; Spanish; $–$$. Barcelona native and Chef-Proprietor Xavier Laurentino opened this venue devoted to authentic Spanish tapas in 2010 after closing his longtime Metairie restaurant Laurentino's, where he perfected his myriad family recipes of Catalonian cuisine. Today Chef Xavier's domain is a 19th-century building he renovated by hand from the ground up and which now embodies the candlelit romantic decor of a Spanish bodega. A self-described flavor junkie (he even took a workshop in Barcelona taught by staff from El Bulli), the chef's stamp of authenticity can be tasted in a lengthy menu of delicious tapas ranging from *patatas bravas* and *pan con tomate* (traditional Spanish "tomato bread") to fresh home-grown piquillo peppers stuffed with salmon mousse, and pan-seared marinated pork loin medallions served under roasted green peppers and melted Gouda cheese. While traditional paella is on the menu, order the Catalan version, a country cousin called *fideua* (feh-du-AH), which replaces saffron rice with angel-hair pasta for a lighter and subtle alternative that better absorbs the flavors and creates a heavenly twist on Spain's national dish. Swirl in a dollop of aioli just like they do in Barcelona, and at first bite you'll feel whisked away to one of those tucked-away tapas joints in that storied Mediterranean city's medieval Barrio Gothic. See Chef Xavier's recipe for **Fideua Valencia** on p. 270.

Basil Leaf, 1438 S. Carrollton Ave., New Orleans, LA 70118; (504) 862-9001; Thai; $$. This beautifully decorated venue with its colorful wall-length mural and artsy, black bent-back chairs may be the first Thai restaurant to offer not only a separate sushi bar but also home delivery. Talk about keeping up with the times. Devotees of Thai food know that it's a wonderfully complex, strongly spiced, and aromatic cuisine that in the hands of the right chef deftly balances spicy, sour, sweet, salty, and bitter with oft-times brilliant results. One of the best examples of this is the Young Coconut entree, which blends fresh coconut meat with sea scallops, shrimp, eggplant, and traditional Thai herbs, served in a red curry sauce with jasmine rice. Another good way to explore the rich ingredients of Thai curry is with any beef or chicken dish prepared using mussaman curry, which blends peanuts or cashews with coconut milk, potatoes, bay leaves, cardamom, cinnamon, tamarind, and sometimes tumeric, cumin, cloves, and nutmeg.

Boucherie, 8115 Jeannette St., New Orleans, LA 70118; (504) 862-5514; www.boucherie-nola.com; Contemporary Southern; $$. Housed in a converted cottage in the Carrollton neighborhood, Boucherie offers an elegant and intimate atmosphere perfect for date night. Chef Nate Zimet presents a sophisticated twist on traditional local ingredients, such as boudin balls with a garlic aioli or steamed mussels with collard greens and crispy grit crackers. Try the crispy duck confit with cucumber dill salad, sauce gribiche and grilled baby leeks on the side, or the applewood-smoked scallops with roasted local squash and buttermilk bilini. Other good choices include the smoked beef brisket with garlicky Parmesan fries, as well as the St. Louis-style barbecued ribs with roasted beets and crispy fried shallots—both of which hearken to Zimet's roots when he sold his popular barbecue fare from a truck outside local nightclubs. And go ahead and splurge on the Krispy Kreme bread pudding. It's ridiculously good. Boucherie is open for lunch and dinner Tues through Sat, but the dining room is small, so reservations are recommended.

Brigtsen's, 723 Dante St., New Orleans, LA 70118; (504) 861-7610; http://brigtsens.com; Contemporary Creole; $$$. Frank Brigtsen, one of the city's most heralded chefs, opened the doors to this converted shotgun cottage in a quiet Carrollton neighborhood in 1986 and has been swamped by loud applause ever since. Small, cozy rooms with whirring ceiling fans create an intimate yet informal dining experience. And Brigtsen can still be found in the kitchen nightly, personally preparing the majority of dinners—infusing Creole/Acadian cooking traditions with his own creativity. After one taste of his pan-roasted pork tenderloin with sweet potato dirty rice and pork debris sauce, you'll be a believer. Also popular is Brigtsen's grilled seafood platter, a lighter alternative to the traditional fried version. Dinner is served Tues through Sat and reservations are suggested.

Cafe Granada, 1506 S. Carrollton Ave., New Orleans, LA 70118; (504) 865-1612; www.cafegranadanola.com; Spanish; $$. Gustatory adventures await diners eager to explore the hot and cold tapas served here including empanadas stuffed with Manchego cheese and roasted bell peppers, shrimp and crabmeat over tangy Catalan romesco sauce, and duck confit with goat cheese and fig salad. While it might be tempting to order paella, Spain's national dish, best bets entree-wise include the Mediterranean-inspired Moroccan braised lamb *tajine*, with plums, apricots, and Moroccan spices, served with roasted almonds in its own reduction sauce. A traditional dish of *escalivada* (pronounced es-skal-ee-BAH-da) combines grilled eggplant, sweet red peppers, zucchini, and sweet onions, which are peeled and served on rosemary ciabatta bread. The version served here amid a warm decor of saffron-colored walls gets kicked up a notch with olive tapenade and goat cheese.

Camellia Grill, 626 S. Carrollton Ave., New Orleans, LA; (504) 309-2679; www.camelliagrill.net; Diner; $–$$. For a full description, please see the French Quarter listing, p. 19.

Ciro's Cote Sud, 7918 Maple St., New Orleans, LA 70118; (504) 866-9551; www.cotesudrestaurant.com; French; $$. Those who are simply mad about Southern French cooking rarely need look much further than the Provencal yellow and forest-green walls of this cozy, country-style retreat dedicated to classic dishes from the region. And with all due respect to Belgian restaurants that typically prepare that country's national dish, mussels, with savoir-faire, the version that arrives at your table here steamed and accompanied by a choice of curry or Provencal cheese is simply to die for. Truly French (and not New Orleans-style French-Creole—there is a difference!) recipes reign supreme and are best explored when opting for the succulent Cornish hen wrapped in bacon, and the duck breast served with peaches, prunes, apricots, and Bourbon sauce on a bed of mashed potatoes. Two other don't-miss favorites include the grilled pork tenderloin with dijonnaise sauce and the grilled rack of lamb with Provencal herbs. Start off with the cold avocado soup, if it's on the menu, and the starter of baked oysters in a blue cheese sauce.

Dante's Kitchen, 736 Dante St., New Orleans, LA 70118; (504) 861-3121; http://danteskitchen.com; Contemporary Creole; $$$. On a temperate evening it's a tough call deciding whether to dine in the lovely tree-flanged courtyard or inside one of this restaurant's numerous colorfully painted rooms. But whichever you choose there likely will be little disappointment when the slow-cooked rabbit leg and dumplings, hands-down one of the best dishes on the menu, arrive at your table. Ditto for the grilled pork steak served with a corn tortilla and oregano *pupusa*, cilantro crème fraiche, and toasted red pepper sauce. This typically crowded venue buzzes at night with hushed conversation that provides a pleasant backdrop for the kinds of recipes that have made this venue a longtime destination for local gourmets. Start off with the escargot and house-made bacon served with goat cheese, basil, and Vermouth, or Dante's Pot Likka (slow-braised beef pan drippings, goat cheese curd, grilled bread, and fig mustard) before moving smartly to one of the small-portion dishes. Highly recommended is the stuffed rabbit loin with parsnip and fig-mustard puree, cilantro, and garlic olive oil.

Hana, 8116 Hampson St., New Orleans, LA 70118; (504) 865-1634; Japanese; $$. A question about Japanese restaurants arises: Where is the sushi novice to go once he has earned his nori wings and is ready to advance past the commonplace roster of crunchy and California rolls and salmon-box preparations? Answer: this place.

The split-level dining room of this pioneering sushi restaurant in New Orleans, from back in the day when there weren't that many in town, can always be counted on to surprise and delight diners with new and creative twists. For proof just take one bite of the mango-salmon roll and try to contain your enthusiasm. Ditto for the lobster and baked scallop rolls. Fans of specially prepared rolls created with unusual combinations and preparations of salmon, yellowfin tuna, and avocado will find they have a friend in the sushi chef behind the counter. A traditional menu of traditional Japanese teriyaki and tempura dishes is available.

Jacques-Imo's, 8324 Oak St., New Orleans, LA 70118; (504) 861-0886; www.jacquesimoscafe.com; Cajun; $$. This is the little soul-food den you've heard about where customers actually walk past the open kitchen to arrive at the covered-deck dining area out back. And, yes, that's Chef-Owner Jack Leonardi wearing a chef's jacket and Bermuda shorts. But peccadilloes such as those don't even scratch the surface of what makes a meal at this popular neighborhood spot so memorable. What does begin to tell the story of this always bustling den is fried chicken so outstanding devotees have described it as a near religious experience, and a national travel magazine dubbed it the best of its kind anywhere in the United States. But the lengthy regular and specials menu featuring old-school soul food and Creole standards (a must-have is the deep-fried roast beef po-boy) also shares the spotlight with an adventurous shrimp and alligator sausage cheesecake, fried grits with tasso shrimp sauce, chicken livers on toast, oyster-Brie soup, fried rabbit tenderloin with Creole mustard sauce, grilled duck, and pork chop stuffed with ground beef and shrimp.

Jazmine Cafe, 614 S. Carrollton Ave., New Orleans, LA 70118; (504) 866-9301; Vietnamese; $. The soaring popularity of Vietnamese food over the past two decades in New Orleans has given rise to an abundance of restaurants serving quality versions of classic dishes from this country. Even better news is that a handful of truly great Vietnamese establishments such as this venue have surfaced recently, offering exemplary renditions of two personal favorites—hot noodle soup and vermicelli noodle salad, the latter of which can be prepared any number of ways and with ingredients ranging from grilled sliced pork, tofu and avocado, and grilled chicken breast to grilled shrimp and seared tuna. An abundance of tasty rice dishes and appetizers including the ubiquitous spring roll and pot stickers are available. Best bets for hungry diners include the sea scallops and asparagus and caramelized shrimp.

Lebanon's Cafe, 1500 S. Carrollton Ave., New Orleans, LA 70118; (504) 862-6200; www.lebanonscafe.com; Middle Eastern; $$. If Italian restaurants can be rated for quality and authenticity on the basis of tomato sauce, perhaps the same might be said about Middle Eastern eateries with regard to hummus. At this venue the creamy quality of hummus, the best-known preparation of tahini,

or sesame seed paste, is flavored with crushed jala-
peños, garlic, lemon and lime, and ground sumac. A
largely artsy, college student and bohemian crowd
can be found inside this budget-friendly establishment, arguably one of the most beautiful Middle
Eastern restaurants in town thanks to its colorful
bazaar mural, dining on a host of Chef-Proprietor Hussain
Sheereef's kabobs and gyros, falafel, baba ganuj, tabouleh,
stuffed grape leaves, kibby, chicken shawarma, rosemary lamb
chops and other dishes he learned to cook growing up in Iraq.
For many diners the best things on the menu are those that can be
eaten with the deliciously warm and daily fresh-baked pita bread
that helps complete any meal here.

Mat & Naddie's Cafe, 937 Leonidas St., New Orleans, LA 70118;
(504) 861-9600; www.matandnaddies.com; Eclectic; $$$. "Where
Freret (Street) meets the river" might mean something to locals,
but out-of-town visitors might have a hard time finding this place.
Instead, head down St. Charles Avenue (away from the French
Quarter and Downtown) to River Road, turn right, and head 4 blocks
to Leonidas Street. It's on the corner to your right. Look for the
pistachio-green wooden building with a short white picket fence
and the blue neon restaurant name above the door. The tidy menu
created by Chef-Proprietor Steve Schwarz offers dishes at this funky
roadside cafe influenced by local, Continental, and ethnic cookery.
The wild mushroom and Gruyère roulade arrives at your table under
a porcini puree and truffle oil garnish, while the sherry-marinated

grilled quail and Manchego waffle is a gastronomic delight accented by sweet capicola garnish and orange-walnut sauce. Start your dinner off right with the appetizer of roasted corn and sweet pepper fritter with crawfish sausage.

Mikimoto, 3301 S. Carrollton Ave., New Orleans, LA 70118; (504) 488-1881; www.mikimotosushi.com; Japanese; $$. It might be easy to miss this little box of a building at night if it weren't for the large, brightly lighted sign outside announcing what may be among the most popular sushi dens in town. Sure, there's a full host of traditional spring roll and vegetable tempura appetizers as well as traditional Japanese entrees featuring tempura, katsu, and teriyaki preparations depending on whether the main ingredient is chicken, beef, or vegetables. But if you were to ask most locals, the primary reason for dining at this establishment, whether for lunch or dinner, is some of the freshest sushi in town. From amberjack and yellow tail to eel, mackerel, squid, and giant clam, the chefs at this longtime popular spot can be counted on to deliver the kind of praiseworthy sushi and sushi rolls that keep this venue on the short list of any bona fide lover of the Japanese staple.

Oak Street Cafe, 8140 Oak St., New Orleans, LA 70118; (504) 866-8710; www.oakstreetcafe.com; Neighborhood Cafe; $. This being New Orleans, perhaps no one should be surprised to drop into a warm and friendly breakfast-lunch spot like this and hear the strains of live music performed by a modern jazz quartet squeezed into the corner. If something as simple as an egg-and-cheese

sandwich arrives at your table tasting as home-cooked as those your grandmother made when you were a kid, count yourself lucky to have stumbled upon a true soul-food breakfast restaurant. From no-fuss egg platters and French-bread breakfast po-boys (with scrambled eggs, sausage patties, and ham, dressed with lettuce, tomato, and mayo) to assorted omelets and biscuits and gravy, virtually everything on the menu is delicious and satisfying. A personal favorite is the Mediterranean Scramble, a flavorful symphony of scrambled eggs mixed with grilled artichoke hearts, onion, Roma tomato, Italian olives, garlic, green onions, and feta cheese. A word of advice: don't miss the corn bread!

One, 8132 Hampson St., New Orleans, LA 70118; (504) 301-9061; Contemporary Creole; $$$. Owners-Chefs Scott Snodgrass and Lee McCullough have fashioned an old shotgun house into a cozy and cosmopolitan, upscale yet friendly affair with an open kitchen that has kicked into high gear since its opening with an evolving, seasonal menu that generates consistently high praise. In a food city like New Orleans where it might seem daunting to any chef to craft new and exciting recipes using local seasonal ingredients, the menu here always comes out blazing with simple yet elegant appetizers like Louisiana crabmeat cakes with mirliton frittes and basil pesto, and liver and mushroom pate served with fennel and roasted pine nuts. While the coq au vin mixed with grilled chicken sausage and served with potato and white truffle croquettes will win the heart of any fan of Provencal-style cooking, it is the *cochon de lait* with red cabbage and pork cracklin over stone-ground grits that convinces even hard-to-please palates that Snodgrass and McCullough are in it to win it.

Panchita's Mexican Criolla Cuisine, 1434 S. Carrollton Ave., New Orleans, LA 70118; (504) 281-4127; Mexican; $. A friend who had recently returned from a visit to Guadalajara was desperate to find a local joint that served a dish called *chilaquiles* he had enjoyed during his stay in Mexico. Word of mouth led our small group to this Mexican food spot specifically for that dish, and afterward the friend proclaimed it as good as, if not better than, what he had enjoyed south of the border. With lightly fried tortillas simmered until soft and then topped with salsa, fried eggs, pulled chicken, and cheese or sour cream, the *chilaquiles* served at this popular, budget-friendly venue were indeed out of this world and a hearty meal worthy of an "Ole!" or two from the group. A sizeable menu chockablock with 10 different nacho plates, nine types of burritos, plus assorted quesadilla, camarone, enchilada, taco, and fajita dishes makes this establishment a hands-down favorite among those looking for variety as well as quality.

Pupuseria La Macarena, 8120 Hampson St., New Orleans, LA 70118; (504) 862-5252; www.pupusasneworleans.com; Central American; $$. Most every culture in the world has its version of soul food, those timeless and heart-warming comfort dishes that never go out of style. El Salvador is no exception. If that country has a national dish, it may arguably be the *pupusa*, a thin, round, and hearty cornmeal "pancake" traditionally filled with pork, beans, cheese, or a combination thereof, and served topped with pickled cabbage slaw. When you eat the version prepared by longtime Salvadoran cook and co-owner Isabel Galvez Ochoa, who runs this family restaurant along with her affable son, Manny, you'll be dining on what may well be the best (and certainly freshest) *pupusas* this side of San Salvador. This cozy riverfront eatery is a gustatory retreat for those seeking out Salvadoran cooking traditions as seen in dishes like sweet tamales, Salvadoran-style enchiladas (with avocado, boiled egg, and grated cheese), adventurous seafood *pupusas*, and fried yucca *con chicharron*. Try Isabel's equally satisfying, creamy homemade refried beans served with cream and fried plantains, and Spanish-style garlic soup.

Riccobono's Panola Street Cafe, 7801 Panola St., New Orleans, LA 70118; (504) 314-1810; Breakfast; $. For years the Riccobono family has been treating local palates to its traditional take on classic American and Italian fare at its various cafes throughout the metropolitan area. But this unique breakfast and lunch spot has carved itself a niche among a largely neighborhood clientele for its specialties, not the least of which include its pecan waffles, Sausalito omelet (with spinach, mushrooms, shallots, and garlic), crab cakes Benedict (a nice spin on traditional eggs Benedict), eggs Pontchartrain with crawfish, great pancakes, and a rocking version of huevos rancheros every bit as good as one regular remembers eating as a child. Weekend mornings typically find large crowds hunkered down inside this comfortable, well-worn venue that is decidedly out of the way but well worth the trouble to find.

Saltwater Grill and Oyster Bar, 710 S. Carrollton Ave., New Orleans, LA 70118; (504) 324-6640; www.saltwatergrillnola.com; Seafood; $$. It's always a nice surprise when the newest generation of seafood restaurants remembers to pay homage to the stock and trade of southeast Louisiana's most cherished culinary traditions. At this venue, opened in 2004 and today run by William McIntyre and Russell Davis, that homage is to this region's venerated fried green tomatoes, which arrive at the table with grilled Gulf shrimp and homemade remoulade sauce. What has helped earn this upstart a growing reputation as a don't-miss casual seafood den are the kitchen's versions of other timeless classics such as Louisiana crab cakes, shrimp and okra gumbo, and bounteous seafood platters brimming with shrimp, oyster, catfish, crab cake, or a combination thereof. A selection of po-boys includes those stuffed with shrimp, catfish, oysters, crab cake, and *cochon de lait*. But it was the marinated portobello mushroom po-boy enjoyed during a recent visit that really put a smile on everyone's face.

Sara's, 724 Dublin St., New Orleans, LA 70118; (504) 861-0565; www.sarasrestaurant.com; Pan-Asian; $$. If this popular and elegantly casual dining spot comes highly recommended, chalk it up in part to the smart and unconventional synthesis of cooking traditions that fuses Indian, Mediterranean, Thai, and French-Creole cooking styles. The quiet and comfortable main dining room invites lengthy visits over meals with good friends not bashful about trying one another's dishes—and what dishes! The crawfish egg rolls, for instance, come with an oyster sweet-chili dipping sauce while the samosas, an Indian favorite, is a pastry turnover served with tamarind sauce and filled with coriander-spiced vegetables. Don't miss the coconut-flavored lobster bisque, which is at once hearty and flavorful. Entree-wise, a duo of strong suits born on the Indian subcontinent is the brilliantly prepared shrimp satay and *saag paneer* (home-made Indian cheese sautéed with baby spinach and spices). Patrons looking for fowl play should try the grilled Muscovy duck breast, served over plum port reduction and jasmine rice. Just make sure you save room for the mango cheesecake dessert if you know what's good for you.

Squeal Bar-B-Q, 8400 Oak St., New Orleans, LA 70118; (504) 302-7370; www.squeal-nola.com; Barbecue; $$. You might come here at first just because of the humorous name but also because you've heard of this joint's out-of-this-world, St. Louis-style dry-rubbed ribs, which are hickory smoked for—count 'em—8½ hours, or the hickory-smoked meat plate that comes with pulled pork, smoked chicken, and/or green onion sausage. Both are not to be missed. But the Young brothers (Brendan, Patrick, and Eugene), who opened this establishment in 2008, have also fashioned a menu chockablock with some of the most creative barbecue-style recipes seen in recent memory. For proof slide your fork into creamy roasted corn-cheese grits that arrive at your tabled topped with a heaping portion of barbecue pulled pork, or try one of the Squeal Taco entrees filled with barbecue pork, brisket, or beef short ribs, spicy Thai shrimp, or jerk chicken. Don't miss the appetizer of flour-crusted duck cracklins with chili vinaigrette served with a chipotle ranch dipping sauce.

Tartine, 7217 Perrier St., New Orleans, LA 70118; (504) 866-4860; www.tartineneworleans.com; Sandwiches; $. If the ham and Brie sandwich or *tartine* (French for buttered bread or open-faced sandwich) savored at this small, neighborhood storefront of bare-wood tables seems every bit as memorable as that enjoyed in France, chalk it up to the fact New Orleans-born Chef-Proprietor Cara Benson attended New York's acclaimed French Culinary Institute, where she no doubt learned among other things the all-mighty importance of fresh homemade bread. Either way, patrons can count on some of the freshest dense-and-chewy French baguettes in town when diving into one of Chef Cara's casually Continental and slightly sophisticated open-faced sandwiches at this hidden gem of a bakery, breakfast, and lunch spot. Among the treats not to be missed include her *tartine* of pork rillettes or homemade pate over

Dijon mustard and sweet onion jam, dotted with herbs and pieces of dates, and salumi, which features mozzarella, basil oil, and eggplant caviar on ciabatta.

Vincent's, 7839 St. Charles Ave., New Orleans, LA 70118; (504) 866-9313; www.vincentsitaliancuisine.com; Italian; $$. Locals have been flocking to this romantic Italian dining den ever since New Orleans native Vincent Catalanotto opened his first restaurant in Metairie in 1989. While there is certainly no shortage of good Italian eateries in the city, it was the wonderful homegrown dishes his Sicilian parents prepared for him and his family as a child that help inspire the rave-worthy menu Catalanotto, along with partner Tony Imbraguglio, put together for diners eager for a taste of Italy. Simple dishes prepared extremely well include appetizers like oysters Almondine and artichoke Vincent, which features Louisiana shrimp and crabmeat over fried artichoke hearts topped with lemon-tarragon cream sauce. Where the kitchen really shines, though, is with its eight pasta entrees ranging from Italian sausage or sautéed Italian oysters over angel-hair pasta to eggplant Parmesan. Chicken, seafood, and veal are given the royal Italian treatment, most notably the veal piccata and veal marsala, fresh Gulf shrimp, and seafood wrapped in pastry and topped with crabmeat cream sauce, and seafood-stuffed pork chop. There's also a location at 4411 Chastant St., Metairie, LA 70006; (504) 885-2984.

Mid-City

Framed by Bayou St. John and rolling red streetcars and tucked between downtown, Carrollton and Lakeview, the enclave that is Mid-City is distinctly serene yet capable of kicking up its heels at the drop of a hat whenever locals decide to turn a restaurant into an impromptu festival of fun. From romantic terraced venues with a French twist and legendary soul food dens to po-boy holes in the wall and chic retreats serving up nouvelle Creole specialties, the restaurants in this part of town boast a character—and, sometimes, eccentricity—all their own. And it's among the main reasons people throughout the metropolitan area flock to this neighborhood when they need to escape the fussy and fastidiousness and become reacquainted with the hand-in-glove feeling of a slower way of life and a cuisine that fits it to a T.

Foodie Faves

Cafe Minh, 4139 Canal St., New Orleans, LA 70119; (504) 482-6266; Vietnamese; $$. Don't make the mistake of thinking this

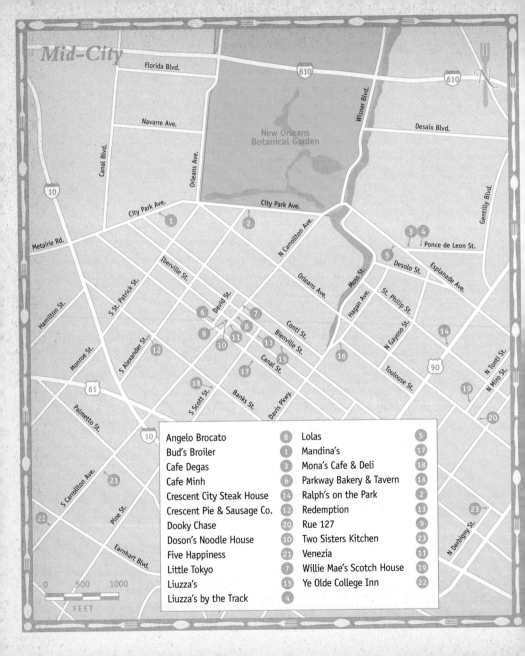

Mid-City

Florida Blvd.

610

610

N

Navarre Ave.

New Orleans
Botanical Garden

Canal Blvd.

Orleans Ave.

Wisner Blvd.

Desaix Blvd.

10

Gentilly Blvd.

Metairie Rd.

City Park Ave.

City Park Ave.

1

2

N Carrollton Ave.

3 4

Ponce de Leon St.

5

Desolo St.

Iberville St.

Orleans Ave.

Moss St.

Hagan Ave.

St. Philip St.

Esplanade Ave.

Hamilton St.

S. St. Patrick St.

David St.

6

7

Conti St.

N Gayoso St.

14

90

N Tonti St.

Monroe St.

S Alexander St.

9

8

10 11

13

Bienville St.

15

16

Toulouse St.

N Miro St.

12

Canal St.

61

17

19

S Scott St.

18

Banks St.

Davis Pkwy.

20

Palmetto St.

10

Angelo Brocato	8	Lolas	5
Bud's Broiler	1	Mandina's	17
Cafe Degas	3	Mona's Cafe & Deli	18
Cafe Minh	6	Parkway Bakery & Tavern	16
Crescent City Steak House	14	Ralph's on the Park	2
Crescent Pie & Sausage Co.	12	Redemption	13
Dooky Chase	20	Rue 127	9
Doson's Noodle House	10	Two Sisters Kitchen	23
Five Happiness	21	Venezia	11
Little Tokyo	7	Willie Mae's Scotch House	19
Liuzza's	15	Ye Olde College Inn	22
Liuzza's by the Track	4		

S Carrollton Ave.

21

Pine St.

23

22

Earnhart Blvd.

N Derbigny St.

0   500   1000

FEET

neighborhood establishment is your run-of-the-mill Vietnamese restaurant churning out copious quantities of spring rolls. From the moment you walk inside and see the stylish, minimalist-hip decor of modern artwork and dark-metal-and-blonde-wood bent-back dining chairs juxtaposed against white-linen tables, it is clearly understood that this is no mere noodle-bowl joint. Opened in 2006, this venue truly takes Vietnamese cuisine to the next level by incorporating the country's French-colonial cooking traditions with a distinctly contemporary Creole flair. Good examples include the smoked duck with five spices that arrives au jus with mung-bean sticky rice, sautéed curry shrimp over angel-hair pasta, and the Asian-marinated oven-roasted pork tenderloin served alongside sweet potato ginger puree and laced with tamarind sauce. Sure, patrons will find more traditional dishes—yes, including the ubiquitous spring roll and pork noodle soup—on the menu, but it would be a shame not to explore the more envelope-pushing, Next Generation recipes on which this popular spot has staked its well-earned popular reputation.

Crescent Pie & Sausage Co., 4400 Banks St., New Orleans, LA 70119; (504) 482-2426; www.crescentpieandsausage.com; Neighborhood Cafe; $$. Just the idea of a Friday "Hit the Deck!" seafood boil, where patrons get a heaping plate of boiled crawfish and "all the fixins" for one low price, should give a pretty good idea of the laid-back fun to be enjoyed at this gourmet pizza and sandwich joint. Regardless of whether you arrive on Friday there are always plenty of good eats on hand ranging from the chicken marsala pizza (with mushrooms, homemade ricotta, onions, Parmesan, and herbs) to the mixed grill of fresh or smoked daily meats, and the Chaurice, a macaroni-and-cheese dish kicked up a notch with the addition of sautéed okra. During a recent visit the brisket sandwich proved a meal in itself and arrived at the table with red onions, mild poblano chili peppers, red pepper aioli, and barbecue sauce for a tangy, garlicky feast of unusual and highly creative ingredient combinations. Wash it down with a bottle of NOLA Brewing's Flambeau Red Ale, one of several homegrown craft beers available.

Dooky Chase, 2301 Orleans Ave., New Orleans, LA 70119; (504) 821-0600; www.dookychaserestaurant.com; Creole; $$. In a city where good—nay, great—soul food restaurants are in abundance, this one is near and dear to the hearts of locals not only for its rotating menu of time-honored Creole staples like the meatless gumbo *z'herbes* (arguably the best in town) but also for the owner, Leah Chase, born in 1923, a multiple award-winning chef and James Beard Foundation inductee who is widely regarded as both a national treasure and the Queen of Creole Cuisine. Over the years the eatery has grown from the best-kept secret of the African-American community to a restaurant of international renown, mostly because of the talents of Leah Chase, the wife of Dooky Chase Jr. and a home-taught cook who is behind such delicacies as chicken breast a la Dooky—stuffed with oysters, baked in a *marchand de vin* sauce, and served with sweet potatoes. Other best bets include fried chicken, red beans and rice, Creole gumbo, and stuffed shrimp.

Doson's Noodle House, 135 N. Carrollton Ave., New Orleans, LA 70119; (504) 309-7283; Vietnamese; $$. This comfortable neighborhood joint opened in 2006 and since then has earned a loyal following among fans of the vermicelli and fried noodle dishes that are so much a mainstay of traditional Vietnamese cuisine. What's nice about this place is the menu offers both brunch- and dinner-size portions of its most popular recipes including beef, chicken, and shrimp noodle soup, as well as vermicelli dishes prepared with grilled chicken, pork, or shrimp, lemongrass, and grilled tofu and vegetables. A recent visit found the pan-fried noodle dishes particularly noteworthy, especially those prepared with chicken and shrimp. Hearty entrees run the gamut from beef with broccoli in garlic sauce to sweet and sour shrimp or chicken, and crispy whole fish.

Five Happiness, 3605 S. Carrollton Ave., New Orleans, LA 70118; (504) 482-3935; http://fivehappiness.com; Chinese; $$. When Five Happiness owner Peggy Lee first visited the Big Easy in the early 1980s, she found that local Chinese restaurants were serving rather bland food. Knowing New Orleanians' love for spicy food, she decided to relocate to New Orleans her California-based restaurant, which specialized in Szechuan and Hunan fare. Since that time, this Mid-City eatery has grown into one of the city's most popular Chinese restaurants. The dining area, divided into three rooms for a more intimate feel, was completely redesigned in 2005, adding sophisticated wall treatments, etched glass elements, and authentic Chinese furniture. Best bets include Szechuan shrimp, pot stickers, hot and sour soup, and the Triple Delight—a combination of chicken, beef, and shrimp sautéed with vegetables in a brown sauce. All the food here is fresh and well-prepared, however, so you really can't go wrong ordering anything. Five Happiness serves lunch and dinner daily. It's best to make reservations for dinner, especially on the weekends.

Little Tokyo, 310 N. Carrollton Ave., New Orleans, LA 70119; (504) 485-5658; www.littletokyonola.com; Japanese; $$. Tucked inside the Mid-City Center, this restaurant has been popular with locals from the day the first location opened in Metairie in the mid-1980s. White-linen tables and bent-back chairs set amid a beautifully artsy decor provide the backdrop for fresh fish shipped to the restaurant three times a week from the Tsukiji Market in Tokyo. A menu chockablock with sushi, sushi rolls, sashimi, soups and noodle dishes, tempura, salads, plus dinner specials keeps loyal customers coming back for more. New to this restaurant? Try the Love Boat Tokyo for Two, which features a sizeable combo of tempura shrimp and vegetables, beef and chicken teriyaki, selected sushi and sashimi, and fresh fruit. What makes this sushi den a standout is that it stays open until midnight or 1 a.m. (depending on the day of the week). There are also locations at 1340 S. Carrollton Ave., New

Orleans, LA; 70118; (504) 861-0688; and 1521 N. Causeway Blvd., Metairie, LA 70001; (504) 831-6788.

Liuzza's by the Track, 1518 N. Lopez St., New Orleans, LA 70119; (504) 218-7888; Neighborhood Cafe; $. When New Orleans family members living out of state blow into town for a short visit, invariably this is the second or third restaurant on their short list of must-eat spots. And for good reason. The menu at Liuzza's, a stone's throw from the New Orleans Fair Grounds Race Track, hits the backstretch of cherished local dishes ranging from its acclaimed (and oh-so-spicy) barbecue shrimp po-boy, fried oyster salad, and superbly seasoned Creole chicken and sausage gumbo to fresh sautéed shrimp and corn chowder with crawfish. This homegrown thoroughbred may look like a downscale neighborhood joint from the inside, but once you've tasted its don't-miss roast beef po-boy with "nostril-searing" horseradish (so good *Gourmet* magazine proclaimed it "the reason to come to New Orleans"), you'll feel like you just won the Triple Crown of gastronomic indulgences.

Lola's, 3312 Esplanade Ave., New Orleans, LA 70119; (504) 488-6946; Spanish; $$. Lovers of Iberian cuisine often rate Spanish restaurants by the intensity of garlic aroma emanating from the kitchen the moment they open the front door—the more intense the garlic smell the more likely the dishes are to be authentic (and good). But this is only one of the reasons loyalists flock to this cozy and always crowded dining den near Bayou St. John. Others have to do with the menu's splendid Andalusian-style recipes from southern Spain like the traditional *ajoblanco* soup and *caldereta*, a lamb stew made with bell peppers, onions, garlic, carrots, hot peppers, and spices. A full complement of classic paellas (meat, seafood, or a combination, and vegetarian) is available as well as garlic shrimp and gazpacho. While the list of tapas is by no means the largest in town, regulars familiar with the menu often jump for the roasted duck breast in fig reduction sauce, a full-flavored exploration of the cooking traditions of España.

Mona's Cafe & Deli, 3901 Banks St., New Orleans, LA 70119; (504) 482-7743; Mediterranean; $–$$. For full description, see Marigny & Bywater chapter, p. 65.

Parkway Bakery & Tavern, 538 Hagan Ave., New Orleans, LA 70119; (504) 482-3047; Sandwiches; $–$$. Yes, "bakery and tavern" may sound like a strange combination, but it's actually not a bakery. It's a sandwich shop, and part of the New Orleans tradition of calling places by what they used to be. This is a great spot to experience any of the traditional po-boy sandwiches. Start with the roast beef (you want it hot and with gravy) or the fried shrimp (dressed with ketchup, not mayo; add your own hot sauce, but remember, just a few drops will do you). And they should both be on French bread. If you're really hungry or sharing, you may want to go for the Parkway Surf and Turf, which is slow-cooked roast beef topped with fried shrimp and covered in roast beef gravy. They do lots of takeout, but if you have a little time to spend in the dining room, you can peruse all the old New Orleans memorabilia hanging on the walls.

Ralph's on the Park, 900 City Park Ave., New Orleans, LA 70119; (504) 488-1000; www.ralphsonthepark.com; Contemporary Creole; $$$. There is a sublime graciousness about this venue, set in a former two-story home constructed in 1860, that every local who dines here remembers along with the outstanding dishes crafted by Chef Chip Flanagan. Maybe it's the elegant white-linen tables and bent-back chairs near window with views of the centuries-old, moss-draped oaks of City Park just across the street. Or perhaps it's gentility of the atmosphere and service created by owner-host Ralph Brennan of the city's acclaimed Brennan restaurant family. This oasis has been a longtime favorite among locals who have discovered the brilliant simplicity of "snack plates" as simple as vinegar fries, served with béarnaise sauce, boudin balls with Creole mustard butter sauce, and *foie gras* served atop a fried peanut butter and jelly sandwich. Palate-pleasing complexities on the entree side of the menu include the grilled double-cut pork chop that arrives with applewood-smoked bacon and bean ragout, and red onion marmalade. Whatever your particular cravings, a don't-miss is the turtle soup.

Redemption, 3835 Iberville St., New Orleans, LA 70119; (504) 309-3570; www.redemption-nola.com; Contemporary Creole; $$. If you think the food here is divine, it might be for good reason. Located in a long-ago church and former home of the restaurant Christian's, the dining room of this new kid on the block, with its beautiful dark-wood tables amid walls of original arched Gothic windows, is alone enough to dazzle first-time patrons. But the "revival cuisine" husband-and-wife owners Tommy and Maria Delaune have cobbled together makes this dining shrine more than just another pretty angel. From the Gruyère and panchetta gravy macaroni to the crawfish potato boulette (served with artichoke hollandaise) and rabbit confit (with truffle bread pudding and roasted oak demi-glace), the food is consistently worth the sometimes lengthy wait and comes highly recommended by virtually everyone who has had the pleasure of walking through the canopied entrance. Culinary high notes include the near-perfect Chateaubriand, seared tuna, Chambord roasted duckling, and charbroiled oysters with crab-butter topping. Make sure to save room for the heavenly dessert of pistachio cheesecake.

Rue 127, 127 N. Carrollton Ave., New Orleans, LA 70119; (504) 483-1571; www.rue127.com; American Contemporary; $$–$$$. Housed in a renovated 19th-century shotgun home, Rue 127 is set back off the street, so it may be a little hard to spot. But it's worth the trouble. Native New Orleanian and CIA graduate Chef Ray Gruezke worked around the country and locally at **Commander's**

Palace (see p. 136) before opening this new American bistro last year. He specializes in using local, sustainably grown produce and the freshest meats and seafood, so the menu changes weekly. We had the perfectly cooked citrus-glazed duck breast with caramelized fennel, potato puree, and Louisiana citrus jus, as well as the grilled scallops with sour cream whipped potatoes, roasted fennel, and oyster mushrooms. Fabulous. The dining room is beautifully lit and furnished, with original artwork on the walls, but it's tiny. So make reservations. You can also eat at the small bar or out front. They have also added lunch service, and if you're staying downtown, you can take the Canal Street streetcar to get here.

Two Sisters Kitchen, 223 N. Derbigny St., New Orleans, LA 70112; (504) 524-0056; Creole; $. It is often said New Orleans is home to more great hole-in-the-wall restaurants than maybe anywhere else in the country—so many that you can barely fall down without landing inside one of them. Hands-down this Creole soul-food den deserves to be in that number. For proof just try the stewed hen, pig-tails, neck bones, shrimp and okra stew, ham hocks, or (a personal favorite) turkey necks with collard greens and corn bread for a taste of true down-home soul food. Time your visit for a Friday or Saturday if you want to enjoy the oh-so-flavorful gumbo that arrives with a side of potato salad, which longtime regulars immediately plop into the middle of the gumbo for a new twist and a new taste of this perennially popular New Orleans staple. Servings are huge so you're not going to walk away hungry. A short list of po-boys is also available.

Venezia, 134 N. Carrollton Ave., New Orleans, LA 70119; (504) 488-7991; www.venezianeworleans.com; Italian; $$. Locals have a soft spot in their hearts for restaurants they remember dining at with their parents when they were growing up. And this family-owned and operated Italian spot, which opened in 1957, is no exception. But people don't just come here for the nostalgia. This establishment has kept pace with the times and today serves up a tour de force of traditional pizzas as well as those with a decidedly nouveau spin if the breaded veal pizza recently enjoyed is any indication. While it's always a temptation for any restaurant to overreach in the recipe department, this venue knows its clients well and therefore can be counted on to make a dish as simple as spaghetti and meatballs rock with flavor and homegrown soul. Ditto for the eggplant Vatican, cannelloni, lasagna, and veal Parmesan. Even the garlic bread is out of this world.

Willie Mae's Scotch House, 2401 St. Ann St., New Orleans, LA 70119; (504) 822-9503; Creole; $. The group of tourists sitting in the front dining room at lunchtime was alternating between reading the menu and their guidebooks that were turned to the write-up about this place. A buzz of excitement filled the air as did the aroma from the kitchen. The tourists had come to this off-the-beaten-path corner restaurant tucked in the 7th Ward for the same reason everyone else does: the fried chicken that so many claim is the best in the city. And this in a city that knows a thing or two about fried chicken. Truth is, the version served here is indeed unbelievably good—can you say, "melt in your mouth"?—and certainly worth the pilgrimage for anyone who wants to taste an exquisite version of this classic Southern staple. Other time-honored recipes on the menu include corn bread and the New Orleans standard-bearer, red beans and rice.

Landmarks

Angelo Brocato, 214 N. Carrollton Ave., New Orleans, LA 70119; (504) 486-1465; www.angelobrocatoicecream.com; Desserts; $. Simply called Brocato's by locals, this Mid-City Italian dessert shop is a New Orleans institution. It was established in 1905 by Angelo Brocato, who fashioned it after the fine ice cream emporiums of Sicily where he learned his trade. Today, walk in the door and feel like you're transported back in time. Glass jars full of colorful candies line the shelves, a man behind the long ice cream case packs a cone with sweet frozen delight, and fans hanging from the high ceiling turn slowly over happy patrons who sit at old-fashioned glass-top tables munching on gelato, cannoli, and spumoni. And it's not just the look of the place that hasn't changed. The third generation of the Brocato family still runs the place using Brocato's original recipes. The ice creams and desserts are all made on-site daily and only with the freshest ingredients. Try the lemon ice (simply delicious) and take home a box of cannoli for later.

Bud's Broiler, 500 City Park Ave., New Orleans, LA 70119; (504) 486-2559; http://budsbroiler.com; Burgers; $. If you feel the need to eat fast food while in New Orleans, stick to this local chain. There's no drive-thru, just fresh charcoal-broiled burgers topped with a secret-recipe hickory sauce that's been made the same way since 1952. Bud's is also one of the few places in town where you can get hot dogs. Locals identify themselves by their favorite menu item number. (I'm a #7 with onions. That's a grilled hot dog, sliced, topped with grated cheddar cheese and chili, served on a toasted hamburger bun.) There are also chicken, smoked sausage, and fish fillets. The fries are good and the shakes are thick and sweet. Now open 24 hours, this original location is tiny inside, but there's lots of room to eat outside under the shade of giant live oak trees. There are other locations Uptown, in Metairie, Jefferson, Kenner, and on the West Bank. See those chapters or the website for details.

Cafe Degas, 3127 Esplanade Ave., New Orleans, LA 70119; (504) 945-5635; www.cafedegas.com; French; $$. Sitting under the lovely covered front deck on a breezy fall or spring evening while savoring a repast of escargot bourguignon and Provencal-style Salade Niçoise over a cool glass of crisp Côtes-du-Rhône is among the better simple pleasures of Big Easy life. Named after the 19th-century French Impressionist Edgar Degas who lived down the street for a brief time, this European-ish restaurant is ideal for lunch or dinner after visiting the nearby New Orleans Museum of Art. Daily specials augment the rotating French-language menu (with English translations). But count yourself fortunate if this romantic venue, popular among hoi polloi and politicians, is serving starters like crispy sweetbreads (with caper and sherry vinaigrette) and duck gizzard confit (with smoked portobello mushrooms and strawberry vinaigrette), or palate-winning entrees including pan-seared rack of veal (with truffles and mascarpone mashed potatoes). Finish your meal European-style by ordering the daily selection of French cheese.

Crescent City Steak House, 1001 N. Broad St., New Orleans, LA 70119; (504) 821-3271; www.crescentcitysteaks.com; Steak house; $$$. Middle-aged and even older locals remember dining at this venue, opened in 1934 and one of the Big Easy's oldest and most cherished chophouses, with their parents back in the day when it was a popular hangout among politicians and the city's movers and shakers. What hasn't changed at this still family-owned establishment over the years, besides the old neon sign still hanging in front of the building, is the New Orleans-style manner in which steaks arrive at the table: sizzling in butter. At this venerated venue a brief and customary roster of appetizers, salads, and potato "sides" share the menu with the prime reason people still come here in droves—USDA Prime beef rib eyes, filets (wrapped in bacon), strip sirloins, T-bones, and porterhouses. Truly the steaks are so mouthwatering good you might want to dine in one of the restaurant's four curtained privacy booths if you're bashful about letting others see that heavenly smile on your face.

Liuzza's Restaurant & Bar, 3636 Bienville St., New Orleans, LA 70119; (504) 482-9120; www.liuzzas.com; Neighborhood Cafe; $–$$. Opened in 1947, Liuzza's is one of the city's most popular neighborhood restaurants. The Frenchuletta is Liuzza's answer to the muffuletta (a cheese, ham, salami, and olive salad sandwich on a large round bun, which was originally Central Grocery's answer to the po-boy). The Frenchuletta is basically the same thing, except that the meats are grilled and it's served on French bread. The closest thing to low-cal here is the spinach salad—topped with half a dozen fried oysters and bacon. (OK, they have grilled tuna, but you can get that at home.) Try the stuffed artichoke, the gumbo, or the breaded eggplant po-boy with red gravy. The preferred drink is beer served in a frosty 18-ounce glass goblet. You can also get a root beer or cream soda in the frosty mug. Liuzza's is closed Sun and Mon, but serves lunch and dinner the rest of the week. They're cash only, but there's an ATM in the bar.

Mandina's Restaurant, 3800 Canal St., New Orleans, LA 70119; (504) 482-9179; http://mandinasrestaurant.com; Creole Italian; $$. Down-home cooking is the name of the game at this locals' hangout. The two-story pink building was originally a corner grocery started in 1898 by Sebastian Mandina, originally from Palermo. It evolved into a pool hall that sold sandwiches, and in 1932 Sebastian's sons turned it into this family-friendly neighborhood dining den, daily serving up Creole, Italian, and Cajun specials, plus burgers, deli and po-boy sandwiches, seafood, chicken, and steaks. The place bustles at lunch, and a lively crowd can always be found on weekend nights hunkered around the dinette tables under the whirring ceiling fans. Try the trout meunière or catfish amandine at half the price charged by upper-crust establishments, as well as the locally famous "loaf"— a whole loaf of French bread gutted and filled with a choice of fried oysters, shrimp, catfish, or half-and-half (shrimp and oysters). There's also a children's menu. Come as you are.

Ye Olde College Inn, 3000 S. Carrollton Ave., New Orleans, LA 70118; (504) 866-3683; http://collegeinn1933.com; Neighborhood Cafe; $–$$. College Inn has been around since 1933, for generations feeding folks in the neighborhood hearty local fare, with po-boy sandwiches and the breaded veal cutlet at the heart of the menu. In 2003 the Blancher family, owners of Rock n' Bowl (a popular bowling alley/concert venue) bought the place and reinvigorated the menu with farm-fresh local produce and a decidedly modern take on traditional dishes. Old favorites like the veal, po-boys, and a mound of handmade onion rings can still be had. But also look for Chef Johnny Blancher's pulled slow-roasted duck appetizer, crawfish salsa, the Creole caprese salad with tomato, mozzarella, smoked Andouille sausage, and basil-infused olive oil, or the oysters, Havarti, and bacon po-boy. The original College Inn was destroyed by Hurricane Katrina, but the staff reopened just five months later in the building next door. The dining room features a family atmosphere, New Orleans-themed murals on the walls, and a friendly staff. See Ye Olde College Inn's recipe for **French Market Coffee Rub** on p. 260.

Lakefront

The City of New Orleans' northern border is brackish Lake Pontchartrain, from which generations of fishers have hauled in their catch of the day. For many, the traditional docking point has been Bucktown Harbor on the 17th Street Canal, which separates New Orleans from Jefferson Parish on the city's West End. Not surprisingly, several fine seafood restaurants have grown up in the area. Adjacent to Bucktown and West End is the inland suburb of Lakeview, which doesn't actually have a lake view, but does have a handful of restaurants worth noting.

Foodie Faves

Deanie's Seafood, 1713 Lake Ave., Metairie, LA 70005; Bucktown & West End; (504) 831-4141; www.deanies.com; Seafood; $–$$$. For complete description, see French Quarter chapter, p. 23.

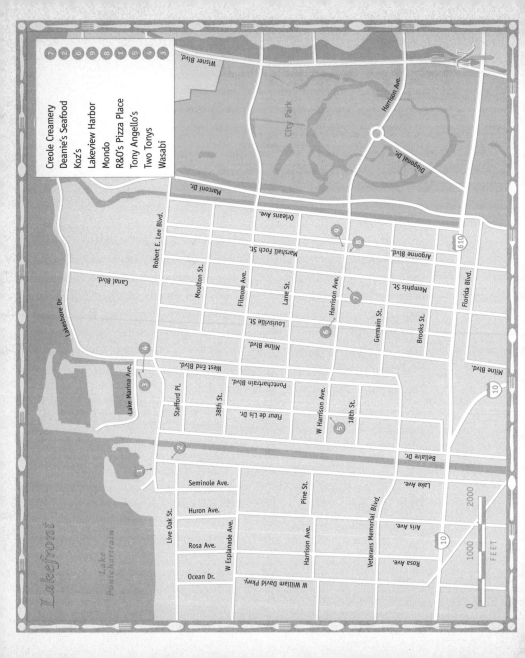

Koz's, 515 Harrison Ave., New Orleans, LA 70124; Lakeview; (504) 484-0841; www.kozcooks.com; Sandwiches; $. **Koz** Gruenig, who ran the Po-Boy Bakery in Gentilly until Hurricane Katrina dumped 10 feet of water on it, brought his popular po-boys back to the city in 2009 when he set up shop in Lakeview. There's nothing fancy here, just tasty po-boys and daily plate specials. Koz has been doing this for a really long time, so all the po-boys are good, although the fried shrimp, hot sausage, and barbecued ham are standouts. Depending on your appetite, you can get an 8-inch, a 12-inch, or a whole loaf. (Yes, that's a sandwich made with an entire loaf of French bread.) For sides, try the baked macaroni or the sweet potato fries. Koz's has a second location at 6215 Wilson St. in Harahan; (504) 737-3933.

Lakeview Harbor, 911 Harrison Ave., New Orleans, LA 70124; Lakeview; (504) 486-4887; www.lakeview-harbor.com; Hamburgers; $$. Lakeview Harbor is the place to go for great burgers in this suburban neighborhood. The ground beef is ground fresh on-site daily, and burgers are beautifully cooked to order. They come with a baked potato, french fries, sweet potato fries, or Tater Tots. The menu also includes other sandwiches, salads, and seafood, steaks, and pizza, but the burgers are the real star here. Although the separation of the bar and restaurant is almost nonexistent, it's actually a very family-friendly place, and there is a kids' menu for those 13 and under. Lakeview Harbor is open for lunch and dinner daily (until midnight weekdays, 1 a.m. Fri and Sat), but it does get crowded at peak hours. The best bet is a late lunch or early dinner.

Mondo, 900 Harrison Ave., New Orleans, LA 70124; Lakeview; (504) 224-2633; www.mondoneworleans.com; Neighborhood Cafe; $$. Superstar Chef Susan Spicer, who helms the famed **Bayona** (see p. 46) restaurant in the French Quarter, created this casual dining cafe in her own residential neighborhood. Mondo offers a comfortable yet stylish atmosphere, a reasonably priced wine list, and a simple, well-crafted menu. The dining room is well lit and attractive, but because it's a neighborhood place, the bar is also a popular place to eat. You can easily make a meal from the starters menu. Highlights include buckwheat noodles with peanut sauce and baby bok choy; chicken liver pate with Creole mustard, pickled vegetables and crostini; ceviche with fresh tortilla chips and guacamole; Italian chopped salad with peppers, pecorino, celery, and olives; and fried eggplant with lemon aioli. For entrees, try the slow-roasted pork shoulder with black beans, plantains, and pico de gallo; or the duck leg confit with lentils, brussels sprouts, and mustard jus. Mondo is open for lunch and dinner, as well as Sunday brunch.

R&O's Pizza Place, 216 Old Hammond Hwy., Metairie, LA 70005; Bucktown & West End; (504) 831-1248; Creole Italian, Seafood; $–$$. People always look as though they're having a good time in this crowded, noisy Bucktown restaurant, and no wonder. The mostly local, family crowd knows that they can expect some of the best pizza, po-boys, and simple specialty dishes in town. The large, airy restaurant has been expanded several times, and each time the customer base has expanded with it. This is not a place for intimate conversation, but if your family wants to go out with a baby who sometimes cries and a brother who talks too loud, no one will even notice. R&O's serves a really good, traditional thin-crust, hand-tossed pizza. The po-boys are also a winner, and the seafood is some of the best-priced you'll find. Try the roast beef po-boy dripping with gravy and mayo or the stuffed crab plate. Lunch and dinner are served daily.

Tony Angello's, 6262 Fleur de Lis Dr., New Orleans, LA 70124; Lakeview; (504) 488-0888; Italian; $$–$$$. At first glance, this signless restaurant could be mistaken for a large house on a corner lot in west Lakeview. But the crowds headed for the door with smiles on their faces give the place away. Inside, a welcoming attitude, subdued lighting, and attentive service make this a popular date spot and always a good experience even before you take the first bite. Sit back and relax with one of the fine Italian wines the restaurant offers by the glass or bottle, and then say the magic words: "Feed me, Mr. Tony." This will be followed by a series of small courses, such as stuffed shells, lobster cup, soft-shell crab, spinach salad, soup, cannelloni, veal with peppers and mushrooms, and eggplant Tina. There are several versions of "feed me" from which to choose, as well as a full a la carte menu. Dinner is served Tues through Sat, and reservations are recommended. "Dressy casual" attire is suggested.

Two Tonys, 8536 Pontchartrain Blvd., New Orleans, LA 70124; Bucktown & West End; (504) 282-0801; Italian; $$. Two Tonys was a perennial favorite among Bucktown restaurants. But it got crowded out by the federal government's new, larger flood protection system developed after Hurricane Katrina. So Chef Tony Montalbano Jr., whose late father, Tony Sr., had founded the original restaurant with him, decided to move to a new location just over the 17th Street Canal in New Orleans' West End. This is good news for fans of the restaurant's excellent renditions of Italian and seafood fare. Start with the Italian fried artichoke hearts with Creole horseradish sauce or the fried eggplant with marinara. Specialties include Pontchartrain veal or chicken, which is paneed and topped with sautéed Louisiana crawfish tails and a roasted pepper cream sauce. On the lighter side, try the perfectly grilled yellowfin tuna, topped with a lite lemon butter sauce. And if you like Two Tonys' all-natural marinara sauce, you can now take a jar of it home with you.

Wasabi Sushi & Asian Grill, 8550 Pontchartrain Blvd., New Orleans, LA 70124; Bucktown & West End; (504) 267-3263; http://wasabinola.com; Japanese; $$. For complete description, see Marigny & Bywater chapter, pg. 72.

Specialty Stores, Markets & Producers

Creole Creamery, 6260 Vicksburg St., New Orleans, LA 70124; (504) 482-2924; www.creolecreamery.com. For full description, see Uptown chapter, p. 136.

Gentilly & New Orleans East

As West End and Lakeview border Lake Pontchartrain on the northwest corner of New Orleans, Gentilly and New Orleans East form the city's northeastern border. Where the West End is upscale, the east end is down-home. Gentilly is a mostly middle-class city suburb that is home to four institutes of higher learning, including the lakefront campus of the University of New Orleans. A hundred years ago, when the area was a resort known as Milneburg, it was the birthplace of jazz. New Orleans East is also predominately a bedroom community—for both people and animals. More than 23,000 acres of fresh and brackish marshlands in the East comprise the Bayou Savage National Wildlife Refuge, the nation's largest urban wildlife refuge. Neither area can boast the number or caliber of restaurants found downtown. But you will find a handful of neighborhood places that have loyal followings for good reasons.

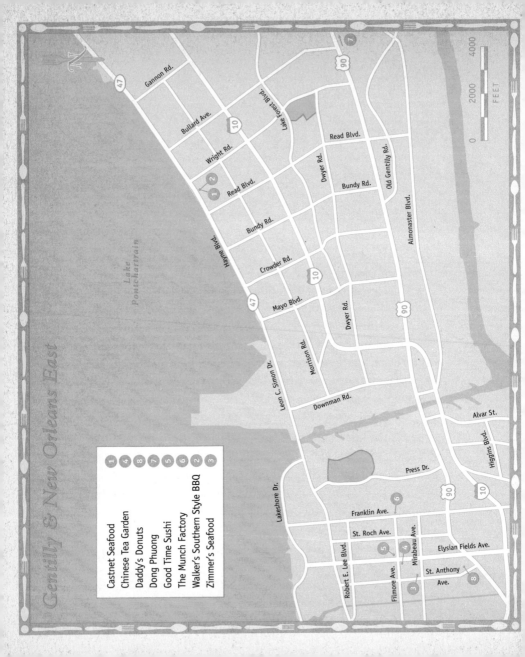

Chinese Tea Garden, 2170 Filmore Ave., New Orleans, LA 70122; Gentilly; (504) 282-1493; www.chineseteagardennola.com; Chinese; $. Chinese Tea Garden serves fresh and hearty food in large portions at great prices. The combo plates, served at both lunch and dinner, generally cost less than $8 and are often big enough to feed two people. If you're on a tight schedule for lunch, service is fast enough to get you in and out in an hour. At suppertime, a loyal following of neighborhood folks can be found eating in or taking out. Most regular customers appreciated the fact that the owner, Mr. Lee, reopened long before any other area eatery following Hurricane Katrina, providing them a place to find a hot meal and a friendly smile after a long day of rebuilding their homes. The egg rolls, cho-cho, pot stickers, and wonton soup are all first-rate. If you like spicy, go for the General Tong's chicken—hot and delicious. Also try the roasted pork and green beans. The Tea Garden is open daily for lunch and dinner.

Dong Phuong, 14207 Chef Menteur Hwy., New Orleans, LA 70129; New Orleans East; (504) 254-0296; www.dpbanhmi.com; Vietnamese; $. There is a thriving Vietnamese community in New Orleans East that was established by refugees in the mid-70s. The community boasts a large number of farmers, fishers, and a variety of Vietnamese-owned businesses. Dong Phuong is the premier Vietnamese bakery and restaurant. The Vietnamese have a long history of French baking, and over the past 30 years, Dong Phuong has become one of the city's top suppliers of French bread. The baguettes are used to make *Banh mi* sandwiches, for sale at the bakery. Most cost about $2.85, although the veggie and pate varieties are—no joke—$1.95. And if you buy 10, you get one free. The bakery offers lots of other fresh baked goods, and the adjacent restaurant serves traditional Vietnamese and Chinese food for breakfast and lunch (both closed Tues). The bakery is quite a ways from downtown, so you may want to go on Saturday morning when you can also visit the Vietnamese farmers' market.

Good Time Sushi, 5315 Elysian Fields Ave., New Orleans, LA 70122; Gentilly; (504) 265-0721; Japanese; $$. This may be the smallest restaurant you ever eat in. But much to the owner's credit, it's still an attractive and welcoming atmosphere—and not at all cramped. Although even if you had to squeeze in, you'd still want to eat here. Good Time Sushi serves very fresh, very well-crafted sushi and sashimi. And the presentation of a recent sashimi  dinner was no less than art. As for the cooked food, try the shrimp tempura dinner, which also has zucchini, sweet potato, broccoli, and a big onion ring. The hibachi fried rice is well-seasoned and tasty, even without meat, and it costs about $3. The staff is so helpful and friendly, you'll feel great about giving them your business. Good Time Sushi is open for lunch and dinner, and does a thriving take-out business.

The Munch Factory, 5339 Franklin Ave., New Orleans, LA 70122; Gentilly; (504) 324-5372; www.facebook.com/TheMunchFactory; Neighborhood Cafe; $$. Don't let the cute name fool you; there's some serious cooking going on here. The Munch Factory serves some of the best traditional New Orleans food (with a decidedly contemporary twist) that this neighborhood has seen in a long time. The charming young owners, Chef Jordon Ruiz and his wife, Alexis, have created a short but flavor-packed menu of soups, salads, sandwiches, and a revolving list of entrees. Try the pork rillettes appetizer—ground pork, lightly battered with French bread crumbs, fried and served with a Creole mustard sauce. Or choose the wonderful potato croquettes—mashed potatoes stuffed with Gouda and bacon, lightly fried. Do not miss the gumbo. The restaurant is open for dinner Tues through Fri and for lunch on Fri), serving shrimp and grits, plus two other entrees nightly. Best bet: the slow-cooked herb chicken topped with a light cream sauce, served with potato croquettes and spiced green beans. Also try the braised short ribs and fish tacos.

Walker's Southern Style BBQ, 10828 Hayne Blvd., New Orleans, LA 70127; New Orleans East; (504) 241-8227; www.cochondelait poboys.com; Barbecue; $. Walker's is one of those places that is so much more than it appears to be. It's in a nondescript building, facing the levee, next to a seafood market/restaurant with which it shares a dining room. But it's also the place that serves the Cochon de Lait Po-Boy, a JazzFest staple that's been touted by the likes of *Esquire* magazine and NPR. Go figure. The sandwich, sold at festival under the catering arm Love at First Bite, features suckling pig, hickory-roasted for 12 hours, then nestled in French bread and finished with Cajun mustard slaw. And that's just one of the offerings at Walker's, along with really good barbecued pork, brisket, chicken, and sausage. That's if you can get in. Another enigmatic aspect of the restaurant is the hours. Walker's is open Tues through Fri from 10:30 a.m. until they run out—which is generally pretty early. They're also supposedly open Sat from 10:30 a.m. to 6 p.m. It's probably best to call ahead.

Zimmer's Seafood, 4915 St. Anthony Ave., New Orleans, LA 70122; Gentilly; (504) 282-7150; www.zimmersseafood.webs.com; Seafood; $–$$. Zimmer's has served Gentilly some of the city's best seafood po-boys (especially the shrimp) for three decades. The shop is at a busy intersection, and locals know to slow down when driving home to avoid hitting any of the throngs of people running into Zimmer's to get dinner before closing. Zimmer's also sells fried seafood plates and boiled seafood by the pound. As for sides, try the stuffed artichoke, marinated crab salad, or Maw Maw's potato salad. There's nowhere to sit and eat at Zimmer's, but you're really close to the lakefront, where it's so relaxing to pass time on a bench overlooking the water. Or even closer, there's a terrific little neighborhood park 7 blocks away (head up St. Anthony toward the lake, take a left on Burbank) that features what's considered a marvel in New Orleans—hills. So, grab a sandwich. Then pick a spot to enjoy the great taste and slow pace that Gentilly has to offer.

Specialty Stores, Markets & Producers

Castnet Seafood, 10826½ Hayne Blvd., New Orleans, LA 70127; New Orleans East; (504) 244-8446. Castnet is a combination seafood market and restaurant. Enter on the left to pick up your raw or boiled seafood, as well as a good selection of fresh and smoked fish. Go in on the right to place your order for cooked food, including seafood po-boys. For sides, go with the potato salad or corn on the cob. There are also seafood platters and home-style specials on Tuesday (breaded veal and macaroni) and Wednesday (spaghetti and meatballs). But the specials run out early. And while you're waiting for your food, you can enjoy a 12-ounce cup of cold beer for—believe it or not—50 cents. Castnet is actually part of a sort of complex. On one side of the market is a snowball stand selling the traditional frozen treat and on the other side is **Walker's Southern Style BBQ** (see p. 189) which shares a dining room with Castnet.

Daddy's Donuts, 2051 Caton St., New Orleans, LA 70122; Gentilly; (504) 283-3388. Daddy's is another food outlet that has opened in

Gentilly since Hurricane Katrina. Run by second-generation donut-maker George Carlton, Daddy's serves delicious fried dough daily from 6 a.m. to 1 p.m. If you want to get them while they're hot, show up at opening or around 8:30 a.m. when the second batch of the day comes out. Best bets are the apple fritters, hot glaze, cream-filled chocolate shells, and the Big Texas, a two-fisted glazed donut that has to be seen (or better, tasted) to be believed. Daddy's also makes the sometimes hard-to-find traditional Russian cake.

Metairie, Kenner, Harahan & River Ridge

The unincorporated community of Metairie/Old Metairie has grown into a full-fledged enclave that today boasts a typically suburban mix of ubiquitous strip malls and large shopping complexes, sprawling subdivisions and civic centers, not to mention Zephyr Field, the metropolitan area's only stadium for minor league baseball. Equally important is how this area over the years has blossomed and given rise to an indisputably reputable roster of specialty food stores and dining establishments that run the field from fine Italian and cherished seafood dens to Latin American and Mediterranean.

In the outlying areas of East Jefferson in Jefferson Parish lies the trio of suburban bedroom communities of Kenner, Harahan, and River Ridge, which offer unique twists on dining opportunities. The City of Kenner, in particular, is home to the Louis Armstrong New Orleans International Airport.

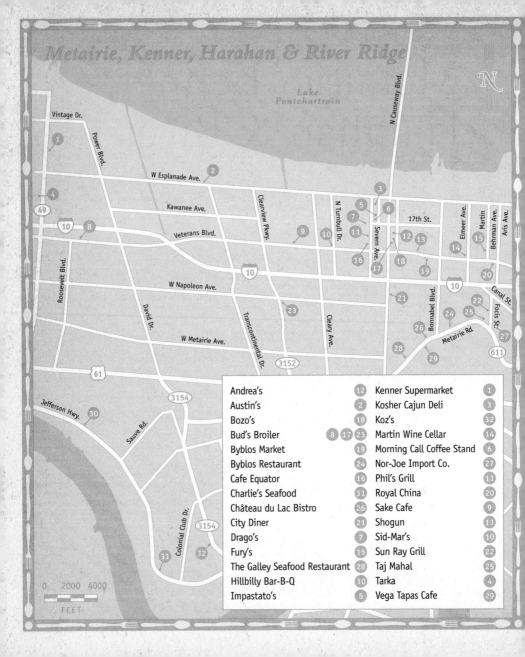

Metairie, Kenner, Harahan & River Ridge

Lake Pontchartrain

N

Vintage Dr.
Power Blvd.
W Esplanade Ave.
Kawanee Ave.
Clearview Pkwy.
N Turnbull Dr.
N Causeway Blvd.
17th St.
Elmeer Ave.
Martin
Behrman Ave.
Aris Ave.
Veterans Blvd.
Severn Ave.
Roosevelt Blvd.
W Napoleon Ave.
David Dr.
Transcontinental Dr.
Cleary Ave.
Bonnabel Blvd.
Canal St.
Focis St.
W Metairie Ave.
Metairie Rd.
Jefferson Hwy.
Sauve Rd.
Colonial Club Dr.

Andrea's	12	Kenner Supermarket	1
Austin's	2	Kosher Cajun Deli	3
Bozo's	18	Koz's	32
Bud's Broiler	8 17 23	Martin Wine Cellar	14
Byblos Market	19	Morning Call Coffee Stand	6
Byblos Restaurant	24	Nor-Joe Import Co.	27
Cafe Equator	16	Phil's Grill	11
Charlie's Seafood	31	Royal China	20
Château du Lac Bistro	26	Sake Cafe	9
City Diner	21	Shogun	13
Drago's	7	Sid-Mar's	10
Fury's	15	Sun Ray Grill	22
The Galley Seafood Restaurant	28	Taj Mahal	25
Hillbilly Bar-B-Q	30	Tarka	4
Impastato's	5	Vega Tapas Cafe	29

0   2000   4000
FEET

Andrea's, 3100 19th St., Metairie, LA 70002; (504) 834-8583; www.andreasrestaurant.com; Italian; $$$. Few chefs so embody the heart and soul of Southern Italy and its vibrant cooking traditions as Andrea Apuzzo, who for the past quarter century has been sharing the flavors and recipes of his beloved native Capri with a customer base so fiercely loyal that many have traveled with him on group tours to his Mediterranean homeland. With membership in a who's who of prestigious cooking organizations, including the James Beard Foundation and The Confrerie de la Chaine des Rotisseurs, Chef Andrea is a noted cookbook author who has prepared dishes for the likes of Queen Elizabeth II, Princess Anne, and President and Mrs. Jimmy Carter. But at the end of the day it's the food that has won this restaurant its die-hard local following, thanks to Chef Andrea's classic treatments of scampi alla Caprese, grilled salmon Florentina, veal scaloppini, and rigatoni *quattro formmagi*. But the award-winning chef is no stranger to adding New Orleans-style twists to time-honored recipes. A good example is the osso bucco that arrives at the table on a plate filled with the local staple (and wonderfully seasoned) red beans and rice. Dining rooms are airy, well-lit, and overall pleasant odes to Chef Andrea's proud Mediterranean roots, with walls in pastel hues featuring European Romantic-style paintings. A relatively new addition to this Metairie venue is Capri Blue, a bright and lively piano bar from which patrons can order from the entire menu.

Austin's, 5101 W. Esplanade Ave., Metairie, LA 70006; (504) 888-5533; www.austinsno.com; Creole; $$. It's not often that an eatery tucked in a strip mall in the 'burbs manages to pull off the feat of doing so many things so well. But this casual-upscale neighborhood gem rarely fails to hit all the notes with the kind of diner who expects his veal Parmagiana to be not just good but damn near perfect. More than 20 entrees running the specter from boneless duck (with cherry demi-glace) and grilled Atlantic salmon (topped with caper-butter sauce) to New Orleans' traditional trout amandine and crawfish crab cakes (served with a crawfish dill sauce) keep hungry hearts and discerning palates alike coming back to this beautifully decorated, romantic oasis of dining plea-

sures. Died-in-the-hoof carnivores will find that the steak selection (petit filet, filet mignon, New York strip, and rib eye) illustrates the truism that simple things done well is the hallmark of any truly good kitchen. Live piano music weekend nights sets the mood for memorable dining and adds a touch of elegance to a consistently rave-earning venue well worth the drive no matter where you live in town.

Bozo's, 3117 21st St., Metairie, LA 70002; (504) 831-8666; www.bozosrestaurant.com; Seafood; $$. Simplicity is the name of the game at this perennially popular and long-standing suburban purveyor of the kind of food that makes New Orleanians tick. In lieu of a lengthy, overwrought menu that attempts to be all things to all diners is an abbreviated roster whose best dishes typically begin with the word "boiled," "fried" or "stuffed." And this is precisely why patrons have been flocking to Bozo's since it opened in 1928 when it was originally located on St. Anne Street in Mid-City. Today this decidedly Spartan venue serves up a tour de force of oysters, shrimp and catfish plates, and po-boys, plus the customary seafood combo platters, in addition to a few specialty dishes such as hamburger steak, grilled chicken breast, chicken and andouille gumbo, and red beans and rice. A nod to the family-run Bozo's origins as primarily an oyster bar (founder Bozo Vodanovich was an oysterman in Plaquemines Parish) is the fact the present-day owners still offer the succulent bivalve on the half-shell "ice cold and freshly shucked." As any New Orleanian will tell you, it just doesn't get any better than this.

Bud's Broiler, 2929 N. Causeway Blvd., Metairie; (504) 833-3770; 2008 Clearview Pkwy., Metairie; (504) 889-2837; http://budsbroiler .com; Hamburgers; $. Additional Kenner location at 2800 Veterans Blvd., (504) 466-0026. For a full description, please see the Mid-City listing, p. 174.

Byblos Restaurant, 1501 Metairie Road, Metairie, LA 70005; (504) 834-9773; www.byblosrestaurants.com; Middle Eastern; $$. From the saffron-colored walls to the large mural painted in soft Mediterranean hues, there is no mistaking the decor of this longtime Metairie venue for anything but a sensual retreat for palates that fancy the flavors of Lebanon and other culinary cultures of the Middle East. Like its sibling of the same name located Uptown, Byblos trumps its hand with a panorama of earthy pleasures like chicken shawarma that arrives at your table broiled and sliced after marinating overnight in olive oil, garlic, lemon juice, and aromatic Lebanese spices. Other tasty entrees run the field from lamb kabobs and shrimp skewers to Mediterranean pasta (sautéed with shrimp and herbs in garlic and olive oil and topped with feta cheese and kalamata olives) to the tour de force veggie platter with a choice of hummus, moussaka, baba ghanoush, *mujadarah*, falafel, tabbouleh, and other noteworthy imports from Lebanon. Diners with small appetites aren't forgotten, as the menu is replete with tidy portions of baba ghanoush (eggplant dip), herbed and seasoned falafel, fried eggplant, *sambousek* (meat pies), Cypriot halloumi cheese (seared in olive oil and flambéed with ouzo), and the ubiquitous yogurt salad. Just make sure you leave room for dessert because the traditional Lebanese *ashta* (an egg-less homemade custard made with rose water and orange blossom in phyllo and topped with syrup and pistachios) is a taste of the Mediterranean not soon forgotten. Another location is at 3218 Magazine St., New Orleans, LA 70115; (504) 894-1233.

Cafe Equator, 2920 Severn Ave., Metairie, LA 70002; (504) 888-4772; www.cafeequator.com; Thai; $$. The soft colors and subdued lighting of this elegant little restaurant are in direct contrast to the wow factor of its authentic Thai food. Start with the Tom Yum Koong spicy shrimp lemongrass soup with fresh mushrooms, cilantro, a splash of lime juice, and chilis. Or try the delicious and flaky Spicy Beef Roll with cucumber sauce, featuring ground beef, water chestnuts, potatoes, white onions, and glass noodles, fried to a golden brown. Best bets for entrees include the authentic Pad Thai or the Tilapia Ginger, which is crispy fried cubes of fish served over sautéed carrots, onion, young ginger, squash, and shiitake mushrooms in a ginger sauce. There are also a number of vegetarian offerings, and all of the food is as beautifully presented as it is tasty. Located across the street from Lakeside Shopping Center in Metairie's busiest shopping district, Cafe Equator is the perfect stop for either a quiet lunch break or an intimate dinner.

Charlie's Seafood, 8311 Jefferson Hwy., Harahan, LA 70123; (504) 737-3700; www.charliesseafoodrestaurant.com; Seafood; $–$$. What makes this casual-dining seafood restaurant special is that it's owned and overseen by a James Beard Award-winning chef. Frank Brigtsen, of the celebrated **Brigtsen's** (see p. 147) fine dining restaurant in New Orleans, grew up eating at Charlie's. So when the restaurant closed a couple of years ago, after more than a half-century in business, he bought it. The menu features only fresh local seafood from wild-caught Des Allemands catfish to Lake Pontchartrain crabs that arrive live. All food is made to order from scratch by Brigtsen's handpicked chefs. Starters include shrimp remoulade with deviled egg, filé gumbo with chicken and andouille sausage, or shrimp calas with homemade tartar sauce and Creole rice fritters. You can't go wrong with any seafood entree, and don't miss the handmade meat pies created by Cane River native Janet Caldwell. If ever there were a reason to visit Harahan, Charlie's is it.

Château du Lac Bistro, 2037 Metairie Rd., Metairie, LA 70005; (504) 831-3773; www.chateaudulacbistro.com; French; $$$. **Brit**tany-born Chef-Owner Jacques Saleun has cobbled together what may be among the most eclectic selections of time-honored (and simply irresistible) French dishes available anywhere in the metropolitan area. With more than 20 years of culinary training in four-star Parisian restaurants under his toque, he opened this venue, located on Metairie Road's "restaurant row," where during lunch and dinner he showcases the talents he brings to bear on classic French entrees that seem to leave discerning customers always coming back for more. It's a fairly good guess this has as much to do with the virtual perfection of his escargot bourguignon and steak tartare (with traditional capers, shallots, and egg yolk) as it does the superb pan-roasted duck breast (with lavender-honey glaze) and straight-from-a-French-farmhouse rabbit and pistachio terrine. Another nod to Chef Jacques' honor-the-classics-and-do-it-brilliantly approach to French cooking arrives at the table in the form of Le Steak Frites, a masterpiece of filet mignon served with béarnaise and accompanied by french fries. Those in the know will want to pony up the extra $10 to have this French staple served with truffles and truffle sauce. It doesn't hurt that this popular spot at night offers a romantic bistro atmosphere complete with candlelit linen tables and Provencal-yellow walls as well as dinner- and glassware in the familiar hues of Southern France.

City Diner, 3116 S. I-10 Service Rd., Metairie, LA 70001; (504) 831-1030; www.citydiner.biz; Diner; $. This 24-hour diner, situated just on the other side of the interstate from Lakeside Shopping Center, is a great place for travelers staying in Metairie to find an affordable, stick-to-your-ribs breakfast (which is served all day) before heading out to see the sights. Try the traditional two-egg breakfast or the short stack of pancakes so big they could probably feed two people. Late-night eaters or those simply in the mood for something heavier will want to check out the crawfish and andouille hash browns made with local crustaceans and spicy sausage, and topped with a Cajun cream sauce. Or dive into the Bottom of the Bowl, featuring sautéed crawfish, shrimp, and crab in a cream sauce, topped with cheese and served in a seasoned toasted bread bowl. But no matter what you choose, you'll be greeted by a friendly staff and the tantalizing smell of something frying on the grill. And whether you're not quite finished partying for the night or just need a little hair of the dog the next morning, City Diner serves beer.

Drago's, 3232 Arnoult Rd., Metairie, LA 70002; (504) 888-9254; www.dragosrestaurant.com; Seafood; $$. Sure, a lot of restaurants have begun offering the perennially popular charbroiled oyster, but the question of the day is invariably this: Are they as good as Drago's? Answer: probably not. Turns out the family-owned restaurant Drago and Klara Cvitanovich opened in 1970 in the Fat City neighborhood of Metairie put charbroiled oysters on the city's culinary map. No matter what else patrons in the two downstairs and two upstairs dining rooms order from the menu, you can rest assured a large platter of at least one dozen (and probably more) charbroiled oysters on the half-shell will find its way to the table. Seasoned with garlic, butter, and herbs, dusted with Parmesan and Romano cheese, then cooked in the shell over an open-flame grill, this sumptuous preparation of New Orleans' favorite succulent bivalve first came to life back in 1990, the result of an "experiment" conducted by second-generation restaurant manager Tommy Cvitanovich. Today the restaurant serves an estimated 900 dozen charbroiled oysters a day. A sizeable menu of largely traditional New Orleans seafood and Creole fare includes fried seafood platters, barbecue drumfish, shrimp and grits (with tasso), and a personal favorite—oysters brochette (wrapped in bacon on skewers, broiled then fried, and served with a Jack Daniels glaze and horseradish sauce). There's also a location at 2 Poydras St., New Orleans, LA 70130; (504) 584-3911. See Drago's recipe for **Herradura Shrimp** on p. 272.

Fury's, 724 Martin Behrman Ave., Metairie, LA 70005; (504) 834-5646; Seafood; $–$$. New Orleans is a place where "old-fashioned" is often still considered a good thing, and the reason for that is nowhere more evident than at Fury's. Walk into this nondescript little eatery, tucked just off Veterans Boulevard, and you'll find traditional no-nonsense Creole and Creole-Italian fare made pretty much the same way it's been served for decades—cooked-to-order using fresh local ingredients—all at very reasonable prices. Try any of the seafood dishes (all prepared with fresh local catches), the crispy fried chicken, or the red beans and rice (served, as is tradition, on Monday). And a vegetarian's taste buds will never be so happy as when they experience the eggplant parmigiana. Fury's is open for lunch and dinner, but the small dining room gets crowded fast. To avoid a wait, try a late lunch or early dinner. The crowd tends to be mostly members of the senior set, and the waitstaff is likely to call you "dawlin'," but all that combines to create a very relaxed and comfortable setting in which to enjoy simple New Orleans food the same way locals have for generations.

The Galley Seafood Restaurant, 2535 Metairie Rd., Metairie, LA 70005; (504) 832-0955; Seafood; $$. Longtime caterers Dennis and Vicky Patania opened this always-crowded habitué for seafood lovers back in 1990, and today its popularity can be measured by the fact that at night it can be difficult to find a parking space. Three dining rooms (one inside, two outdoors) are typically filled with a cast of regulars and newcomers alike who come to enjoy the bounty of fresh boiled shrimp and crawfish that helped put this Old Metairie venue on the map. From traditional seafood platters brimming with deep-fried oysters, boiled shrimp, catfish, and soft-shell crab to a phalanx of po-boys stuffed with a bounty of the local waters, the Galley over the years has earned its stripes in part for both the quality of ingredients and consistency with which dishes are prepared. Lately the Patanias' son, Dominic, has taken the reins and today oversees the ever-expanding, rotating roster of 15 to 20 daily specials that is helping inject the restaurant with new and exciting dining possibilities. During a recent visit the lobster ravioli (with lobster sauce) and blackened redfish proved standouts worthy of a repeat performance. Another new addition is steak. A lively crowd and atmosphere make this dining den a fun place to spend the evening with friends.

Hillbilly Bar-B-Q, 208 Tullulah Ave., River Ridge, LA 70123; (504) 738-1508; www.hillbillybbq.com; Barbecue; $. If you're in River Ridge and into good barbecue, you've got to check out Hillbilly. All the meats are smoked to perfection with hickory wood imported from the owner's hometown of Paducah, Kentucky. Best bets include the pork ribs, beef brisket, and smoked chicken. Although, the daily specials—such as Friday's boneless pork loin with macaroni-n-cheese and green beans—are pretty mouthwatering as well. And if you're ever going to try it, this is the place to get alligator sausage or smoked boudin. Also, ask for a side of cold corn salad with sweet corn, Roma tomatoes, green onions, seasonings, and a dash of mayo. They also sell their barbecue sauce by the bottle. Hillbilly is open for lunch and dinner, but they sometimes run out of the most popular items, such as the ribs. So going early is recommended.

Impastato's, 3400 16th St., Metairie, LA 70002; (504) 455-1545; www.impastatos.com; Italian; $$. No one could ever accuse this traditional Italian restaurant of having no personality. Several of the walls are completely covered with photographs—some of celebrities, many simply of happy patrons, and a number of members of the Impastato family. There's also a very impressive collection of sports memorabilia including signed helmets and jerseys from some of the NFL's biggest stars, past and present. But the real star here is the food created by Sicilian-born owner and Chef Joe Impastato, who has been in the business for half a century. The pasta is made in-house, so fresh and delicious it would be a memorable meal just on its own. But combine it with the shrimp scampi, crawfish au gratin or veal parmigiana, and you'll find yourself asking for more bread so you can sop up every last bit. And considering the quality of the food, the prices are unbelievably good. There's even an early-bird special of five courses for $25. Serving dinner only, the restaurant rounds out your experience with the excellent service of attentive, tuxedoed waiters, and the musical croonings of a guy who looks like he could have opened for Sinatra. *Molto buono!*

Koz's, 6215 Wilson St., Harahan; (504) 737-3933; www.kozcooks .com; Sandwiches; $. For a full description, please see the Lakefront listing, p. 181.

Morning Call Coffee Stand, 3325 Severn Ave., Metairie, LA 70002; (504) 885-4068; Coffee; $. No trip to New Orleans is complete without a cup of *café au lait* (coffee with steamed milk) and a trio of beignets (square hole-less donuts topped with a mountain of powdered sugar). So if you can't make it to Cafe du Monde in the French Quarter, the next-best thing is Morning Call, which is located right behind Lakeside Shopping Center on 17th Street (despite its official Severn Avenue address). The Original Morning Call opened in the French Quarter in 1870 but moved to the suburbs about 40 years ago. The cool-looking wooden counters found inside are from the original location. Stop first at the newsstand next door for some reading material, then sit down to enjoy *café au lait* and beignets, which will be pretty much the best $4 you'll spend on vacation. There are a few lunch items on the menu, but stick to the basics that have been serving locals well for more than a century. The shop is open 24 hours and is cash-only, but there's an ATM in the dining room.

Phil's Grill, 3020 Severn Ave., Metairie, LA 70002; (504) 324-9080; www.phils-grill.com; Hamburgers; $. In a city best known for its devotion to seafood, it takes real vision—not to mention guts— to open up a new burger joint much less keep it open. But that's precisely what Phil de Gruy did in 2007, and today his typically packed suburban eatery is going like gangbusters, thanks chiefly to an imaginative idea he brought to the table: let customers "build" their own burgers. Sounds simple but there is nothing ordinary about Phil's build-your-own-burger concept that gives fans of this American staple "over 1 million possible combinations!" Patrons first choose the burger (Black Angus beef, chicken, turkey, or homemade veggie) and type of bun (white, sun-dried tomato, whole wheat, or jalapeño) before proceeding to their choice of sauce (ranging from barbecue and blue cheese to garlic aioli and chipotle), toppings, cheese, and, finally, how they want it cooked. The Black Angus on sun-dried tomato bun with aioli and sautéed mushrooms is downright otherworldly. Less fussy patrons can choose from 10 specialty burgers that include the Bayou Bengal, an alligator meat burger with tangy "tiger sauce" and shredded jalapeño Jack cheese. A roster of salads and sides are available.

Royal China, 600 Veterans Blvd., Metairie, LA 70003; (504) 831-9633; Chinese; $$. Just in case you get a hankering for Chinese food while in New Orleans, check out this small restaurant just across the parish line in Metairie. Royal China, known to locals as Ms. Shirley's, is one of the finest Chinese restaurants in metro New Orleans and one of the only places to get dim sum. Always-present owner Shirley Lee has created a relaxed and inviting family setting in which diners enjoy such standouts as pan-fried shrimp dumplings, crawfish with black bean sauce, lemon chicken, and scallops with broccoli. Or you can make an entire meal from the excellent dim sum menu, which features nearly 50 different items—all cooked fresh to-order—including crabmeat shiu mai, baked pork bun, and even chicken feet. There's also a sizable vegetarian menu. Royal China is open for lunch and dinner, but not in between, and it gets crowded. Early lunch or dinner is recommended. The restaurant also has a thriving take-out business.

Sake Cafe, 4201 Veterans Blvd., Metairie, LA 70006; (504) 779-7253; www.nola.com/sites/sakecafe; Japanese; $$. For a full description, please see the Uptown listing, p. 128.

Shogun, 2325 Veterans Blvd., Metairie, LA 70002; (504) 833-7477; www.shogunneworleans.com; Japanese; $$. When a friend moved to the city in 1980, he decried the total absence of bona fide sushi bars, which were already a staple in his native Los Angeles. As if by divine intervention, this venue opened the following year and became an answered prayer as well as the city's first (and still oldest) sushi bar. Along the way this airy and pleasant establishment introduced countless thousands of Big Easy residents to the centuries-old joys of eating small pieces of raw fish pressed onto cooked vinegared rice and tied with a dried strip of pressed seaweed known as nori. Although this suburban dining den boasts a full menu of Japanese dishes that can be enjoyed in one of its spacious dining rooms (not to mention a separate hibachi grill with six tables), sitting at the sushi bar and establishing a de facto short-term dining "relationship" with one of the L.A.- or New York-trained sushi chefs is a uniquely cosmopolitan pleasure that never seems to wear out its welcome or allure. Whether you're a newbie playing it safe with a California roll, a mid-level sushiphile discovering the wonders of salmon box and handheld eel rolls, or a culinary *bon vivant* eager for the chef to surprise you with one of his personal creations, Shogun consistently brings to the sushi bar some of the best game—er, fish—in town.

Sid-Mar's, 3322 N. Turnbull Dr., Metairie, LA 70002; (504) 831-9541; www.sidmarsrestaurant.com; Seafood; $$. Even before you walk in the door, you'll be greeted by the heady aroma of boiling seafood at this perennial New Orleans favorite. Established in 1967 by Sidney and Marion Burgess, Sid-Mar's was originally located in Bucktown, a small community on the shores of Lake Pontchartrain from which much of its fresh seafood was harvested. After the restaurant was destroyed by Hurricane Katrina, it moved to its current suburban location where it continues to serve fresh local seafood in a bright and airy dining room filled with pictures of old Bucktown. Start with the gumbo or stuffed artichoke, then move on to a po-boy sandwich or any of the seafood entrees. If you're really bold, tackle the Fisherman's Platter with oysters, shrimp, catfish, stuffed crab, and soft-shell crab. Broiled or grilled seafood with steamed vegetables is also available, as is a children's menu. Lunch is the best deal with numerous offerings for under $9.

Sun Ray Grill, 619 Pink St., Metairie, LA 70005; (504) 837-0055; www.sunraygrill.com; Eclectic; $$. For a full description, please see the Warehouse District listing, p. 101.

Taj Mahal, 923 Metairie Rd., Metairie, LA 70005; (504) 836-6859; Indian; $$. Tucked like a secret at the end of a spur off Metairie Road, this purveyor of Indian cuisine has for more than a quarter century been satisfying both the novice and seasoned palates of those in the mood for tandoori, *vindaloo*, *korma*, *tikka masala*, and other flavorful preparations from the subcontinent halfway around the world. From buttery mild to fiery hot, the kitchen staff can accommodate virtually anyone's heat threshold when preparing classic Indian chicken, lamb, shrimp, and vegetable dishes with curry or chutney. The venue's brilliant rendering of mulligatawny, a lentil soup prepared with spiced chicken flavored with cumin, curry leaves, and lemon, arrives at the table piping hot and is a wonderful representation of Indian "soul food," especially on a cold day. Ditto for *samosas*, a traditional crispy pastry filled with flavorfully spiced potatoes and peas, and the tandoori-roasted farmer's cheese known as *paneer tikka*. Adventurous diners already familiar with traditional Indian fare will probably want to steer their palates to the side of the menu offering *dosas*, a subtle preparation of light crepes (made with rice and lentils and served with coconut chutney), which come filled with a choice of potatoes and onions, noodles and spring vegetables, or pasta and cheese. A dozen types of Indian bread run the gamut from poori and naan to an assorted breadbasket sure to please even the pickiest foodie. A popular daily buffet is usually packed with customers.

Tarka, 3207 Williams Blvd., Kenner, LA 70065; (504) 471-6141; Indian/Pakistani; $$. Among Kenner's newest kids on the block is this humble dining retreat specializing in the cuisine of Pakistan and northern India. Pakistani chefs often first cook an exotic blend of spices—for instance, cumin, coriander, clove, cardamon, garlic, and cinnamon—together in olive oil to better draw out the essences before adding it to a recipe, a process known as *tarka* (hence the restaurant's moniker). The result is a dish possessing a subtle and oh-so-nuanced complexity quite distinct from cuisine found in that country's cross-border neighbor India (although both cultures do share many common cooking traditions). While this Spartan eatery does offer the ubiquitous mix of Indian-style tandoori, kabob, and *tikka* dishes, your best bet is to let Tarka's Pakistani chef work his magic on dishes from his homeland for which this venue is becoming increasingly popular among those in the know, which include *biryani* chicken, goat, lamb, shrimp, fish, and vegetables. Marinated overnight and steam-cooked with a delicious blend of basmati rice, tomatoes, and *tarka*-style fresh herbs and spices, the Pakistan-born *biryani* cooking style at Tarka, opened in 2010, is a palate-awakening and horizon-broadening discovery of a centuries-old culinary motif not yet widely represented in the New Orleans area.

Vega Tapas Cafe, 2051 Metairie Rd., Metairie, LA 70005; (504) 836-2007; www.vegatapascafe.com; Mediterranean; $$. It's near impossible to miss this ode to haute Spanish cuisine—the façade features a lovely motif of trencadis (broken mosaic tile) accented by a pair of wildly colorful, Gaudi-esque "towers" on the roof. All of which foreshadows the adventurous dining experience to come when gourmands step inside and find themselves enveloped by this chic venue's Mediterranean burnt-orange walls and rotating exhibit of original abstract paintings by local artists. In a city that has witnessed a near explosion of tapas restaurants in recent years, Vega can rightfully claim to be the first kid on the block when former local chef and then-owner Suzanne Vega opened the doors to this establishment in 1996. Today owner and Chef Glenn Hogh has taken the high road—literally—throughout Spain and back to offer diners his versions of the eclectic tastes he discovered during frequent travels throughout the Iberian Peninsula. Whether it's a simple salad of baby greens taken to the next level with a mix of Granny Smith apples, creamy Brie, and caramelized leeks in a cider vinaigrette, a classic *patatas bravas* served with aioli, classic mac-'n-cheese with smoked duck sausage and Gruyère, or the roasted Spanish pequillo peppers that arrive at your table stuffed with veal and Idiazabal cheese from the Basque region of Spain, Chef Glenn keeps the Vega menu a vibrant, dynamic, and sexy feast for the senses. A black-clad waitstaff adds a touch of cosmopolitan cool. Adjacent to the main dining room is a separate, cozy bar whose staff effortlessly turns out traditional cocktails as well as the hippest Flavor of the Month as prescribed by European and East Coast trendsetters.

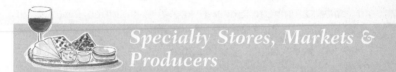

Specialty Stores, Markets & Producers

Byblos Market, 2020 Veterans Blvd., Metairie, LA 70002; (504) 837-9777. If, like many international travelers, you often return home from journeys abroad eager to re-create in your kitchen the dishes you savored in faraway lands, this is the place for you if your globe stomping has taken you to the Middle East, Turkey, and other parts of the Mediterranean. The panoply of goods here from the region is so comprehensive it's hard to imagine a market where roasted Turkish pistachios, Saudi date-filled cookies, Palestinian Nabulsi cheese from Israel's West Bank, and Lebanese fava beans all share the same shelf. A large selection of Middle Eastern cooking staples—for instance, hummus, tabbouleh, tahini, baba ghanoush, and zucchini puree spread—share the aisles with cardamom tea, a small selection of Turkish hookahs, jars of olives, and much more. In the back of the airy and browse-worthy market is a deli offering a brief but always tasty menu of regional fare including falafel, hummus, *kibeh*, chicken shawarma salad, beef and lamb gyro, as well as chicken and beef kabobs.

Kenner Supermarket, 3750 Williams Blvd., Kenner, LA 70065; (504) 469-1993. This location is actually two venues in one—a market filled with aisles of Latin specialties and a restaurant whose menu boasts some of the best Central American fare in town. Customers are greeted by a deli window filled with freshly prepared to-go foods ranging from guava- and cheese-stuffed pastries and pork-filled *pupusas* to fried plantains and spicy meat empanadas. DIY cooks of Latin dishes will find aisles of Central American foodstuffs including bottles of Salsa Lizano, jars of chimichurri sauce, sofrito tomato cooking bases, plus a large selection of their favorite pre-ground espresso coffee from Costa Rica, Colombia, and elsewhere south of the border. A full-scale deli in back stocks various cuts of meat as well as bags of fresh *chicharrón*, Latin America's superior version of the pork rind. On one side of the market is a restaurant specializing in made-to-order Mexican and Central American favorites such as *carne asada*, corn tamales with sour cream, yucca *con chicharrón*, fried plantains with cream, corn meat pies, Honduran-style chicken tacos, and not-to-be-missed *tortas* made with a choice of barbecue beef, chicken, or ham.

Kosher Cajun Deli, 3519 Severn Ave., Metairie, LA 70002; (504) 888-2010; www.koshercajun.com. Those looking to keep kosher during their visit to New Orleans will want to check out this deli and grocery featuring the largest selection of kosher products in the state. Three blocks from Lakeside Shopping Center, it can be a little difficult to find because it's set back off the street. But it's worth the effort. The deli features the expected chopped liver, nova salmon, and knishes, as well as real standout corned beef and pastrami. The full-service kitchen, operated under strict rabbinic supervision, offers freshly prepared breakfast, lunch, and dinner to eat in the newly enlarged dining area or to take out. The grocery is well-stocked and includes products for special dietary needs, such as sugar- and lactose-free. There's even a gift area where travelers who'd like to take the New Orleans experience home with them can pick up one of Mildred Covert's popular local recipe books on kosher Cajun and kosher Creole cooking.

Martin Wine Cellar, 714 Elmeer Ave., Metairie, LA 70005; (504) 896-7300; www.martinwine.com. A few years back a local traveler returning from a trip to Prague tried to no avail to find a bottle of the Beckerovka liqueur he had enjoyed while in the Czech Republic. Then he called the Metairie location of this longtime purveyor to see if they could order it. No problem. Within two weeks there was not one but 10 bottles of the Czech Republic's national liqueur on the store shelves. Since opening its doors in 1946 at a now-defunct Uptown location, this premier wine and gourmet food establishment has prided itself on providing connoisseurs with what may well be the metropolitan area's largest retail selection of everyday and hard-to-find wines, spirits, liqueurs, champagne, and cognac. Whether searching for 18-year-old

Flor de Caña rum from Nicaragua, a budget-friendly case of Cristolino cava from Spain, or a bottle of 2002 Saint-Emilion Grand Cru to impress a dinner host, chances are this beloved repository of libations great and small carries it—or can get it. A deli counter with seating offers a tasty mix of tasty sandwiches and salads while the aisles in back are stocked with a breathtaking range of gourmet foodstuffs. Additional locations are at 3500 Magazine St., New Orleans, LA 70115, (504) 899-7411; and 2895 Highway 190, Mandeville, LA 70471, (985) 951-8081.

Nor-Joe Import Co., 505 Frisco Ave., Metairie, LA 70005; (504) 833-9240; www.norjoe.com. You are just as likely to see local chefs as you are regular customers browsing the well-stocked aisles of gourmet Italian and Mediterranean products that have earned this venue a soft spot in the hearts of local foodies. Opened in 1994, this off-the-beaten-track "destination" boasts more than 20,000 items ranging from olives, prosciutto, and myriad Italian cheeses to harder-to-find items like truffles, dried porcini, canned escargot, champagne wine mustard, grappa, and more types of pasta than you can shake a Genoa salami at. A deli counter in back packages all types of aged cheese and cured meats to go. Further proof that owners Joseph Giglio and Norma Jean Schiffman have created a died-and-gone-to-heaven spot for any fan of Mediterranean foodstuffs can be found under the front counter, where staff keeps a $350 bottle of 300-year-old balsamic vinaigrette. Shoppers on a budget needn't fret, though: also for sale is a 100-year-old bottle for a mere $185.

West Bank & St. Bernard

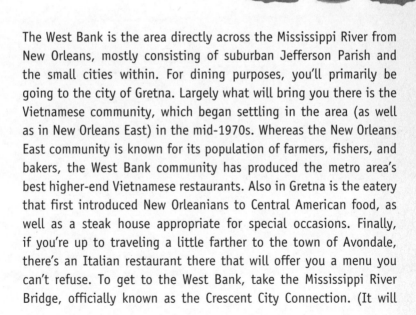

The West Bank is the area directly across the Mississippi River from New Orleans, mostly consisting of suburban Jefferson Parish and the small cities within. For dining purposes, you'll primarily be going to the city of Gretna. Largely what will bring you there is the Vietnamese community, which began settling in the area (as well as in New Orleans East) in the mid-1970s. Whereas the New Orleans East community is known for its population of farmers, fishers, and bakers, the West Bank community has produced the metro area's best higher-end Vietnamese restaurants. Also in Gretna is the eatery that first introduced New Orleanians to Central American food, as well as a steak house appropriate for special occasions. Finally, if you're up to traveling a little farther to the town of Avondale, there's an Italian restaurant there that will offer you a menu you can't refuse. To get to the West Bank, take the Mississippi River Bridge, officially known as the Crescent City Connection. (It will

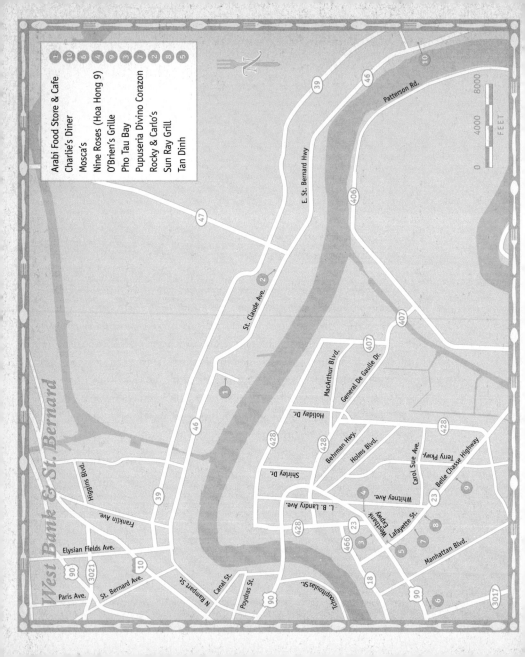

West Bank & St. Bernard

1. Arabi Food Store & Cafe
10. Charlie's Diner
6. Mosca's
4. Nine Roses (Hoa Hong 9)
9. O'Brien's Grille
3. Pho Tau Bay
7. Pupuseria Divino Corazon
2. Rocky & Carlo's
8. Sun Ray Grill
5. Tan Dinh

N

FEET
0   4000   8000

cost you a $1 toll to get back.) This will lead you to the Westbank Expressway, which will take you to everywhere else you want to go.

The hardscrabble residents of St. Bernard Parish embody the post-Katrina pioneering spirit of locals working at times against all odds to rebuild their homes, livelihoods, and community. Home to the Chalmette Battlefield (site of the famous 1815 Battle of New Orleans), historic plantations, picturesque fishing villages and scenic bayou roads, and the Islenos Museum, which celebrates the earliest Spanish settlers to this region from the Canary Islands, "da' parish," as it's affectionately called, has never wanted for good home-style places to eat. Unfortunately many of them are now gone while slowly but surely new venues are cropping up to take their places. But near and dear to the hearts of locals are those beloved, long-standing establishments that have not only withstood the test of time but also the ravages of Katrina.

Foodie Faves

Arabi Food Store & Cafe, 650 Friscoville Ave., Arabi, LA 70032; St. Bernard; (504) 277-2333; Neighborhood Cafe; $. This grocery store and sit-down (or take-out) lunch spot popular among locals and those in the know from elsewhere around the metropolitan area may not be fancy, but it serves up what may be among the best muffulettas in town. In fact, this classically New Orleans Italian-style sandwich is well worth the drive alone if you have a little time

on your hands. Here's why: The tangy olive salad is mixed with just the right amount of extra-virgin olive oil while the deli meats, cheeses, and bread always taste fresh, fresh, fresh. Mostly diner-style lunch fare is the name of the game here, but you would be doing yourself a disservice by not ordering the wonderfully messy roast beef po-boy for which this establishment has earned a not insignificant reputation among longtime patrons.

Charlie's Diner, 6129 E. St. Bernard Hwy., Violet, LA 70092; St. Bernard; (504) 682-9057; Neighborhood Cafe; $. **Oftentimes** it's when you're hungry and returning from a day trip deep into the easternmost end of St. Bernard Parish that a stop at this family-friendly venue makes perfect sense. It was on such an occasion that a simple lunch of pan-fried fresh andouille and boudin sausage, served with seasoned grilled onions and a honey-Creole mustard dipping sauce, seemed about as perfect—and delicious—as anything enjoyed in this bend of the bayou in recent memory. While you're not likely to be blown away by the decor, what will help make your meal truly memorable is one of the deep-fried oyster or shrimp po-boys that grace the lengthy menu. Namely because these two seafood staples are caught in local waters and arrive fresh at the docks at the old fishing villages of Shell Beach and Yscloskey just a shout down the road from this perennially popular family venue.

Nine Roses (Hoa Hong 9), 1100 Stephens St., Gretna, LA 70053; West Bank; (504) 366-7665; Vietnamese; $–$$. Pho is just the beginning of the adventure at Nine Rose, which must have the longest menu of any area restaurant. There are literally hundreds of items. The restaurant serves authentic Vietnamese fare, as well as Chinese food (as most local Vietnamese eateries do). Nine Roses opened in the early 1990s when most New Orleanians would have asked, "Banh what?" It caters primarily to the Vietnamese community, members of which can often be seen sitting around the spacious dining room's large tables. Because of this, your waitress may not speak English very well (although probably still better than you speak Vietnamese), so please don't expect her to explain the entire menu to you. If you're not that familiar with Vietnamese food, stick to the spring rolls and maybe the *Bo Nuong Vi*—a beef dish you cook at table with a little burner. It's delicious and fun. Note: The route to Nine Roses can be confusing. Get good directions.

O'Brien's Grille, 2020 Belle Chasse Hwy., Gretna, LA 70056; West Bank; (504) 391-7229; www.obriensgrille.com; Steakhouse; $$$–$$$$. The West Bank has never been known for having an abundance of fine dining restaurants. So O'Brien's was a welcome newcomer when it opened in 2008. The outside doesn't look like much, but the dining room features white tablecloths, good lighting, and a romantic atmosphere. The menu specializes in steaks, which they certainly know how to cook properly, but also features pork, fish, and seafood offerings. Best bets for starters include the Oysters O'Neil, which are local and baked, topped with bread crumbs and blended cheeses, then finished with a hot sauce hollandaise. Or try the grilled scallops, served with grilled corn maque choux and a Creole beurre blanc. The food and service here are generally very good, but be prepared—it is a little pricier than folks are used to at most West Bank restaurants. O'Brien's is open for lunch weekdays and dinner Mon through Sat.

Pho Tau Bay, 113 C Westbank Expy., Gretna, LA 70053; West Bank; (504) 368-9846; Vietnamese; $. Pho Tau Bay is basically a down-home Vietnamese restaurant located in the unassuming U-shaped strip mall where Expressway Lanes bowling alley used to be. A number of the mall businesses have Vietnamese names, which sort of makes you feel like you're not in New Orleans any more, Toto. Pho Tau Bay serves the Vietnamese basics: *pho, bun, banh mi,* and the like. The food is hearty, the portions are generous, and the check is small. The place is family-run and the staff is friendly and helpful. The dining room is generally packed, so don't get upset if the staff seems rushed. Pho Tau Bay has what may seem like odd hours. It opens early at 9 a.m. (mostly to accommodate the Vietnamese community), but closes early at 8:30 p.m. And it's not open at all Sun and Thu. But if you like good basic Vietnamese food, and you can get there when they're open, you'll be glad you did.

Pupuseria Divino Corazon, 2300 Belle Chasse Hwy., Gretna, LA 70053; West Bank; (504) 368-5724; Central American; $. **After** Hurricane Katrina, the metro New Orleans area became home to a large migration of new Hispanic residents who came to find work rebuilding the city. But in the late 1980s, when Gloria Salmeron, a native of El Salvador, opened her Gretna *pupuseria*, Latin people and food were relatively rare here. So, she served a mixture of Central American food along with a more familiar Mexican menu. But once locals got to know the food, they loved it and the business took off. A major renovation following the storm included closing in the porch, greatly expanding the dining area without losing the eatery's cozy and comfortable feeling. That's probably because the warmth of the place comes from the staff. Specialties include excellent *pupusas*, tamales, and ceviche, but everything on the menu is fresh and made from scratch. So you really can't go wrong with anything. Plantains with beans and cream make a memorable finish.

Sun Ray Grill, 2600 Belle Chasse Hwy., Gretna, LA 70056; West Bank; (504) 391-0053; www.sunraygrill.com; Eclectic; $$. **For full** description, see Warehouse District chapter, p. 101.

Tan Dinh, 1705 Lafayette St., Gretna, LA 70053; West Bank; (504) 361-8008; www.facebook.com/tandinh; Vietnamese; $. **Tan Dinh** is another good Vietnamese restaurant with an extensive menu (though not as long as Nine Roses') where the food is good and relatively inexpensive. As for level of sophistication, it is some-where between Nine Roses and Pho Tau Bay. Try the shrimp spring rolls (*goi cuon tom*), the marinated roasted duck with jus sauce (*vit nuong chao*), the fried shrimp with lime sauce (*tom rang muoi*), or the charbroiled pork with jasmine rice (*com thit nuong*). The quail is also very popular. Tan Dinh offers a lot of specialty drinks. Have the Vietnamese coffee with condensed milk (as long as you don't need to be asleep in the next several hours) and have the soda *chanh* (fresh-squeezed limeade with club soda) no matter what. Tan Dinh is closed on Tues.

Landmarks

Mosca's, 4137 US 90 West, Avondale, LA 70094; West Bank; (504) 436-9942 or (504) 436-8950; http://moscasrestaurant.com; Italian; $$$. Since 1946, this perennial favorite has followed generations-old family recipes to create classic Italian cuisine. And in those 60-plus years, not much has changed around the place. Legend tells us it all started when Provino Mosca cooked for "businessman" Carlos Marcello (That's all I'm saying about Marcello. Look him up if you want to know more.), who liked what he ate. So he set up Mosca in business at the same location where the restaurant stands today. You'd never know it to look at the rather modest exterior, but Mosca's always was and still is a meeting place for the rich and powerful. It's also the spot to find great Italian food. You must have the baked oysters (a dish created here). Also try the shrimp in white wine sauce or any of the chicken dishes. Mosca's serves dinner only and is closed Sun and Mon. Make reservations (but you'll probably still wait). Mosca's only takes cash.

Rocky & Carlo's, 613 W. St. Bernard Highway, Chalmette, LA 70043; St. Bernard; (504) 279-8323; www.rockyandcarlos.com; Neighborhood Cafe; $. Smothered pork chops, mountains of steaming chicken and sausage jambalaya, immense corn flour-crusted oyster platters, liver and onions just the way Mama used to make it, T-bone steaks so huge they literally hang off the plate. This venerated cafeteria-style diner will never be confused with a health club smoothie bar, but that's precisely why this bustling eatery is so cherished by its largely local customers. Check your heart-healthy diet at the door and take a place in line to order your New Orleans- or Sicilian-style dish from one of several menu marquees. Typically it's while watching the food preparers toiling feverishly behind the counter that first-time visitors first notice the portions—they're huge. Like most of the refreshingly affordable dishes, the long-stringed baked macaroni and cheese (be a local and order it slathered in garlicky red gravy), for example, comes piled high on the plate and is enough to feed two or three people. Other note-worthy dishes include fried chicken, veal cutlet, and this venue's famous Wop Salad (sorry, dawlin', political correctness hasn't made its way this far down in da' parish yet).

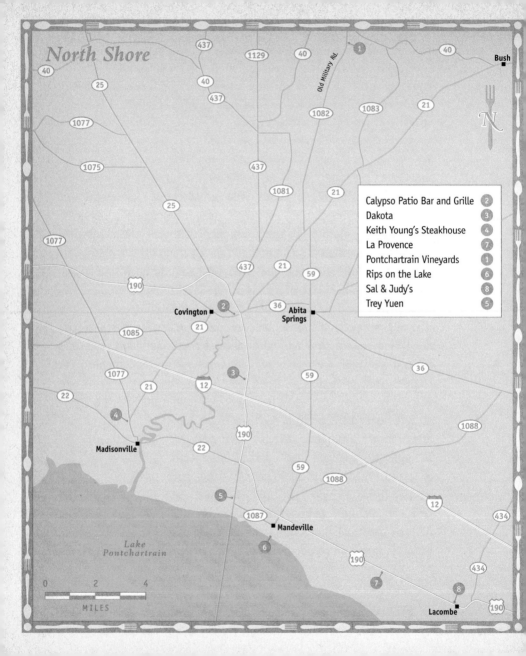

North Shore

Once a 19th-century resort enclave of rural beauty and tranquility to which fashionable New Orleanians flocked to recover from illness, escape their Creole decadence, or to evade yellow fever epidemics, the north shore in recent decades has blossomed (others say exploded) in population, business growth, and opportunity. As a result, this once sleepy region located across Lake Pontchartrain a half-hour north of New Orleans is now fully vested with not only upscale subdivisions and tony retail enclaves but also dining on both a small and grand scale.

Foodie Faves

Calypso Patio Bar and Grille, 326 Lee Lane, Covington, LA 70433; (985) 875-9676; www.calypsopatio.com; Caribbean-American; $$. Unfortunately too many eateries these days think it's cool (and smart marketing) to fasten Caribbean-ish words to the moniker in the hopes of luring devotees of the region's cuisine while offering little in the way of true West Indies-style food. Fortunately, this place does not fall into that category. While the menu at this breezy and typically lively joint does offer such repasts as the ubiquitous coconut shrimp, the dish is darn good. Ditto for the Calypso Egg Rolls filled with marinated chicken, onions, peppers, cream cheese, and pico de gallo, which is served with a mango barbecue and honey-ginger dipping sauce that would be right at home in St. John or Barbados. To sample a dish seemingly right out of the Latin-Caribbean, try the West Indies-spiced seared tuna, served tostado style over a black-bean salad drizzled with an avocado-wasabi cream and raspberry-chipotle glaze.

Dakota, 629 N. Highway 190, Covington, LA 70433; (985) 892-3712; www.restaurantcuvee.com/dakota/index.htm; Contemporary Creole; $$$$. In an era where too many fine-dining establishments have given way to the culture of casual when it comes to dress code, it's refreshing when a venue such as this makes no bones about the fact that while a jacket and tie are not required, such attire certainly would not be at odds with the elegant aesthetic so much a part of this establishment's appeal. Plus, looking sharp for dinner will likely only enhance the gastronomic experience of any gourmand's first-ever spoonful of the deliciously silky lump crabmeat and Brie soup, the Parmesan-crusted tilapia fillet topped with lump crabmeat, or the soft-shell crab that arrives at your table stuffed with crab, shrimp, and crawfish, served atop roasted pecan rice and topped with a Creollaise sauce. Eager to feast on pure culinary wizardry? Try this venue's bold version (and vision) of paella in which lobster, shrimp, scallops, and mussels are served in white wine broth with a saffron-rice cake and crisp chorizo.

Keith Young's Steakhouse, 165 Hwy. 21, Madisonville, LA 70447; (985) 845-9940; www.keithyoungs.net; Steak house; $$$$. Since 2005 this low-slung chophouse in bucolic Madisonville has been churning out hand-cut, cooked-to-order steaks for a discerning north shore clientele that now includes numerous transplants from New Orleans. The steak side of the menu offers a surprisingly small list of the usual suspects—filets, petit filets, strips, and rib eyes. But they are cooked to perfection and arrive with a choice of toppings that include crab and mushrooms, sautéed onions, bleu cheese, and bordelaise sauce. A roster of New Orleans-style seafood features pan-seared scallops, jumbo lump crab cakes, soft-shell crabs, and grilled yellowfin tuna. But what set tongues wagging during a recent visit were the lamb chops and especially the pair of pan-seared duck breasts that arrived topped with fruit chutney and served over sautéed spinach, a testament that this well-rounded venue's forte is not limited to beef alone.

Rips on the Lake, 1917 Lakeshore Dr., Mandeville, LA 70448; (985) 727-2829; Creole; $$$. There is no spinning the fact this place gets mixed reviews. But on a good day when the kitchen is revving on all cylinders and you're hunkered down at a table on the upstairs terrace overlooking a simply glorious sunset over Lake Pontchartrain, you'll swear the blackened pan-seared tuna or the jumbo soft-shell crab, topped with lump crabmeat and topped with hollandaise sauce, is worth the price of admission. If in doubt, simply order a round of sunset cocktails accompanied by the appetizer of sautéed jumbo lump crab cakes with cilantro-lime mayonnaise and fresh greens.

Sal & Judy's, 27491 Hwy. 190, Lacombe, LA 70445; (985) 882-9443; Italian; $$. Garlic-lovers will be keeping vampires at bay for weeks following a meal at this retreat of true-to-your-school rural Sicilian cooking overseen by Italian immigrant and Chef-Owner Sal Impastato ever since the day he opened it in 1974. The decor and menu haven't changed much since then, but locals wouldn't have it any other way. Prepare yourself for mouthfuls of Sicilian splendor when Chef Sal starts rocking the kitchen with his shrimp scampi, crabmeat-stuffed artichokes, chicken cacciatore, and baked lasagna—so good some loyalists claim it's the best food on the north shore and the best Italian restaurant in the metropolitan area. For a real taste of how he blends his Italian culinary roots with local ingredients, you have only to try the spaghetti with sautéed oysters and the oh-so-flavorful casserole of baked oysters Cinisi (named for Sal's hometown in Italy), which arrives mixed with mushrooms, Italian sausage, onions, cheese, and white wine. If it's hard to get a table, chalk it up to the fact Chef Sal for nearly 40 years has simply been doing what he does better than most anyone else around.

Trey Yuen, 600 N. Causeway Blvd., Mandeville, LA 70448; (985) 626-4476; http://treyyuen.com; Chinese; $$–$$$. According to a good-natured joke repeated by the owners of this family-run restaurant, "it takes five Wongs to make it right." And if anyone should know, it is indeed the Wong brothers and chefs-in-arms— James, Frank, John, Tommy, and Joe. What is no joke is that the siblings have been featured in numerous PBS *Great Chefs* series and in 1999 prepared a complete-course dinner for President Clinton at the White House. This first "fine dining" Chinese restaurant in the metropolitan area is also among the most beautiful ever seen, featuring imported rosewood ceilings, carved wall panels, antique furnishings, and inlaid mother-of-pearl dining chairs. While the menu is extensive, best bets include the fried soft-shell crab (served in a reduction sauce of soy and vinegar with ginger, garlic, and crushed peppers), fresh Louisiana alligator stir-fried with Szechuan peppers, and crawfish in spicy lobster sauce.

Landmarks

La Provence, 25020 Hwy. 190, Lacombe, LA 70445; (985) 626-7662; www.laprovencerestaurant.com; French; $$$–$$$$. Anyone who has spent time in Southern France will feel right at home inside this Old Provencal auberge that reflects the soul of that region right down to the muted yellow walls, exposed beams, terracotta tile floors, archways, and high-back chairs. The traditional (and flavorful) cooking style of Provence has been in supremely capable hands ever since New Orleans superstar Chef John Besh (see **August** [p. 86], **Besh Steak** [p. 76], **Lüke** [p. 83], **American Sector** [p. 92], and **Domenica** [p. 79]) purchased the venue shortly before the restaurant's original longtime owner and beloved culinary figure Chef Chris Kerageorgiou passed away. Today a small farm along with a vegetable and herb garden, located just behind the restaurant, literally guarantees the regularly changing menu comprises only the freshest ingredients. Consider yourself blessed indeed if you arrive during an evening when Executive Chef Eric Loos, who has trained under and worked with Besh for years, offers entrees including bouillabaisse, escargot bourgogne, slow-roasted lacquered duckling, Chef Chris' Quail Gumbo, sirloin of Mangalitsa pig, *soup au pistou,* or the grilled lamb sausage. See Chef Loos' recipe for **Malfatti of Creole Cream Cheese with House-cured Bacon** on p. 266.

Specialty Stores, Markets & Producers

Pontchartrain Vineyards, 81250 Old Military Rd., Bush, LA 70431; (985) 892-9742; www.pontchartrainvineyards.com. Home of the popular Jazz'n the Vines outdoor concert music series, the area's only fully operational winery has been near and dear to the hearts of locals almost from the time proprietor and winemaker John

Seago opened it in 1992. Today the vineyard's national and international award-winning wines can be found in fine-dining dens, stores, and homes throughout the metropolitan area. But what makes this sweet spot such a charming lure is the opportunity to sample the liquid fruits of Seago's labors, produced on more than 11 acres of fertile sandy loam soil, by stepping inside the French provincial-style wine-tasting room overlooking the vineyards. The main varieties grown are Blanc du Bois (white) and Cynthiana/Norton (red). Don't miss trying the white Roux St. Louis 2007 or the red Criolla Rossa 2005. Most of the wines produced are available for purchase.

Cocktail Culture

Drinking has been a favorite pastime in New Orleans since her early colonial days. There were none of those straitlaced Puritans who landed on the Atlantic coast here. The fun-loving Creoles who found themselves living in a city built on a swamp, populated by alligators, with the threat of disease and natural disaster always on the horizon, quickly developed the attitude of eat, drink, and be merry, because who knows what tomorrow may bring. This philosophy lives on to the current day, and New Orleans graciously offers a wide variety of establishments in which to enjoy such a tradition. Some bars are worth visiting for a certain specialty drink, others for atmosphere, and some because people have been imbibing there for more than a century and joining in is a very cool way to become part of history. Below are a Top 20, and while there are lots of other bars in the city, these all offer something particularly special. Finally, while you may be accustomed to partaking of alcohol only at the proper cocktail hour, while you're here, keep in mind the unofficial motto of New Orleans: "It's five o'clock somewhere." Cheers!

Arnaud's French 75 Bar, 813 Bienville St., New Orleans, LA 70122; French Quarter; (504) 523-5433; www.arnaudsrestaurant .com. If a rendezvous is in your plans, the French 75 Bar is the perfect setting. Step inside this intimate and sophisticated lounge, adjacent to the main dining room of the storied Arnaud's restaurant, and you could easily be walking into the New Orleans of a hundred years ago. Snag a small table in a discreet corner and enjoy a vintage cocktail created behind a century-old bar. The place is named for the French 75 cocktail, which legend says was created during World War I. A battle-weary fighter pilot found that drinking champagne no longer had enough kick, so he asked the bartender if there was something he could do about that. The barkeep added a little lemon juice, sugar, and a shot of cognac. The result was a cocktail, the pilot reported, that hit you like a 75 mm how-itzer shell. You can find out if that's true nightly, beginning at 5:30.

Bacchanal, 600 Poland Ave., New Orleans, LA 70117; Bywater; (504) 948-9111; www.bacchanalwine.com. Located in an unadorned corner building in this 9th Ward Neighborhood, Bacchanal is one of the most relaxing places in the city. Try to arrive by 7ish to beat the crowds. First, stop in the wine shop up front and choose your favorite grape, which they'll put in a bucket of ice for you if it needs chilling. There are some very nice cheeses, which you also may want to try. Then take your treasure out to the patio. Actually, it's really a backyard. (Think of a great backyard where you could have the best party ever.) Grab a seat, then sit back and enjoy your wine and cheese among the trees, while listening to live jazz, inhaling the aroma of whatever gourmet meal the chef has on the grill tonight, and experiencing what it feels like to just be. Bacchanal hosts the kind of night that ends with you moving here.

The Bombay Club, 830 Conti St., New Orleans, LA 70112; French Quarter; (504) 586-0972; www.thebombayclub.com. At first glance, the Bombay Club—with its leather wingback chairs and classic portraits hanging on wood-paneled walls—looks like a traditional British gentleman's club. You half-expect to see at the end of the bar an old man wearing a monocle and recounting tales of his days in North Africa. But the decor is simply the backdrop of an atmosphere that is reminiscent of 1940s supper clubs. Ask to sit in one of the curtained booths where you can have some privacy, while you listen to live jazz music and peruse the leather-bound cocktail menu that is a veritable history of the art, featuring drinks from as far back as the 1860s. There's also an exclusive selection of cognacs, cordials, single-malt scotches, ports, and bourbons. Or you could go straight to the signature martinis served in vintage glassware, considered by many the best in town. The Bombay Club is open nightly. Jackets preferred for gentlemen.

The Bulldog, 3236 Magazine St., New Orleans, LA 70115; Uptown; (504) 891-1516; http://bulldog.draftfreak.com. The Bulldog is a tavern with 50 beers on tap and 100 more bottled. It was named one of the Top 100 Beer Bars in the United States by Beer Travelers website and is just a fun place to relax and have a brew. Inside there's a long crowded bar, lots of animated conversation, and not much light. Outside there's a large patio, shaded tables, and a cascading fountain created by water flowing from a line of open beer taps. Happy hour is celebrated Mon through Fri from 2 to 7 p.m. with deals on pints and pitchers, as well as two-for-one mixed drinks and wine. There's also an adventure called the Beer Journey. Those who have successfully completed the labyrinth of imbibing all 50 beers on tap (not all on the same night, of course) get their name enshrined on a plaque. Plus they get their choice of Bulldog logo attire. The Bulldog is open every day from lunchtime 'till.

The Carousel Bar, Hotel Monteleone, 214 Royal St., New Orleans, LA 70130; French Quarter; (504) 523-3341; http://hotelmonteleone .com. The Hotel Monteleone opened in 1886 and eventually became one of the Vieux Carre's premier lodgings. In fact, in a bygone era it had been said that the French Quarter began in the lobby of the Monteleone. Adjacent to that lobby is the Carousel Bar, a quintessentially New Orleans place where drinking is turned into an amusement park ride. Opened in 1949, the bar is round with a carousel top and chairs whose backs are emblazoned with pictures of animals—and the whole thing continuously revolves, making a full revolution every 15 minutes. In the early days, musicians such as Louie Prima and Liberace performed here; Ernest Hemingway

Made in NOLA

Here are a few quality New Orleans brands to look for at local bars: **Abita Beer,** 166 Barbee Rd., Abita Springs, LA 70420; (985) 893-3143; www.abita.com. Founded in 1986, the Abita Brewing Company is located 30 miles north of New Orleans, in the rural St. Tammany Parish town of Abita Springs. The brewery was an immediate success with local beer drinkers and within eight years had to move to a larger facility. More than 109,000 barrels of ales and lagers (as well as 6,000 barrels of root beer) are brewed in small batches each year. The beer is cold filtered with no additives, stabilizers, or preservatives. Only the best German and American yeasts, Pacific Northwest hops, and British and North American malted barley are used. But the real secret to this great-tasting beer is the water—taken directly from the pure artesian springs for which the town of Abita has been known for a century. Flagship beers produced year-round include Abita Amber, Golden, Jockamo, Light, Purple Haze, Restoration, and Turbodog. There are also seasonal varieties based on local produce. Most New Orleans bars carry Abita beer. And if you're on the North Shore, you can tour the brewery, including a stop at the tasting room.

NOLA Brewing, 3001 Tchoupitoulas St., New Orleans, LA 70130; (504) 896-9996; www.nolabrewing.com. Like a lot of locals after Hurricane Katrina, Kirk Coco was determined to come back to New Orleans and contribute to the rebuilding of his city. The Big Easy, once the Deep South's cradle of brewing, had all but completely lost that tradition with no major breweries still operating within city limits. So Coco decided to bring back that brewing tradition by creating the New Orleans Lager & Ale Brewing Company in 2008, locating his plant in the city's Irish Channel neighborhood. Brewmaster Peter

Caddoo, who had worked for one of those old line New Orleans breweries, Dixie, came onboard, combining his expertise with the finest English, Belgian, German, and American hops, as well as unique yeast blends and malts from around the world. The result was a fine menu of craft beers, including the year-round NOLA Blonde and Brown Ales, Hopitoulas, and the 7th Street wheat (which began life as a summer beer but proved so popular, it's been promoted to year-round distribution). Lots of local bars carry NOLA beer, and the brewery offers free brewhouse tours, including tastings, every Friday at 2 p.m. Call for details.

Old New Orleans Rum, 2815 Frenchmen St., New Orleans, LA 70122; (504) 945-9400; www.neworleansrum.com. Old New Orleans Rum was the brainchild of an unlikely bunch—a group of local artists and musicians. Their leader, painter James Michalopoulos, had been inspired by a friend who served her guests alcohol she had created from fruits found in her garden. From that experience, Michalopoulos came up with the idea of using local sugar cane to make rum. Years of trial and error followed. Then in 1995, Celebration Distillation bought an old cotton warehouse in the 9th Ward to serve as the home of Old New Orleans Rum. The fermentation process was perfected, and in 1999, Old New Orleans Crystal, the distiller's first white rum, went on sale. Next came Old New Orleans Amber, followed by Cajun Spice Rum. Over the years, the rums have won both national and international awards, while the distillery's workforce has remained largely made up of artists and musicians (along with a few engineers). Old New Orleans Rum can be found all around town, and the distillery offers tours Mon through Sat. They even provide transportation from the French Quarter, if you call ahead.

even mentioned the bar in one of his short stories. Today, it's full of locals swapping old stories and tipsy tourists trying to figure out where their seats have gone while they were in the restroom. Try one of the two famous drinks invented here: the Vieux Carre Cocktail featuring rye, cognac, and vermouth, or the rum- and juice-based Goody. The bar turns daily, 11 a.m. to 2 a.m.

The Columns Hotel, 3811 St. Charles Ave., New Orleans, LA 70115; Uptown; (504) 899-9308; www.thecolumns.com. There is no more civilized activity than sipping a martini or other cocktail of choice while sitting on the Victorian porch of the elegant Columns Hotel, one of the last remaining examples of turn-of-the-20th-century Louisiana plantation architecture. If you're determined to have a mint julep while you're in town, this is the place to do it—while feeling the gentle night breeze on your face and watching the streetcars clank down oak-lined St. Charles Avenue. As many locals as hotel guests can be found any given night passing a *trés* genteel time on the porch or in the ornate Victorian Lounge with its imported paneled mahogany ceiling, original stained-glass chandeliers, and 12-foot 300-pound solid mahogany doors. The Victorian Lounge is open nightly.

Cooter Brown's, 509 S. Carrollton Ave., New Orleans, LA 70118; Uptown; (504) 866-9104; www.cooterbrowns.com. Cooter Brown's has long been considered the place to find the city's best selection of beers, as well as a great spot to watch the game. This popular Riverbend bar offers more than 400 brands of domestic and imported bottled beers, as well as 40 beers on tap at the front bar and, on game day, another 20 on tap at the back bar. Sports fans will delight to discover Cooter Brown's two 8-foot drop-down screens, which complement the 17(!) flat-screens broadcasting all Sunday NFL games, as well as the Big 10 and all the other Direct TV sports packages. As if that weren't enough, the bar's Celebrity Hall of Foam and Beersoleum allows you to bend an elbow with 100 of your all-time favorite dead celebrities. Three-dimensional celebrity caricatures don the walls, each holding a beer. John Wayne has his manly grip on a Lone Star beer; Alfred Hitchcock guzzles a Rogue's Dead Guy Ale; and Judy Garland hoists a Hexen Brau ("witch's brew").

Crescent City Brewhouse, 527 Decatur St., New Orleans, LA 70130; French Quarter; (504) 522-0571; www.crescentcitybrewhouse.com. Nowhere is the German contribution to New Orleans more pleasingly obvious than at the French Quarter's only microbrewery, the Crescent City Brewhouse. At this 17-barrel, state-of-the-art brewery and bar in the French Quarter, German brewmaster Wolfram Koehler crafts a fine selection of distinctive lagers with no chemicals or stabilizers. And talk about old school: Koehler uses only the standards set by the Bavarian Purity Law of 1516, as well as four natural ingredients—water, malt, hops, and yeast. But you don't have to know any of that to belly up to the bar and do your own personal beer-tasting, while listening to the live music performed nightly and, if you like, checking out the changing exhibits of local art. Try the malty and aromatic Vienna-style Red Stallion or the dark full-bodied Munich-style Black Forest. And don't forget to ask about the brewmaster's monthly Special Brew. There is also a restaurant. The brewhouse opens at lunchtime every day.

El Gato Negro, 81 French Market Place, New Orleans, LA 70116; French Quarter; (504) 525-9752; http://elgatonegronola.com. This terrific little Mexican restaurant and bar is directly across from the French Market and shouldn't be missed. It's the perfect place for an afternoon cocktail. Look for the wrought-iron tables, shaded by thatched grass umbrellas, where you can sit and watch the throngs shop while you enjoy a refreshing beverage. Try the sangria (so good you'll even eat the fruit), or delicious margaritas made with fresh-squeezed fruit juices and agave tequila (with top-shelf brands available). If you want to show who's boss, order the Macho Man Margarita—48 ounces(!) of cielo featuring Patron Silver, Patron Citronge, and a fresh house mix. To top it all off, when you want to grab a little grub to keep the tequila from getting the best of you, the food here is fresh, authentic, and *delicioso*. Order the guacamole or something else they make at tableside. You'll be glad you did. El Gato Negro opens daily at lunchtime.

Feelings, 2600 Chartres St., New Orleans, LA 70117; Marigny; (504) 945-2222; www.feelingscafe.com. The cozy courtyard of the Patio Bar at Feelings Cafe is a wonderfully romantic place to have a drink. The long, narrow bar is located in the rear quarters of the old D'Aunoy Plantation that houses the restaurant. Right outside its French doors is the property's original antebellum courtyard, which has been cleverly closed in while still conveying the feel of being outdoors in old New Orleans. Sit and enjoy the view of the original brick floor and plaster walls covered by lush banana trees and palms, while listening to soft music from the piano bar. If you stay for dinner, ask to be seated upstairs, above the bar, overlooking this beautiful courtyard. Feelings is open nightly and Sun for brunch.

Lafitte in Exile, 901 Bourbon St., New Orleans, LA 70116; French Quarter; (504) 522-8397; http://lafittes.com. Lafitte's claims to be the oldest gay bar in America and they could very well be. The origins of this gin joint start down the block at another bar, Lafitte's Blacksmith Shop. Housed in a mid-18th-century building, the blacksmith shop is said to be the oldest continuously operating bar in the country, and it was a gay bar with regulars such as Tennessee Williams back in the day. Then one day, I think it was during the Reagan administration, management decided to go straight. So, all the gay folks moved down the street and started Lafitte in Exile, which, not surprisingly, is a much more fun place to hang out. The people are cool and the drinks are very well priced. Lafitte's is open pretty much all the time, and happy hour lasts from Mon at 1 p.m. to Fri at 9 p.m. They also have movie and karaoke nights. And don't miss the view from the upstairs balcony.

Landry's, 8000 Lakeshore Dr., New Orleans, LA 70124; West End; (504) 283-1010; www.landrysseafood.com. Unless you've snagged an invite to the New Orleans Yacht Club, this West End seafood restaurant is about the only place you're going to see the sunset over Lake Pontchartrain. During happy hour, the restaurant places chairs along the rail of its expansive back porch for just this purpose. Relax and watch the gulls fly by and the sailboats head in for the night, while the sun dips and you sip one of the drink specials served Mon through Fri from 4 to 7 p.m. The mai tai and mango mojito are house specialties, and they are only $5 during happy hour, as are martinis. Select wines are $4 and premium drafts are $2. A limited food menu is also available.

Loa, International House Hotel, 221 Camp St., New Orleans, LA 70130; Central Business District; (504) 553-9550; www.ihhotel.com. In a city that happily spends a lot of time in the past, the luxurious International House Hotel manages to lure locals and visitors alike with its fashion-forward design and air of quiet sophistication. This is especially true in Loa, the hotel's sensuously chic bar, adorned with rich fabrics and imposing chandeliers, softened by candlelight—giving the impression that the room contains hidden power. The name itself suggests the same. In voodoo, Loa are the divine spirits that provide humanity a connection to its creator. And you will certainly feel a connection to the earth with the bar's inventive cocktails, inspired by the fresh seasonal offerings from the local farmers' markets and created by expert mixologists who are as attentive as they are skilled. Just ask your bartender to serve you his current favorite cocktail and it's sure to be the start of an interesting night.

Ms. Mae's, 4336 Magazine St., New Orleans, LA 70115; Uptown; (504) 218-8035; www.facebook.com/theclubmsmaes. Ms. Mae's is where you find the proof that cheap drinks are the great equalizer.

Anybody and everybody can be found at this ultimate dive bar at one time or another, imbibing in $2 well drinks, $3 doubles, and Miller High Life or Pabst Blue Ribbon for $1.50. Located at the corner of Napoleon Avenue, this 24-hour bar is the place to go when both your cash flow and standards are low. But people love the place. In 2007 a fire broke out and firemen had trouble getting people to evacuate because they were watching a Saints game. In 2011, when it was announced that after decades, drink prices were being raised from $1 to $2, the controversy made the local paper. Go to Ms. Mae's and have fun, but keep an extra $20 in your pocket for a cab home, because nobody leaves Ms. Mae's sober. It's not allowed.

Napoleon House, 500 Chartres St., New Orleans, LA 70130; French Quarter; (504) 524-9752; http://napoleonhouse.com. By 1821, Napoleon's empire had shrunk to the tiny island of St. Helena, where he was exiled. His reign over the hearts of many French expatriates, however, had not diminished. In New Orleans, no less than former mayor Nicholas Girod and pirate Jean Lafitte sipped absinthe and hatched plots to rescue their hero. Ships were readied, the mayor enlarged his home to properly accommodate an emperor, and who knows what would have happened if Napoleon hadn't had the bad taste to die before the mission could be completed. Today, the mayor's 200-year-old house is a National Historical Landmark where generations have gathered to practice the art of civilized drinking. Walls covered with peeling plaster and yellowed oil portraits create a well-earned time-worn look that, along with the piped-in classical music and subdued lighting, are part of the pub's shadowy charm. Be sure to order a Pimm's Cup, the house specialty. This tangy gin concoction is equally good when sipped sitting next to the open French doors on a rainy afternoon or over a candlelit table on a hot summer night.

Orleans Grapevine, 720 Orleans Ave., New Orleans, LA 70116; French Quarter; (504) 523-1930; http://orleansgrapevine.com. This charming wine bar and bistro is housed in a beautifully renovated 19th-century French Quarter building. The interior is warm and inviting with exposed brick walls and subdued lighting. Or you can choose to sit outside to enjoy one of the 70 wines available by the glass or about 350 by the bottle. But the best time to go is during happy hour, from 4 to 6 p.m., when wine-tasting flights are offered. Each day three wines that share characteristics, varietal, or country of origin are offered. Whether you want to learn more about wine or just want to enjoy, these flights are a lovely way to pass the late afternoon. And beginning at 5 p.m., you can complement your wine with baked Brie, a cheese board, or other small-plate offerings.

Pat O'Brien's, 718 St. Peter's St., New Orleans, LA 70116; French Quarter; (504) 525-4823; www.patobriens.com. Pat O's, as locals call it, is the home of the original Hurricane, a fruit punch and rum powerhouse guaranteed to knock even the most seasoned drinker off his game. The drink was developed during World War II, when whiskey was hard to come by, but rum was in great supply. It got its name from the glass in which it is served, which is shaped like a hurricane lantern. Pat O's has been synonymous with fun since the 1933 repeal of Prohibition turned this former speakeasy legit. Whether you decide to sit at the piano bar or outside around the courtyard fountain, get here early to avoid waiting in line. If it does start to get too crowded for you, grab your drink and go next door to Preservation Hall, where live jazz is played continuously from 8 to 11 p.m. nightly. This dilapidated French Quarter landmark is like a living museum that exists only to preserve and honor this art form in its purest rendition.

Pirate's Alley Cafe, 622 Pirate's Alley, New Orleans, LA 70116; French Quarter; (504) 524-9332; www.piratesalleycafe.com. This popular spot is located on an old cobblestone alley, adjacent to the city's traditional dueling grounds, where pirates used to hang out, and you can drink absinthe. Do you really need to know anything more than that? OK, it's also next door to the house where William Faulkner lived when he wrote his first novel, and the alley right outside its doors was the black market where privateers like Jean Lafitte sold their ill-gotten booty. The alley may not be on your map. It runs between the St. Louis Cathedral and the Cabildo, from Jackson Square to Royal Street. The folks in there are very cool. Stop in and have the absinthe if you dare, or the secret-recipe Toxic Baby if you don't mind not being able to remember the night.

Tracey's, 2604 Magazine St., New Orleans, LA 70130; Uptown; (504) 899-2054; http://traceysnola.com. Established in 1949,

Tracey's was the original Irish Channel bar. It was the first in the neighborhood with air conditioning, color TV, and always cold beer. The bar had been closed for a number of years when it was reopened in 2010 by the folks who used to run the popular Parasol's po-boy shop for years. The place is big and airy. You can enjoy a pitcher of beer or an Irish whiskey at the long bar or at shaded tables outside. Tracey's also boasts 18 televisions, often showing a variety of different sporting events at the same time. From the ceiling hang numerous green and white second-line umbrellas that have been used during the huge St. Patrick's Day celebration and parade. This is a traditional Irish bar where people really enjoy drinking, watching a game, and hanging out with friends. There are also really good sandwiches here. Tracey's bar is open daily 11 a.m. 'till.

Tujague's, 823 Decatur St., New Orleans, LA 70116; French Quarter; (504) 525-8676; www.tujaguesrestaurant.com. Since 1856, Tujague's has been the place that New Orleanians of all walks of life, from dock workers to politicians, have come together to rub elbows and quietly make deals. Nowhere more so than in the dimly lit Tujague's bar where you'll encounter strong drinks and no bar stools. You need to be cool to drink in this place. Don't even think about ordering something like a Sex on the Beach, unless you want to get kicked out—or simply ignored. Just lean against the old cypress bar, as patrons have done since before the Civil War, and maybe catch your reflection in the bar back mirror that adorned a Paris bistro for almost a century before being shipped here in 1856. Ask for a Sazerac or a Ramos Gin Fizz, then throw it back, and taste history. Tujague's bar is open nightly.

Farmers' Markets

Since Hurricane Katrina, the number of farmers' markets in and around New Orleans has increased dramatically, perhaps due in part to a renewed appreciation for homegrown produce and products, as well as the desire for a healthier approach to life that second chances seem to inspire. Whatever the reason, local residents, farmers, fishers, and artisans are regularly coming together and sharing some of the best the region has to offer. Following is a cross section of markets in and around New Orleans.

New Orleans

Crescent City Farmers Market, various locations; (504) 861-5898; www.crescentcityfarmersmarket.org. The Crescent City Farmers Market operates at three different locations on three different days each week, year-round: the original Saturday morning market in the downtown Warehouse District, Tuesday morning market Uptown, and the Thursday afternoon market in Mid-City. The Saturday morning market is held in the William B. Reily Company parking lot (or in the adjacent warehouse if it rains), at 700 Magazine St. (corner of Girod Street). It features the best of regionally grown produce, seafood, baked goods, and other local products, as well as cooking demonstrations, contests, and live music. Arrive early for the best selection. The Warehouse District market takes place Sat from 8 a.m. to noon.

On Tuesday, the Crescent City Farmers Market heads Uptown to 200 Broadway St. at the river. Under the big, brightly colored tents, you'll find all the same great produce and products, as well as the Green Plate Special. Every month a local chef (some from big restaurants) becomes the market's chef-in-residence, who designs and prepares for each Tuesday a different healthy and affordable meal based on the market's fresh ingredients and products. Have lunch there or bring it home for dinner. The Uptown market is open Tues from 9 a.m. to 1 p.m.

Thursday, it's over to Mid-City, where the Crescent City Farmers Market sets up in the parking lot of the American Can Co. apartment complex, at Orleans Avenue and Bayou St. John. Find produce, seafood, and products. Then after the market, check out the Can Co.'s retail outlets, including a coffee shop, wine bar, and an Italian cafe. The Mid-City market runs Thurs from 3 to 7 p.m.

The French Market, Barracks Street & the river, French Quarter; (504) 522-2621; www.frenchmarket.org. The French Market, an open-air bazaar-type marketplace, has been operating at the back of the French Quarter for more than 200 years. Part of it is a flea market with myriad vendors selling everything from $5 sunglasses to artisan jewelry. But the other part is a newly renovated farmers' market featuring a modest offering of fresh produce, as well as a variety of eateries offering gourmet cheeses, Cajun sausage, fresh-squeezed juices, coffee, seafood, pralines, sweet potato pies, fruit smoothies, bread pudding, and local spices. The **Hollygrove Market and Farm** (see below) brings its produce to the French Market on Sat from 11 a.m. to 6 p.m. The flea market is open daily 7 a.m. to 7 p.m. The farmers' market operates daily 9 a.m. to 6 p.m.

Hollygrove Market and Farm, 8301 Olive St., Hollygrove; (504) 483-7037; http://hollygrovemarket.com. The Hollygrove farm is an urban farm used to facilitate the development of community gardens, to teach area young people to farm, and to demonstrate environmentally sustainable practices such as recycling and composting, sustainable gardening, cistern irrigation, and chicken cooping. The retail market is the point-of-sale for fresh produce from a variety of local growers. The market also sells at the French Market and other locations around the city. Check the Hollygrove website for additional sites. The Olive Street market is open Tues from noon to 6 p.m. and Sat from 10 a.m. to 2 p.m.

Sankofa Farmers' Market, 5500 St. Claude Ave., corner of Caffin, Lower 9th Ward, (504) 875-4268; www.sankofafarmersmarket.org. The word "sankofa" is from the Akan language from Ghana, meaning "go back and take." It is associated with the idea of reconnecting with the forgotten wisdom of the past in order to make life better in the present. This is an apt name for one of New Orleans' newest farmers' markets, which acts as a community anchor in its Lower Ninth Ward neighborhood. It declares as its mission "to encourage healthier eating and support farmers and fishermen by providing locally grown fresh produce and seafood to residents of Greater New Orleans." The fledgling market offers a wide variety of fresh seasonal produce, pastured poultry, wild-caught Louisiana shrimp, honey, herbs, pecans, lots of plants and seedlings, jams and jellies, salsa and salad dressings, and baked goods. Also look for grilled burgers and other cooked food—because no event in New Orleans is complete if people can't eat.

Vietnamese Farmers' Market, 14401 Alcee Fortier Blvd., New Orleans East. Every Saturday morning at 6 o'clock in a strip mall parking lot, the Vietnamese Farmers' Market gets under way in New Orleans East. A thriving Vietnamese population inhabits the area where they began migrating as refugees in the mid-1970s. Many of the community's farmers and fishers offer their fresh produce, fowl, and fish for sale at the market, along with plants, traditional Vietnamese conical hats, and assorted other products. While in the neighborhood, you may want to eat at one of the Vietnamese restaurants and bakeries in the area. The market operates Sat from 6 to 9 a.m.

West Bank

Gretna Farmers Market, Huey P. Long Avenue and Second Street, Old Downtown Gretna; www.gretnafarmersmarket.com. The large covered pavilion in Old Downtown Gretna is the weekly site of the Gretna Farmers Market where local producers and homemade food vendors come to sell their wares. There are always a lot of free samples at the Gretna market. And Aug through Oct, the market is combined with the Gretna Arts Walk, during which area artists and craftspeople create and sell art on-site. The Gretna Farmers Market takes place Sat from 8:30 a.m. to 12:30 p.m.

Camellia City Market, Robert and Front Sts., Olde Towne Slidell; (985) 285-3599; http://camelliacitymarket.org. Located about 30 minutes north of New Orleans, across Lake Pontchartrain in the city of Slidell, this is a true farmers' market focusing on regional produce and produce-related goods, with some local entertainment thrown in just to keep things interesting. Of course, produce changes seasonally, but also look for all types of fresh-baked breads, biscuits, scones, and pralines. Prepared foods include hot sauces, smoked meats, pickles, and jams. There's also a variety of herbs and other plants, free-range fowl eggs, and organic products from goat milk soap to doggie treats. In spring and summer, the market operates every Sat from 8 a.m. to noon. Check website for off-season hours.

Covington Farmers Market, two locations, Covington; (985) 892-1873; www.covingtonfarmersmarket.org. Covington is a little over an hour away from New Orleans, north of Lake Pontchartrain. There are markets every Saturday and Wednesday mornings. On Saturday, along with the usual, expect a live musical performance and free samples of something tasty from a local guest chef. On Wednesday, there's always something to inspire you to declare, "Lunchtime!" as well as more music. The Covington Farmers Market is held on the side lawn of City Hall, 609 N. Columbia St., Sat from

9 a.m. to 1 p.m.; and at the Covington Trailhead, 419 N. New Hampshire St., Wed from 10 a.m. to 2 p.m.

Mandeville Trailhead Community Market, Mandeville Trailhead, 675 Lafitte St., Mandeville; (985) 624-3147; www.cityof mandeville.com/department/division.php?fDD=10-15. Mandeville is a little less than an hour away from New Orleans, north of Lake Pontchartrain. The Mandeville Community Market is a family event with produce and food vendors, as well as artisans. Look for children's activities, workshops, artwork, and live music. The Mandeville Market takes place Sat from 9 a.m. to 1 p.m.

River Parishes

German Coast Farmers Market, two locations, www.german coastfarmersmarket.org. The German Coast is a rural area about 45 minutes or so upriver from New Orleans, where German immigrants settled during Louisiana's colonial period. Their arrival came much to the relief of the Creoles living in New Orleans, who most assuredly would have starved to death had it not been for these industrious farmers. This market is truly a community event. Along with local produce and products, look for cookbook exchanges, plant swaps, contests, live music, pony rides, gardening advice, and holiday celebrations—but not all on the same day. The market is held on both sides of the river. The East Bank market takes place at Ormond Plantation, 13786 River Rd. in Destrehan, Sat from 8 a.m. to noon. The West Bank market is held at the St. Charles Plaza Shopping Center, 12715 Hwy. 90 in Luling, Wed from 3 to 6:30 p.m.

Recipes

Roasted Tomato
& Watermelon Gazpacho

Chef Steve Himelfarb serves this popular dish at Cake Cafe in Marigny. He says that this light chilled soup, featuring fresh seasonal ingredients, is a great way to beat the summer heat.

Serves a big party

For the roasted tomatoes and juice:
3 pounds Roma tomatoes, cut in quarters

Lightly salt and pepper tomatoes, then roast at 400 degrees for an hour and a half. This will yield approximately ⅔ quart tomatoes and juice.

Ingredients

⅔ quart roasted tomatoes and juices from tomatoes (see above)

½ watermelon, seeded and cut up

3 cucumbers, peeled, seeded, and chopped

2 yellow bell peppers, seeded and chopped

⅓ cup lime juice

⅓ cup olive oil

1 bunch cilantro, chopped

1 jalapeño, seeded and chopped fine

4 tablespoons chopped garlic

Salt and pepper to taste

Blend all ingredients with a hand mixer to a chunky consistency.

Taste. Add more tomatoes, if you prefer a bolder flavor. (If you don't have another hour and a half for roasting, canned tomatoes are fine.)

Keep very cold on ice in cooler. Will not last long.

Garnish with cilantro and serve with a crusty piece of toasted ciabatta.

Courtesy of Chef Steve Himelfarb of Cake Cafe (p. 61)

French Market Coffee Rub

Chef Johnny Blancher loves to use this flavorful rub at Ye Olde College Inn, a Mid-City staple since 1933. *"Rub it on ribs, St. Louis or baby back. Rub it on chicken thighs or even burgers,"* he says. *"Versatile, complex but simple!"*

Prep time: 5 minutes

Rubs down approximately 6 pork ribs or 24 boneless chicken thighs

Ingredients

- **1 pound brown sugar**
- **5 ounces fresh ground French Market coffee beans (my favorite is the Viennese blend)**
- **5 ounces coarse kosher salt**
- **5 ounces finely ground black pepper**
- **2.5 ounces garlic powder**

Combine all ingredients in a large mixing bowl then work with a whisk or hands to remove lumps and mix ingredients thoroughly. Rub liberally on your choice of meat. For ribs, spread olive oil on the ribs before applying dry rub.

Courtesy of Ye Olde College Inn (p. 177)

Collard Greens

These delicious down-home collard greens keep customers clamoring for more at The Store, Chef Reuben Laws' Central Business District breakfast and lunch cafe.

Serves 6

Ingredients

5 lemons, juiced

1 cup Dijon mustard

5 tablespoons honey

2 tablespoons red pepper flakes

¼ cup Crystal hot sauce

½ cup Worcestershire sauce

2 large yellow onions, diced small

¼ cup olive oil

1 pound bacon, diced

2 tablespoons minced garlic

5 to 6 heads fresh collards, washed, cut, and dried (or 3 pounds frozen collard greens)

Salt and pepper to taste

Combine in bowl the lemon juice, mustard, honey, pepper flakes, hot sauce, and Worcestershire. Mix well, then set aside.

In a large, heavy pot, sweat onions in oil until tender (approximately 4 minutes). Add bacon and cook approximately 4 more minutes on medium-low. Add garlic and continue to cook for about 1 more minute.

Add greens; if fresh, cook for 12 to 15 minutes on low, covered. If frozen, cook for about 5 minutes on medium-low.

Add lemon-mustard mixture from bowl and simmer for 15 minutes over low heat, stirring occasionally.

Add salt and pepper to taste to finish!

Pairs well with pork and shrimp.

Courtesy of The Store (p. 88)

Slim Goodies' Jewish Coonass

Slim Goodies is a fun Uptown diner that embodies the New Orleans philosophy of not taking ourselves too seriously, as expressed in the self-deprecating humor employed to name its meals. This dish features two potato latkes topped with fresh grilled spinach, two eggs any way you like them, and Slim's own crawfish étouffée.

Coonass was originally a derogatory nickname for Cajuns. However, over the generations most Cajuns have come to embrace the moniker, even commonly referring to themselves as Proud Coonasses.

Serves 5

For the latkes

3 cups shredded potatoes	2 tablespoons chopped parsley
1 cup bread crumbs	3 eggs
¼ cup chopped red onion	1 teaspoon salt
3 tablespoons grated carrots	1 teaspoon pepper

Combine all the ingredients in a bowl, mix well, and shape into patties the size of your palm ¼ inch thick. Fry until golden brown.

For the étouffée

1 medium white onion, chopped

3 stalks celery, chopped

1 small green bell pepper, chopped

3 toes garlic, chopped

1 stick salted butter

1 pound crawfish

1 teaspoon black pepper

1 teaspoon cayenne pepper

1 teaspoon white pepper

1 teaspoon salt

3 dashes Tabasco sauce

Simmer the onion, celery, bell pepper, and garlic in the butter until onions are clear. Add crawfish. Turn on low flame and simmer for 5 minutes. Add the black pepper, cayenne pepper, white pepper, salt, and Tabasco. Simmer for 20 minutes on low with lid on. When étouffée is ready, place two latkes on each plate. Top with grilled spinach (optional), étouffée, and two eggs any style.

Courtesy of Slim Goodies (p. 129)

Jerry's Jambalaya

Mother's, Home of the World's Best Baked Ham, has been serving some of the city's best po-boy sandwiches and down-home New Orleans food in the Central Business District since 1938. This recipe was the first-place winner in the 1985 La Fete Jambalaya Cook-off.

Serves 6

Ingredients

2 ounces butter
1 cup diced onions, divided
¾ cup rice
2 cups chicken stock, divided
3 bay leaves, whole
8 ounces smoked sausage, sliced
8 ounces chicken, diced in large chunks
½ cup diced celery
½ cup diced green pepper
1½ tablespoons finely minced garlic

1 teaspoon chopped fresh thyme
1 teaspoon chopped fresh basil
1 teaspoon chopped fresh oregano
¼ teaspoon white pepper
¼ teaspoon cayenne pepper (or to taste)
1½ tablespooons flour
6 ounces Creole tomato sauce (see recipe)
½ cup chopped green onion tops
Salt and pepper to taste

In a medium saucepan (use the type of pan that will also go into the oven), melt butter, add ½ cup onions and sauté until onions are clear. Add rice, 1 cup chicken stock, and 1 bay leaf. Bring to a boil, then remove from stove and place in a 450-degree oven for 5 to 7 minutes. Remove from the oven and hold. Rice should be approximately half cooked.

In a heavy pot, render fat out of the sausage. Remove sausage, sauté chicken in the same pot, and remove. Sauté remaining onions with celery, green pepper, garlic, and seasonings (thyme, basil, oregano, white pepper, cayenne pepper) in remaining fat. Dust with flour (sprinkle about 1½ teaspoons on top of vegetables to thicken and flavor) and cook for 5 minutes. Add remaining chicken stock, cook 2 minutes, and add sausage and chicken, precooked rice, Creole tomato sauce, green onions, and remaining bay leaves. Simmer for 30 minutes or less or until done, but not too dry. Salt and pepper to taste.

Creole Tomato Sauce

The following recipe is a basic tomato sauce that is difficult to make in small quantities. You can make the whole amount and freeze the remainder for other uses, such as on pasta dishes.

Yields 5 cups

Ingredients

3 pounds ripe Creole tomatoes
   or 3 pounds canned whole
   or diced tomatoes
¼ cup olive oil
¾ cup French shallots, diced
6 medium cloves garlic, diced

1 teaspoon fresh thyme
1 teaspoon fresh oregano
2 teaspoons white pepper
¼ cup red wine
1 teaspoon sugar
Salt and pepper to taste

Boil whole tomatoes for one minute, then remove skins, cut in half, remove seeds, and dice. You should have about 7 cups. Heat olive oil in medium saucepan, add shallots, and cook for 2 minutes. Add garlic, thyme, oregano, and white pepper. Sauté until shallots are clear. Add diced tomatoes and bring mixture to a boil. Add red wine and sugar. Reduce heat and simmer for 45 minutes to 1 hour, or until tomatoes begin to break up. Salt and pepper to taste and purée in a blender or food processor.

Courtesy of Mother's (p. 85)

Malfatti of Creole Cream Cheese with House-cured Bacon

Creole cream cheese, made from buttermilk, skim milk, and rennet, has been a staple in the New Orleans area for generations, so it's not surprising to see its incorporation by Chef Eric Loos of La Provence into a dish featuring malfatti, a type of gnocchi, and a Provencal-style house-cured bacon for a spectacular dish.

Serves 10

Ingredients

1 pound Creole cream cheese

1 egg

1 lemon zest grated finely

1 pinch grated nutmeg

1 pinch salt

½ cup powdered Parmesan

2 cups flour

1 pinch white pepper

1 pound bacon, cut into lardons

1 shallot, peeled and minced

2 cloves garlic, minced

1 teaspoon chili flakes

1 tablespoon chopped thyme leaves

2 cups chicken stock

2 tablespoons whole butter

1 pound jumbo lump crabmeat

2 tomatoes, peeled, seeded, and diced

A few shavings fresh peeled Parmigiana Reggiano to garnish

Bring a 1-gallon pot of lightly salted water to a simmer (about 180 degrees) with no bubbles. The closer the water is to the top of the pot, the better it will help to not splash your hand in the process.

In a food processor, blend the cream cheese, egg, lemon zest, nutmeg, and a pinch of salt until smooth. Stop the processor, then add the Parmesan cheese and mix until smooth. (Clear the edges of the processor between each addition). Stop the processor then add the flour and pepper and mix until smooth. Place resulting dough in a piping bag with a ½-inch opening. Immediately pipe dough straight down into the simmering water, cutting the dough with a pair of kitchen shears as it exits the tip into ¾-inch lengths (like little barrels) as clean as possible. This will help the dumpling hold its shape while cooking. Dip the scissors in the water to keep the blades clean and keep cutting for 1 minute. Cook for approximately 3 minutes after the last dumpling drops. Check the center of the biggest dumpling to make sure that it is cooked all the way through. Shock it in an ice bath. Repeat the process until all of the dough is used. Drain on a perforated pan, lightly oil, and store the dumplings on parchment paper in the refrigerator until needed.

In a sauté pan over high heat add in the bacon and let it render until crispy on the outside. Add in the shallot, garlic, chili flakes, and thyme and cook just until the aroma fills the air. Add in the chicken stock and butter and bring to a simmer. Add in the dumplings, crabmeat, and tomatoes, turn the heat to a very low simmer, and warm through. Serve in a bowl garnished with the shaved Parmigiana Reggiano.

Courtesy of Chef Eric Loos of La Provence (p. 231)

Crawfish Maque Choux

This traditionally braised, single-pot dish (pronounced "mock shoe") served at Commander's Palace reflects Executive Chef Tory McPhail's keen gift for blending contemporary ingredients like local crawfish into southern Louisiana's rich culinary amalgam of French Acadian and local Native American cooking cultures.

For the stock

5 pounds live crawfish

1 ounce garlic, diced small

1 white onion, diced small

2 bunches celery, diced small

1 green pepper, diced small

1 pinch cayenne

1 pinch salt

Crush live crawfish in pot and add cold vegetables. Sauté until slightly cooked, about 2 minutes. Add 1 gallon cold water. Bring to a boil and skim, simmering for 30 minutes.

Strain stock through fine china cap of cheesecloth. Set aside.

For the roux

1 cup vegetable oil or peanut oil with a high smoking point

1 cup flour

½ bunch celery, diced small

1 green pepper, diced small

1 ounce garlic, diced small

1 onion, diced small

While stock is cooking, make roux. In a heavy gage saucepot, heat oil. When oil comes to smoking point, add half the flour. Stir constantly; do not let burn. Add other half of flour and stir. Note: be very careful not to burn yourself.

After 5 minutes or so flour should be dark brown, the color of chocolate. Pull off heat; add vegetables. Vegetables will caramelize and stop cooking; cook and stir down the roux.

Put back on heat and slowly add strained stock to roux, constantly stirring. Bring sauce to boil and simmer for 15 minutes, constantly skimming. Season to taste.

For the Maque Choux

3 ounces oil

1 ounce minced garlic

3 cups fresh corn, shucked

2 green peppers, diced small

1 yellow pepper, diced small

1 red pepper, diced small

2 cups diced onion

2 cups sliced fresh okra

3 tablespoons Creole seasoning

3 pounds crawfish tails

Steamed rice

2 bunches green onion, for garnish

¼ pound crisp bacon pieces, for garnish

In a large sauté pot, heat oil. Add garlic and let toast to golden brown. Do not let burn. Add corn, peppers, diced onions, okra, and Creole seasoning and cook until tender. Add crawfish tails and sauté until hot. Add sauce (the roux), taste for seasoning. Serve with steamed rice and garnish with green onions and bacon crisps.

Courtesy of Commander's Palace (p. 136)

Fideua Valencia
(Spanish Creole Pasta)

Leave it to a Catalan native like Barcelona Tapas' Chef Xavier Laurentino to handcraft Catalonia's upscale answer to paella, where saffron rice is replaced with angel-hair pasta for a more succulent and flavorful rendering of Spain's national dish. A mix of seafood, shellfish, chicken, and other delicious ingredients, this hearty and brilliant example of one-pot cooking from the Iberian Peninsula is the Old World predecessor to this city's ubiquitous jambalaya.

Serves 2

Ingredients

Pinch Spanish saffron

1 tablespoon olive oil

4 ounces ¼-inch chopped onion

2 ounces ½-inch chopped green pepper

5 garlic cloves, peeled and minced

2 ounces snap beans cut in 2-inch lengths

4 ounces ½-inch chopped tomato

2 ounces sweet peas

4 ounces chicken breast cut in 1-inch cubes

4 ounces andouille sausage cut in thin slices

2 cups chicken stock or water

8 ounces angel-hair pasta broken in 2-inch lengths

2 ounces peeled shrimp (medium size)

4 ounces calamari chopped in ½-inch rings

Salt to taste

In a dry saucepan heat up the saffron until it changes color. Place it in a mortar, pound it to a fine powder, and reserve. In a paella pan, heat the olive oil and sauté the onions until clear. Add the green pepper, garlic, snap beans, tomatoes, and sweet peas and sauté for 5 minutes on high flame. Add the meats, and sauté for another 5 minutes. Still on high flame, add the chicken stock to barely cover all ingredients. Bring to a rapid boil and add the saffron powder, salt, and the pasta. Cover for a couple of minutes until pasta softens and then mix well with the rest of the ingredients. Keep it on high until it boils again, then cover and set heat to low and let it simmer slowly for about 10 minutes. Turn flame to high, and add the seafood. Bring it back to a boil, then lower heat and let it simmer until liquid is absorbed. Allow it to rest for 5 minutes before serving.

Courtesy of Barcelona Tapas (p. 144)

Herradura Shrimp

Although Drago's is renowned for its charbroiled oysters, literally anything this longtime cherished seafood den puts to the kitchen fires is destined to be a hit, including this tequila-infused dish starring one of the city's most cherished shellfish: shrimp. You won't find a better version of this dish anywhere in the city.

Serves about 6

Herradura mix

½ to ¾ cup sun-dried tomatoes (cut into strips)

2 ounces Chardonnay

2 sticks whole butter

2 whole yellow onions, diced ¼-inch cut

2 teaspoons Vegetable Magic (Chef Paul Prudhomme's Magic Seasonings)

¼ teaspoon cayenne pepper

2½ ounces Herradura tequila

Marinate (until rehydrated) sun-dried tomato strips in chardonnay. In heavy saucepot, melt butter on medium heat. Add onions and caramelize. Add marinated tomatoes and heat thoroughly. Add Vegetable Magic and cayenne pepper; mix well. Deglaze the pan with tequila and burn off the alcohol (be very careful). Allow to cool. This mix will hold up to 3 days, refrigerated.

Ingredients

3 pounds large Louisiana shrimp, peeled and deveined, tails still on

1 quart chicken broth

1 recipe Herradura mix

6 tablespoons pine nuts

4 to 6 teaspoons minced garlic

¼ cup chopped green onions (⅛- to ¼-inch cut)

15 to 20 basil leaves

1½ sticks whole butter

1 quart fresh tomatoes, diced

Sauté shrimp in chicken broth. Add Herradura mix and all other ingredients and reduce by a quarter.

Plate and serve with a grilled marinated (in olive oil and red-wine vinegar) portobello mushroom or serve over angel-hair pasta.

Courtesy of Drago's (p. 201)

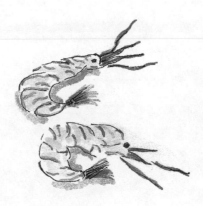

Appendices

Appendix A: Eateries by Cuisine

Appendix B: Dishes, Specialties & Specialty Food

Index